A HISTORY

OF THE

BAPTISTS

IN THE

SOUTHERN STATES

EAST OF THE MISSISSIPPI

BY B.F. RILEY, D.D.
(Originally published in 1898)

Charleston, AR:
COBB PUBLISHING
2017

A History of the Baptists in the Southern States, East of the Mississippi, was originally published 1898 by the American Baptist Publication Society. This edition was published 2017.

The text of this book is exactly as it appeared in the original edition. All footnotes are from the original edition, except for a handful which were added to give definitions of archaic or obscure words. These are marked with the word "Editor" at the end so you know they are new to this edition.

Published in the United States by:
Cobb Publishing
704 E. Main St.
Charleston, AR 72933
www.CobbPublishing.com
CobbPublishing@gmail.com
(479) 747-8372

ISBN: 979-8-3303-2082-0

Contents

PREFACE

In the preparation of this volume I have sought to adhere as far as possible to the intention of the series and to embrace as much as I could of the history of the Baptist denomination within the district indicated by the title. Throughout the volume, the relative importance of matter has controlled the fullness or meagerness of detail with which it has been treated. Because of the impossibility of comprehending within a work of restricted compass everything that might be of interest to the general reader, the author has been forced to leave untouched much valuable material.

It will be observed, from the plan of the work, that the history has been gathered around the most eventful epochs or periods that have distinguished the annals of the Baptist denomination in the older States of the South. The history has been unfolded under such subjects as admit of easy application to all the States alike. By means of such treatment, the essential facts of a general denominational history of the States of the South, east of the Mississippi, are easily presented.

Indebtedness is acknowledged mainly to such works as: *The Minutes of the Southern Baptist Convention* from 1845 to the present time; Cathcart's *Baptist Encyclopedia*; Armitage's *History of the Baptists*; Semple's *History of the Baptists of Virginia*; Spencer's *History of the Baptists of Kentucky*; Paxton's *History of the Baptists of Louisiana*; Campbell's *History of the Georgia Baptists*; and Boykin's *History of Georgia Baptists, with Biographical Compendium*; Vedder's *Short History of the Baptists*; Newman's *American Church History (Baptists)*; Carroll's *Religious Forces of the United States*, in the "American Church History Series"; Cook's *Story of the Baptists*; Hervey's *Story of Baptist Missions*; Tupper's *Foreign Missions of the Southern Baptist Convention,* also his *Decade of Foreign Missions, 1880 to 1890*; Taylor's *Virginia Baptist Ministers*; Foster's *Mississippi Baptist Preachers*; Borum's *Baptist Preachers of Tennessee*; J.L.M. Curry's *Struggles and Triumphs of Virginia Baptists*; Broadus' *Memoir of James P. Boyce*; and Sampey's *Southern Baptist Theological Seminary.*

For special kindnesses shown, the author is indebted to Drs. Lansing Burrows, of Georgia, and H.F. Sproles, of Mississippi, Mr. J.L. Furman, of Louisiana, and the late W.G. Whilden, Esq., of South Carolina.

B.F.R.
University of Ga., Jan., 1898.

1

CHAPTER I
EARLY TRACES

About the year 1682 a body of respectable and well-to-do immigrants left their homes in the southwestern portion of England, and under the lead of Humphrey Blake, a brother of the famous British admiral, set sail for America. Landing upon the Carolina coast near the present site of Charleston, they proceeded a short distance up Cooper River and built their temporary homes upon its western bank. The respectability of these immigrants led so competent an authority as Grahame, in his "Colonial History of the United States," to denominate them a "most valuable addition" to the Carolina population. From the same source we learn that Mr. Blake so generously shared in the convictions of the dissenters, whose leader he became, that he "devoted his fortune" to the furtherance of the scheme to emigrate to America in order that they might escape threatened persecution, the terrors of which were not a little enhanced by the apprehended accession of the Duke of York to the throne.

Among the colonists who landed near Charleston was Joseph Blake, a nephew of the leader of the party, who though not a Baptist, was nevertheless in profound sympathy with the denomination in its views respecting religious freedom. His wife, Lady Blake, was a most earnest Baptist, as was also her mother, Lady Axtell. Joseph Blake was destined to play a conspicuous part in the future history of the province. Already the friend and trustee of Lord Berkeley, one of the lords-proprietors of the province, he was afterward chosen, together with Paul Grimball, a Baptist, and five others, to revise "The Fundamental Constitution" originally framed by the celebrated John Locke. The conduct of Mr. Blake, from the beginning to the close of his career as governor of the province, showed that he was an uncompromising advocate of religious freedom.

About the time of the occurrence of the events just noted, William Screven fled from Kittery, Maine, with a party of persecuted folk and joined the colony upon Cooper River. Indications favor the presumption that it was the result of a mutual understanding that these harmonious bodies of colonists were thus brought together. One of the most significant facts is that the locality of the combined colonists was named Somerton. In his history of the English Baptists, Ivimey mentions the congregation at Somerton, in Somersetshire, England, as co-operating with other congregations in publishing a Confession of Faith in 1656. This Confession was signed by twenty-five persons, among whom was William Screven, of Somerton. Twenty-five years later we find William Screven at Kittery, on the Piscataqua River in Maine, engaged in holding religious meetings in his own house. There is little doubt of the identity of the William Screven of Old England with that of New England.

Subjected to a vigorous persecution, Mr. Screven left New England for the South and reached Charleston about the close of 1682. To a constitution and subscription of a church covenant adopted at Kittery, September 25, 1682, the First Church of Charleston traces its origin. The earliest available records indicate that the settlement of the colony under Screven at Charleston, was regarded as being only a transfer of the seat of worship of the persecuted flock which had been gathered on the Piscataqua. In a historical sketch of the First Church of Charleston, which was inserted in the original minute book of the Charleston Association, it is particularly stated that most of the members came with William Screven from the Piscataqua region. These Baptists on Cooper River, derived partly from England and partly from Maine, were the first to settle in the South. The strong probability is that while they observed social worship in some form at Somerton, their seasons of stated worship were held Sunday after Sunday in Charleston.

Every Sunday morning the families of the Somerton settlement would descend the river in their boats, following the outgoing tide, spend a large portion of the day worshiping in Charleston, and in the afternoon row leisurely back up the river to their homes. The time for beginning worship in the morning was made to depend upon the capricious subsidence of the tide, and it was as liable to take place at high noon as at ten o'clock. Prior to the erection of a meeting-house in Charleston, worship was held "at the house of one William Chapman on King Street." There is little doubt that the Baptists were the first to erect a church edifice in Charleston.

Naturally enough William Screven became the pastor of the original Baptist church established by the combined colonists at Somerton and thereabouts. He served in this capacity until 1706, when he retired to the head of Winyaw Bay, purchased land and built a home where Georgetown now is, and though quite an old man, continued to labor as a missionary in the destitute settlements about him. Upon the retirement of Mr. Screven from the pastorate of the church, a preacher from England, named White, was called to succeed him. Mr. White's pastoral career at Charleston was a brief one, for he soon died. In their perplexity, the membership turned again to their venerable ex-pastor for a supply. About the same time Mr. Screven received a call from the First Church of Boston, to which he made reply, "Our minister that came from England is dead, and I can by no means be spared." In spite of the infirmities of age, Mr. Screven served the church seven years longer, and died October 10, 1713, at the age of eighty-four.

Shortly after the colony under Humphrey Blake left England, another under the direction of Lord Cardross, a nobleman from the north of England, came to Carolina, bringing with him a company of North Britons, most of whom were Baptists, and settled at Port Royal Island. But encountering the hostility of the neighboring Indians and especially that of the Spanish settlement at St. Augustine, they removed their residence some time before 1686 to the mouth of the Edisto River.[1] Many of these became members of the First Church of Charleston, thereby greatly increasing its strength and efficiency.

In 1700 the population of Charleston and the adjacent region numbered about 5,500, the larger portion of which was within the city proper. At that date all the facilities for divine worship and all the schools connected with the province were confined to the limits of Charleston. The outlying population afforded an excellent field for missionary labor, and right zealously was the opportunity seized upon by the Baptists, who were the pioneers of missions in South Carolina.

The English Society for the Propagation of the Gospel in Foreign Parts did not enter this field until 1707, but wherever their representatives went they found that they had been preceded by the Baptists.[2]

At the period of Mr. Screven's death there was in the Carolina province a population of about 15,000, fully one-half of which was slaves. The virgin soil was productive of the most gratifying harvests, the forests yielded an abundance of the finest timbers for distant markets, the woods abounded in game, and the streams and seas were filled with excellent fish. Industry and thrift in commercial quarters were equaled only by the diligence of the local missionary.

William Peartt, who was second in the order of pastoral succession to Screven, was a most assiduous and enterprising advocate of church extension. He was pastor of the church at Charleston for a period of

---

[1] Hewitt, *History of South Carolina and Georgia*, Vol. 1, page 89.
[2] Humphrey, pages 88, 95, 108, etc.

ten years, during which time he was instrumental in the erection of houses of worship on Edisto Island, on Ashley River, and in Stono, sixteen miles distant from Charleston.[1]

As opportunity would offer, the Charleston pastor would minister to these mission stations in person, or else authorize some of its gifted members to do so. In this way William Tilley, first as a licentiate of the mother church in Charleston, and afterward as an ordained minister, rendered valuable service on Edisto Island. None of these stations became organized churches until some years after this period.

VIRGINIA

Although Virginia was settled as early as 1607, a Baptist church was not organized until 1714, more than a century afterward. That there were Baptists scattered throughout some portions of Virginia seems quite clear. There were dissenters in the province as early as 1648, but it is claimed that they were for the most part Congregationalists.[2] In the Assembly of 1661-62, there was an act passed which seems to have been directed against the Baptists:

> *Whereas, Many schismatical persons, out of their aversion to the orthodox established religion, or out of the newfangled conceits of their own heretical inventions, refuse to have their children baptized,*
>
> *Be it therefore Enacted, That all persons that in contempt of the divine sacrament of baptism, shall refuse when they may carry their child to a lawful minister in that county, to have them baptized, shall be amerced two thousand pounds of tobacco, half to the informer, half to the public.*

Notwithstanding the English Act of Toleration was adopted in 1689, it did not become operative in Virginia for twenty years. When the provisions of the Act began to assume practical shape, in the early years of the eighteenth century, the Baptists of the province began to show themselves, especially in the Isle of Wight.

Responding to the first note of encouragement, a small body of Baptists in Isle of Wight County appealed to the London Association for missionaries. Two missionaries, Robert Nordin and Thomas White, were sent out from London in response to this demonstration from Virginia, but the latter of these died before he reached the shores of

---

[1] Manly, *Two Centuries*, page 94

[2] Newman, *American Church History*, Vol. 2, page229.

America. Mr. Nordin, however, reached the province safely, and at once threw himself zealously into the work of evangelization. In anticipation of the advent of pastors from England, a body of Baptists seemed already to have been formed at Burleigh, on the south bank of the James. The constitution of the church, which is now known as Mill Swamp, was promptly effected, the organization taking place in 1714. Later, Nordin was reinforced from England by two other missionaries, Messrs. Jones and Mintz. From Burleigh, in the county of Isle of Wight, these ardent missionaries crossed over into the county of Surrey, and constituted another church at Branden. This is believed to be the same which is known today as Otterdam's Church.

About 1743 Baptist missionaries from Maryland entered the northern portion of Virginia, which was now becoming thickly populated. The prime movers in this evangelistic undertaking are supposed to have been Edmund Hays and Thomas Yates, of the Sater's Baptist Church, Maryland. In the midst of the expanding settlements in Berkley, London, and Rockingham counties, these Maryland missionaries found a fruitful field for evangelistic effort. These ministers were succeeded in this portion of Virginia by Revs. Loveall, Heton, and Garrard, the last named of whom removed from Pennsylvania in 1754. With consuming zeal they went from house to house in the different settlements delivering the message of salvation. As opportunity would offer they would appoint occasions for holding public services, which were almost invariably attended with remarkable demonstrations of interest. Not infrequently persons would ride the distance of forty miles in order to hear the gospel. Vast crowds would assemble under the shades of wide-spreading trees, bush arbors, and even under spacious stock sheds, in order to listen to preaching. As a result of this missionary energy, Opecon, Mill Creek, Ketocton, and other churches along the northern border were constituted and promptly became members of the Philadelphia Association.

At this period two valuable accessions were gained from the Pedobaptists in the persons of Shubal Stearns and Daniel Marshall. Mr. Stearns came to the Baptists from the New Lights, or Separates, and was converted under the preaching of Whitefield about the year 1740. As a New Light he engaged in preaching for a number of years, when his attention was directed to the examination of the New Testament upon the matter of baptism. The result led to the renunciation of his former views and to his union with a Baptist church. He was immersed by Wait Palmer, at Tolland, Connecticut, on May 20, 1751, and was at once ordained to the work of the ministry. After continuing for a brief period in New England, Mr. Stearns removed to Virginia, where he labored in the counties of Berkley and Hampshire. Subsequently he settled in Guilford County, North Carolina, where we shall have occasion to hear of him at a later period.

Daniel Marshall was reared a Presbyterian, in the ranks of which denomination he served as deacon for a period of nearly twenty years. Brought under the influence of Whitefield's preaching, he was fired with new zeal and earnestly craved the opportunity of breaking the bread of life to the Mohawk Indians near the headwaters of the Susquehanna. He undertook a mission to the Indians, but hostilities among the savage tribes prompted his removal to Connogogig, Pennsylvania, and thence to a point near Winchester, Virginia. Being led to an impartial investigation of the faith and order of the Baptists, he became united with a Baptist church, was immersed, and straightway licensed to preach. Like Stearns, he tarried for a period in Virginia, then moved toward the South and settled at Hugwarry, North Carolina. Marshall was a brother-in-law to Stearns.

The earliest Baptist churches of Virginia, like most of those first organized in the South, were deeply infected with Arminianism. This was due to the fact that many of the earliest preachers in the South came direct from England and were the exponents of the principles of the General Baptists of Great Britain. While the ordinances of baptism and the Lord's Supper were stoutly insisted upon by these early preachers, faith and conversion were not demanded as prerequisites.

To the Philadelphia Association the Baptists of the South are chiefly indebted for a correction of this laxness in doctrine. This Association deputed Benjamin Miller and Peter P. Vanhorn to travel southward among the Baptist churches "and to set things in order among them." By some, these men of God were received with distrustfulness, but generally they were most cordially welcomed by the churches, and listened to with marked attention. The result of their protracted tour through the States of the South was a general abandonment of flabbiness of practice and an adoption of the views of the Regular Baptists.

MARYLAND

When we turn to Maryland to seek for the first traces of the Baptists in that province, we find a condition of affairs entirely different from that which exists in the province oi Virginia. In Maryland, the earliest Baptists were favored with far greater freedom than was enjoyed by their brethren on the west side of the Potomac. The civil and religious spirit of that early period finds expression in an enactment of the Assembly of Maryland in 1649:

> *That no persons professing to believe in Jesus Christ shall be molested in the respect of their religion, or the free exercise thereof, or be compelled to the belief or practice of any other religion against their consent, so that they be not unfaithful to the proprietary, or conspire against civil government. That persons molesting any other in respect of his religious tenets shall pay treble damages to the party aggrieved and twenty to the proprietary. That the reproaching any with opprobrious epithets of religious distinctions shall forfeit ten shillings to the person aggrieved. That any one speaking reproachfully against the Blessed Virgin, or the Apostles, shall forfeit five pounds, but blasphemy against God shall be punished with death.[1]*

At the time of the enactment of this law, Maryland was under Roman Catholic domination. It is a matter of surprise to find expressed such liberal sentiments toward dissenters. This becomes more remarkable still when we bear in mind that at this time the Baptists were stoutly opposing the encroachments of Rome in different portions of Maryland. In 1709 a representative of the General Baptists, named Henry Sater, reached Maryland from England and interested himself at once in the propagation of Baptist principles. The result of his labors was the constitution of a church at Chestnut Ridge, in 1742, which was the first Baptist church founded in Maryland. This church, to which was given the name Sater's, is located about ten miles north of Baltimore, where worship is maintained to the present time. The church thrived almost from the beginning, the membership increasing so rapidly that within twelve years after its constitution it was enabled to send forth a colony to organize a church at Winter Run, in Harford County. This church, which bore the name of Harford, was ministered to by Rev. John Davis, who died in 1809, greatly honored for his works' sake.

The members of the Sater's Church manifested considerable missionary zeal in the early portion of its history in bringing about the or-

---

[1] Chalmer, "Political Annals," Vol. 1, page 218.

ganization of Baptist churches in the northern portion of Virginia. Its later history, however, has not been so prosperous because of a defectiveness in faith which has well-nigh sapped its life. Very soon after the organization of these two churches, Baptist interests in Maryland began to drift toward the city of Baltimore. The First Baptist Church of that city was organized on January 15, 1785. Its original members, only eleven in number, were a colony from the Harford Church, with the exception of the pastor, Rev. Lewis Richards. The Harford Church was the parent also of two other organizations, the churches at Taneytown and Gunpowder. The Second Church of Baltimore was constituted by Rev. John Healey in 1797. Two years previous to this, Mr. Healey, in company with five others, came from England to Baltimore. This eminently useful man of God enjoyed the rare distinction of being pastor of the same church for the period of more than fifty years. He also enjoyed the honor of organizing the first Baptist Sunday-school in Maryland, and indeed in the South. Almost from the beginning, Baptist interests in Maryland were centered in the city of Baltimore.

NORTH CAROLINA

The exact date of the first settlement of Baptists in North Carolina, we have no means of knowing. In his *History of North Carolina,* Moore gives the date of 1653 as being that of the advent of Baptists into the province. Without indicating the period of their first appearance in North Carolina, Morgan Edwards, who is excellent authority, states that there were Baptists in the province in 1695, and Doctor Hawks, the Episcopal Church historian, mentions the names of a number of Baptists in the eastern counties of North Carolina in connection with a period preceding the eighteenth century. The question of their first entrance into the province has given rise to much speculation. The suggestion is not without basis of reason that Baptist churches existed in North Carolina before they did in Virginia. The religious liberty enjoyed by the inhabitants of North Carolina exceeded that of many other colonics. While this freedom so widely and wholesomely prevailed in this province, the dissenters of Virginia were sternly repressed by the dominating establishment and by statutes that were cruel and exacting. The Carolinas were not divided until 1729, and yet we find Baptists at Charleston as early as 1683, almost a half-century before. Is it probable that a region so inviting as was North Carolina would have been neglected by Baptists while they flourished on the same coast both north and south, in the one instance for almost fifty years and in the other nearly a decade and a half, and under the most oppressive conditions? Still we are not able to find an organic body of Baptists in North Carolina earlier than 1727, at which time a church, said to be the first, was constituted on Chowan River in Perquimans County by the Rev. Paul Palmer. It has usually been assumed that the North Carolina Baptists were emigrants from Virginia when, for reasons already given, a reversal of the presumption would be more credible. For from the period when the church was established upon the Chowan to 1755, a period of twenty-eight years, the prosperity of the North Carolina Baptists was phenomenal. They not only grew rapidly in numbers, but they were remarkably aggressive. During the same period the Baptists of tidewater Virginia were a struggling and unprogressive folk.

Paul Palmer, the reputed "father of the Baptists of North Carolina," hailed from the Welsh Tract Church, Pennsylvania, and was a correspondent of John Comer, of Newport, R.I. The probability is not without strength that this remarkable man was attracted to North Carolina because of the unmolested enjoyment of freedom on the part of the Baptists of that region.

Like those of the colonies already noticed, save that of South Carolina, the Baptists of North Carolina were General Baptists who held that the provisions of the gospel were general in their nature. Screven and his followers at Charleston were Particular Baptists, or Calvinists, who held rigidly to the doctrines of predestination and particular election. When in 1728 the tide was turned against the General Baptists, who had hitherto prevailed, and the Particular Baptists assumed denominational direction in America, which result was largely due to Whitefield and the Calvinists, Philadelphia and Charleston became two great centers of Calvinistic influence. We have already noticed the action taken by the Philadelphia Association in commissioning Miller and Vanhorn to travel southward to correct the evils growing out of the Arminian principles held by the General Baptists. This action was taken by the Philadelphia Association in the autumn of 1755. The Charleston Association had taken the same step in the spring of 1755 when that body sent John Gano and Robert Williams upon the same mission. The combined efforts of these evangelistic commissioners were eminently successful. The year 1755 marks the date of the reformation of the Baptist churches of North Carolina.

The church formed by Palmer in 1727 was followed by the constitution of the Meherrin Church by Joseph Parker in 1729, and by the organization of another at Sandy Run in 1740, which was made up of a colony from the Meherrin Church, and by still another under the auspices of William Sojourner in 1742, in Halifax County. Ten years later we find that the number of churches had increased to sixteen.

When Gano, Williams, Miller, and Vanhorn reached North Carolina they found the Baptist churches in a most deplorable condition. To baptism and the Lord's Supper were added, as of about equal authority, the rites of love-feasts, laying on of hands after baptism, washing of feet, anointing the sick, the right hand of fellowship, the kiss of charity, and the public consecration of children without christening. Induced by degrees to abandon these doctrinal appendages, the churches were ultimately persuaded to adopt the London Confession of Faith.

The stoutest opponent of this reformatory movement was Joseph Parker, who, in the lead of the Meherrin Church, vehemently protested against the adoption of the views of the Particular Baptists. But with such overwhelming power did the reformation proceed, that even as doughty an opponent as Parker succumbed, and Calvinism was permanently established among the Baptist churches of North Carolina. Special distinction is to be accorded to the Baptists of this province because of their relation to the prestige enjoyed by the denomination in the South.

Under the leadership of Shubal Stearns and Daniel Marshall, North Carolina became the center and power of influence of the great movement for liberty on the part of the Separate Baptists. This spirit of freedom which came to pervade the ranks of the denomination throughout South Carolina, Georgia, Virginia, Kentucky, and Tennessee, emanated from the counties of Guilford, Randolph, and Orange, in North Carolina, where lived and labored Daniel Marshall and Shubal Stearns. The fact must not be overlooked that it was the Separate Baptists who bore the brunt of the long and terrible struggle waged for religious freedom on the part of the Baptists of the South.

GEORGIA

While Baptist principles were making initial headway in Maryland, Virginia, and the Carolinas, seed was being sown by diligent hands in the province of Georgia.

In January, 1733, an English ship, with thirty-four families containing 126 persons, touched at Charleston, South Carolina. The passengers on board this good ship, "Anne," were under the direction of James Oglethorpe, whose destination was the yet unoccupied territory of Georgia, which was still unnamed except in the sealed charter in the possession of Oglethorpe. From Charleston the vessel conveyed the party of colonists to the present site of Savannah, where they established their first homes in these primitive wilds. Among the original inhabitants of Georgia were a few Baptists, who upon arrival were dispersed here and there without the formation of a church. Among the Baptists who first reached this new province were William Calvert, William Slack, Thomas Walker, Nathaniel Polhill, John Dunham, and Sarah Clancy, of whom the last two named accompanied Oglethorpe. This number was gradually increased by accessions from England and from the northern colonies of America.

The original settlement of Georgia was based upon the idea of benevolence. Oglethorpe proposed to found in these Western wilds an asylum for the poor but respectable Englishmen, in which plan he was supported by an association of his countrymen. In order to provide for the penniless children in these inhospitable wilds, it was proposed privately by John Wesley and James Oglethorpe to erect an orphans' home in the neighborhood of Savannah. For some reason the project was never undertaken by these worthy gentlemen, but in 1740 Whitefield established such an asylum at Savannah. It was this enterprise which evoked from Rev. Mr. Lewis, of Margate, England, the sneering remark, "There are descendants of the Moravian Anabaptists in the new plantation of Georgia." No formal declaration of Baptist principles was heard from the colony, however, until some years later.

In 1751, a young Englishman, who was just twenty-one years of age, was made the superintendent of the Whitefield Orphan Home. In the person of Superintendent Bedgewood were combined the elements of a good classical education and the gifts of an effective speaker. Shortly after his assumption of the snperintendency of the Orphan Home, Nicholas Bedgewood was led to embrace Baptist sentiments, but it was not until 1757 that he made a public profession of faith. Doubtless this was due to the fact that there was no Baptist church at this period in the province of Georgia. But during the year named, 1757, we find him going to Charleston and requesting baptism at the hands of Oliver Hart, who at that time was pastor of the First Baptist Church of that city. His ordination to the ministry following two years later, we find Mr. Bedgewood preaching, as he had opportunity, in the region of the Orphan Home. In 1763 he began to gather in the fruits of his labors, for during that year he baptized a number of candidates, among whom was Benjamin Stirk, who afterward became a useful minister. It is most likely that Mr. Bedgewood was authorized by the First Church of Charleston, of which he was a member, to administer the ordinances to such as professed faith in Christ under his preaching. It was a custom of the early Baptist churches of the South to make incursions into unevangelized regions, as the colonists would continue to increase, and establish what was known as "branch churches." These mission posts were nursed by the parent organization until they became sufficiently strong for independent existence.

After his baptism Mr. Stirk began to preach and proved a most zealous and successful missionary. Removing to Tuckaseeking, twenty miles into the interior, he preached to such as he could gather from time to time into his own house. Having become a member of the Euhaw Church, on the Carolina side of the Savannah River, he was not long in establishing a mission station at Tuckaseeking, which became a "branch" of that church. Mr. Stirk spent the remainder of his life in this region, preaching with unabated zeal until his death in 1770.

The little band of Baptists at Tuckaseeking having learned the following year that Mr. Botsford, a licentiate from the First Church, Charleston, was visiting the Euhaw Church, sent an invitation to him to visit them. Accompanied by Rev. Francis Pelot, who was at that time pastor of the Euhaw Church, Mr. Botsford visited the little flock and preached to them on June 27, 1771. He was a missionary who was laboring under the auspices of the First Church, Charleston, but it seems that up to this time his evangelistic efforts had been confined to the eastern side of the Savannah. Being pressed by the isolated band at Tuckaseeking to abide with them, he consented to serve them for the period of a year by being permitted to give a portion of his time to preaching to the settlements on both sides of the river.

While the cause was being thus nourished in the southern portion of the province, an interest was being developed on the eastern border in the neighborhood of Augusta. Rev. Daniel Marshall, who had been baptized thirty-five years before at Winchester, Virginia, and who had spent most of the intervening period in North Carolina, was prompted by apostolic zeal to follow the tide of civilization westward, and had settled on Kiokee Creek, about twenty miles northwest of Augusta. Previous to his settlement in Georgia, he had lingered for a while at Horse Creek, South Carolina, whence he had made several visits to the settlements on the west side of the Savannah, preaching as he could, sometimes in outhouses[1], and at others under the great trees of the forest. On one occasion, while conducting religious service in a grove and while upon his knees offering the opening prayer, he was suddenly interrupted by a heavy hand being laid upon his shoulder with the exclamation, "You are my prisoner." Rising from the posture of devotion, the venerable man of God, with benignant face and snow-white hair, stood front to front with a stern officer of the law. The devout preacher was informed that he was a transgressor of the law in that he had "preached in the parish of St. Paul!" In brief, Mr. Marshall had violated the enactment of 1758 which provided that worship in the colony should be "according to the rites and ceremonies of the Church of England." Thereupon he was forced to give security for his appearance in Augusta on the following Monday to answer for a violation of the law. Having undergone his trial with meekness and patience he was ordered to leave the province of Georgia and to visit it no more in the capacity of a preacher. With fervor and stern courage he boldly replied, "Whether it be right to obey God or man, judge ye"; and fearlessly disregarding the existing statute, the prisoner-preacher continued persistently to proclaim the gospel.[2] The sequel of the scene of the arrest was that of honest indignation on the part of all present, to which sentiment Mrs. Marshall gave earnest expression with solemn denunciation of the law, quoting with fluency passage after passage of Scripture. The stern constable, Samuel Cartlege, was so impressed by the inspired words to which she gave utterance, that he was pricked to the heart, and was ultimately led to Christ. Five years later Mr. Marshall baptized this same constable, and afterward he so commended himself that he became a deacon of the church at Kiokee. Later still, Mr. Cartlege was ordained a preacher, and for half a century zealously proclaimed the gospel.

The Kiokee Church was the first regularly organized Baptist church in the province of Georgia. Its constitution took place in 1772 under the following Act of incorporation:

> *An Act for incorporating the Anabaptist church on the Kioka, in the county of Richmond.*
>
> *Whereas, A religious society has, for many years past, been established on the Kioka, in the county of Richmond,*

---

[1] Outbuildings, such as barns and sheds.—Editor.
[2] Sketch by Rev. Abraham Marshall, *Analytical Repository*, 1802.

called and known by the name of "The Anabaptist church on Kioka":

Be it Enacted, That Abraham Marshall, William Willingham, Edmund Cartlege, John Landers, James Simmes, Joseph Ray, and Lewis Gardener be, and they are hereby declared to be, a body corporated, by the name and style of "The Trustees of the Anabaptist church on Kioka."

And be it farther Enacted, That the trustees [here the names already given are repeated] of the said Anabaptist church shall hold their office for the term of three years; and on the third Saturday of November in every third year, after the passing of this Act, the supporters of the gospel in said church shall convene at the meeting-house of said church, and there between the hours of ten and four elect from among the supporters of the gospel in said church seven discreet persons as Trustees, etc.

Seaborn Jones, Speaker.
Nathan Brownson, President Senate.
Edmund Telfair, Governor.
December 23, 1789.[1]

Mr. Marshall became the first pastor of the church and continued his labors in connection with it until his death. Contemporaneous with Mr. Marshall as true yoke-fellows were Sanders Walker, Solomon Thompson, and Alexander Scott.

At first the early Baptists of Georgia were somewhat annoyed by the differences which existed between the General and Regular Baptists, but these differences were eventually settled by casting out the Arminian features of the General Baptists.

KENTUCKY

When we consider the earliest traces of the Baptists of Kentucky, we discover that they were the first actual settlers of that territory. These pioneer Baptists came over from North Carolina. A brother of the archetype of the hunter and wilderness wanderer, Daniel Boone, was a Baptist preacher.

When the daring Boones ventured across the Alleghenies which walled off the West and boldly invaded the beautiful and fertile regions beyond, they found that "it was a fair and smiling land of groves

---

[1] Watkin's *Digest*, page 409, and *Digest* of Marbury and Crawford, page 143.

and glades and running waters, where the open forests grew tall and beautiful, and where innumerable herds of game grazed, wandering carelessly to and fro along the trails they had trodden during countless generations." So far as the members of the household of the Boones were Christians, they were Baptists, though the great Indian fighter was never a member of any church.

The first Baptist preacher who entered Kentucky before the settlements began, excepting 'Squire Boone,' was Thomas Tinsley. He was doubtless the first to preach the gospel in the region of "the dark and bloody ground," and, so far as can be ascertained, was the first to preach in all the region of the West.[1] It is not known from what quarter Tinsley came, though it is supposed that he removed from Virginia. William Hickman and George Stokes Smith who became conspicuous in the early annals of Kentucky Baptists, removed from Virginia and settled in the new territory in 1776. Mr. Hickman was not a preacher until sometime after his arrival. He was induced by Thomas Tinsley to enter the sacred work, and proved to be one of the most active and efficient ministers of the early Baptist preachers of Kentucky. Among the colonists who continued to cross the mountains to make their homes in Kentucky was a goodly sprinkling of Baptists. Like their fellow pioneers they were partly actuated by a daring spirit and partly lured by the fertility and grandeur of this newly discovered region.

Unlike most of the regions first settled by the whites in the South, Kentucky was not occupied by the Indians except as a common hunting-ground for the tribes which inhabited the domains north and south of it. At certain seasons roving war parties or hunting bands from beyond the Ohio and the Tennessee would visit this attractive section. Naturally enough these wild tribes met with determined and bloody opposition the intrusion of the white settlers upon their favorite hunting-grounds. For the space of twenty years a perpetual conflict was waged between the two races. Depredations of every possible character prevailed. Crops were destroyed, stock was killed or driven off, homes were pillaged and burned, and the inhabitants cruelly butchered. Lurking savages would spring from the most unsuspected quarters to wreak their vengeance upon the whites. This perhaps is sufficient explanation of the fact that though Kentucky was settled as early as 1774, it was not until 1781 that a church was constituted. The dis-

---

[1] Spenser, *History of Kentucky Baptists*, Vol. 1, page 13.

turbed condition of the region was such that it was impossible for the settlers to assemble without serious interference from the savages.

On June 18, 1781, eighteen Baptists met in the wilderness under a green sugar-tree and constituted the first church in Kentucky, and indeed in the entire West. This church, which was named Severn's Valley Church, was constituted by Rev. Joseph Barnett, of Virginia. Rev. John Gerrard was at once chosen pastor. A few weeks later, on July 4, 1781, came the organization of Cedar Creek Church, and a little later still this was followed by the constitution of Gilbert's Creek Church. The spirit of church organization spread rapidly. It was not long before every populous community was favored with the presence of a Baptist church. This served to accelerate immigration from the older sections of the South into this favored region.

At first the places of worship of these pioneer saints were primitive enough. During the milder seasons, they were God's own temples, the groves, while during the cold or rainy periods of the year the rude dwellings of the pioneers were the meeting-places of these plain but pious worshipers. Imagine a structure built of round logs of uneven size and length, and sheltered partly with the skins of wild animals, and partly with broad strips of bark, and one has a conception of the home common to the first settlers of Kentucky. No tools, no implements of industry could be had, save an occasional long-handled, light-headed frontier axe. It being impossible to obtain lumber, wooden floors were out of the question, hence these clumsy houses were built flat upon the ground, and mother earth was the floor. The furniture within partook of the roughness which prevailed without. In these rude cabins the hardy settlers of Kentucky lived, and for many years worshiped. Surrounded by brute and human foes, they owed their lives to sleepless vigilance and resolute hearts. Within these cabin homes the primitive worshipers would gather, while one or more would keep sentinel at the door dividing attention between the message of the preacher and the surrounding forest.

The garb of the primitive worshipers was equally as rude as their dwellings. In a region where the arts were scant, recourse was had to any means, however ludicrous, for covering the body. The men made up their wardrobes partly from Indian costume, from whatever material came within reach. Leather leggings, moccasins, coats and vests of skins of animals with the fur turned inward, caps of soft fur taken from the buffalo and rolled about flexible strips of wood and tied with leather thongs to hold the parts together—these constituted the ordinary garb of the first Kentucky settlers. The garb of the women was even more rude and grotesque, if possible, than that of the men. Their quaintly cut garments were entirely of dressed buffalo hides and deer skins.

Besides those whose names have already been mentioned, there were conspicuous in these early annals of Baptist history in Kentucky, William Marshall, who was among the first Baptist preachers to become a permanent resident of the territory, Benjamin Lynn, John Whitaker, and James Skaggs. At the close of the year 1780 there were only six Baptist preachers in Kentucky. Indeed, they were the only preachers in the territory, for the Baptists, for a period of years, were without a rival in this newly inhabited district. The spirit of the early Kentucky churches was seriously impaired by the infection of Arminianism, which was introduced by the General Baptists. The laxness engendered by such a spirit was greatly enhanced by the gross immoralities which seemed to prevail throughout the circuit of settlements of the new region. While there were more than 20,000 inhabitants in the territory, no one had as yet been received into a Baptist church upon profession of faith. It was not because the early ministry was wanting in diligence, for they traversed the region in all directions, preaching as they went. It was a period of gross disorder which was to be followed by a reaction in 1785, such as has rarely been witnessed in the history of Christianity.

TENNESSEE

Doubtless the Baptists who moved first into Tennessee were refugees from North Carolina and came as fugitives from the battle of Alamance—the precursor of the revolutionary struggle. At any rate we find that Baptists were in East Tennessee prior to 1770. These pioneer Baptists are said to have founded two churches, but they were driven out by the Indians about 1774. It was equally true of Tennessee as of Kentucky, that Baptists were the first Christians within the territory, and were the first to proclaim the gospel in that wild region. No definite information earlier than 1781 can be obtained from existing records concerning the early occupation of Tennessee by the Baptists. At that time there were as many as six churches in the territory, the associational connection of which was across the border in North Carolina. Indeed five of that number were members of the Sandy Creek Association in the province of North Carolina. In 1786 we find these early churches acting in connection with a few others in the constitution of the Holston Association. We gather from Asplund's *Register* for 1790, that at that time the churches of the Holston Association had a membership of 889. Ten years later, the same Association embraced thirty-seven churches, the total membership of which was 2,500. The increase of Baptist strength was commensurate with the growth of the population in the territory.

Writing of these early times in Tennessee, and commenting upon the pioneer Baptist preachers of that period, James R. Gilmore (Edmund Kirke) in his *John Sevier as a Commonwealth Builder*, says: "Their theory of morals was condensed into one phrase, 'Thus saith the Lord.' What he commands is right; what he forbids is wrong; and the Bible is his infallible word. A faith, how simple, and yet how sublime!"

Impelled by a common motive, it was not unusual for an entire church membership to emigrate bodily from Virginia, or the Carolinas, into the new and inviting region of Tennessee. After locating in a given portion of the country and after providing rude shelters for their families, the next care of the colonists was to erect a place of worship at some convenient point. Here, as elsewhere, in the pioneer regions of the South, the cramped quarters of winter worship were abandoned for the freedom of the groves when the warmth of springtime came.

During the week the preachers would till the soil, and on Sunday occupy the pulpits. Among the first preachers who came into the Territory of Tennessee were Tidance Lane, who had been baptized in North Carolina by Shubal Stearns, James Keel, Thomas Murrell, Messrs. Mott and Talbott, Isaac Barton, William Murphey, John Chastine, and William Reno, all of whom came either from Virginia or North Carolina.

While the Baptist standard was being planted in East Tennessee, consecrated missionaries, such as Ambrose Dudley and John Taylor, from Kentucky, were operating in the middle and western portions of the new territory. It was chiefly through the agency of these missionaries that the first churches, the Red River and Sulphur Fork, were constituted in Tennessee.

MISSISSIPPI

In 1780 seven Baptist families emigrated from South Carolina to the Mississippi Territory and settled at the mouth of Cole's Creek, about twenty miles above Natchez. These daring emigrants hailed from the region of the Great Pedee River, South Carolina, where since the beginning of the Revolution they had been special objects of vengeance to the Tory raiders, in consequence of their loyalty to the cause of freedom. Not only were the homes of these devoted sons of liberty frequently plundered, but they themselves were hunted by the Tories from their hiding-places in the swamps of the Great Pedee. Attracted partly by the reports of the fabulous fertility of the soils in the Natchez region, and partly by the fact that they would enjoy exemption from the perpetual harassments of such a wily foe as the Tories of South Carolina, they turned their faces westward. At the head of this intrepid band of pilgrims was Richard Curtis Sr. Making their way overland to the Holston River, they constructed boats in which to sail down the Tennessee, Ohio, and Mississippi rivers to their destination just above Natchez. After encountering hostile tribes of red men on the route, in consequence of which several of the party were killed, the survivors finally reached the scene of their future homes. After providing temporary dwellings, the next care of the colonists was to arrange for seasons of stated worship. Fortunately Richard Curtis Jr., had been licensed to preach before leaving South Carolina, and naturally enough he was called upon to officiate in the services. From these informal meetings came Salem Church.

At this period the Natchez district was nominally under the dominion of the English, having been purchased in 1777 by the British Superintendent of Indian Affairs from the Choctaws; but religiously it was under the control of the Spanish Catholics, whose settlements were scattered here and there over the broad area. Many of these were led to attend upon the worship of the Baptists because of its freedom from formality, and because of the heartiness in which it was engaged. Encouraged by such favorable demonstrations, Mr. Curtis by degrees extended his preaching tours farther into the interior. His labors were greatly blessed, and after some months a number of conversions occurred. Being without an ordained minister, the perplexing question arose as to who should baptize the new converts, inasmuch as no ordained minister was available. Referring the matter to the parent church in South Carolina, from which these members had come, they received the following answer: "There is no law against necessity, and under the present stress of circumstances the members ought to assemble and formally appoint one of their members, by election, to baptize the young converts." Very properly, Richard Curtis Jr., who had been serving the colony with such efficiency as a missionary, was appointed to administer baptism to the candidates.

From this event sprang a sensation which came well-nigh proving serious to the incipient colony. Among the candidates baptized by Mr. Curtis was a Spanish Catholic named Stephen d'Alvoy. This gave offense to the Catholic community, and doubtless punitive measures would have been taken; but as the region was under the domination of Great Britain, of course the Romanists were utterly without authority to inflict punishment. Had the matter been allowed to rest, no trouble would have come of it. But a little later the colony was reinforced by a small band of Georgians, among whom was a Baptist preacher named Harigail who, with more zeal than discretion, began a wholesale denunciation of the corruptions of Romanism. Meanwhile the territory had passed temporarily into the hands of the Spanish. The conduct of Harigail, coming in close connection with the active labors of d'Alvoy, and directly following the provocation awakened by the baptism of the latter, the Spanish authorities resolved upon making an example of Curtis and d'Alvoy, whom they regarded as chief offenders. A plan was accordingly concerted for sending them to labor as convicts in the mines of Mexico; but having learned of the atrocious scheme, these unoffending men concealed themselves until preparations could be made for their flight. The region was thrown into consternation by such high-handed proceedings on the part of the Spanish officials. But still intent upon vengeance, the Spanish made an effort to seize the offending Harigail, and would have succeeded but for the friendly disclosure of the plot by a gambler, who was in turn seized and confined in prison for several months. Barton Hannah, another Baptist preacher, was also imprisoned, but his courageous wife demanded his release with the threat of a general uprising of the people if she was denied, so that the governor deemed it prudent to release him. Meanwhile arrangements were made for the flight on horseback of Curtis and d'Alvoy across the country to South Carolina. So terrorized was the population by the demonstrations of revenge on the part of the Spanish authorities, that for a time no one was found who was daring enough to encounter the peril of conveying to the concealed fugitives the horses and equipment for their journey. A brave woman, Mrs. Chloe Holt, finally assumed the perilous undertaking and put them in possession of the provisions, money, and horses, thus enabling them to make good their escape.

Louisiana

In no portion of the territory east of the Mississippi were there greater barriers to the introduction of evangelical religion than in Louisiana. According to the notorious "Black Code" adopted in 1724, while Bienville was the French governor of the province, no form of worship other than that of the Roman Catholic was tolerated.[1]

Baptists entered Louisiana from Mississippi as early as 1798. The first preacher that ventured across the border-line of the territory was Rev. B.E. Chaney, who removed from the Cole's Creek community, in Mississippi, to St. Feliciana Parish. Beginning missionary labor in that region, he was promptly arrested by the Roman Catholic authorities, but obtained his freedom upon promise to desist from further efforts to preach within the province. He died soon after this occurrence.[2]

The next interest seems to have been the establishment of a Baptist church within nine miles of Baton Rouge where a colony of South Carolina Baptists had settled. Rev. Ezra Courtney, himself a South Carolinian, who had removed to the southern border of Mississippi in 1802, where he founded a church, at a later date served also the group in the Baton Rouge community. Here again was encountered Roman Catholic interference. Mr. Courtney was duly admonished to cease preaching in the province, and was informed that persistency on his part would ultimately lead to imprisonment. But procuring the favor of the *alcalde*[3] he was permitted to prosecute his work, the result of which was the establishment of a church within a short distance of Baton Rouge.

The next interest in the eastern portion of the State, originated in the Pearl River region where, in 1813, Mount Nebo and Peniel churches were constituted as the result of the labors of young missionaries from the adjoining Mississippi territory. These were admitted into membership with the Mississippi Association in 1813, and the following year Hephzibah Church, in Louisiana, was organized and admitted into the same Association. About 1816 the Mississippi Society for Baptist Missions, domestic and foreign, was organized, which society sent Rev. James A. Ranoldson as a missionary into the growing communities of Louisiana. Mr. Ranoldson extended his labors as far south as New Orleans, where a church was organized in 1818. This church,

---

[1] Gayarre's *History of Louisiana*, Vol. 1 (Appendix)
[2] F. Paxton's *History of Louisiana Baptists*, page 36.
[3] The Spanish magistrate.—Editor.

however, soon became extinct and it was twenty-two years before another effort was made to establish a church in the Crescent City.

In 1818 the Louisiana Association was formed with a total membership of five churches. The growing importance of New Orleans as a commercial center attracted the attention of the Home Mission Board of the American Baptist Triennial Convention as early as 1814. Rev. James Ranoldson was its first missionary to this part of the Southwest. He continued his labors for a number of years in the midst of a population three-fourths of which was Roman Catholic. But all efforts at organization failed for a long period of years.

In 1842 Rev. Russell Holman, of Kentucky, was sent as a missionary to New Orleans by the Missionary Board of the Triennial Convention. During the year following a church, the First, comprising ten members, was constituted. In 1854 another church, the Coliseum Place, was constituted, with Rev. W.C. Duncan as pastor.

ALABAMA

There were settlements of whites in Southern Alabama as early as 1803, but we find the presence of Baptists in the territory not earlier than 1808. The first representatives of the denomination came from Tennessee on the North, and across the eastern border from Georgia. It seems that the colony from Tennessee preceded the advent of those whose presence is discovered upon the Tombigbee River, in the Southern portion of the territory. Revs. John Nicholson, John Canterbury, and Zaddock Parker were the pioneer preachers who first proclaimed the gospel upon the northern frontier of Alabama. Through the agency of Mr. Nicholson, a church was organized on Flint River, near the present site of Huntsville, on October 2, 1808, being the first that was constituted in the territory. Shortly after this period, William Cochrane, a licentiate from Georgia, began preaching in the Tensas settlement in Southern Alabama. Later he was reinforced by such efficient laborers as James Courtney, Joseph McGee, Jacob Parker, and Alexander Travis. These men were distinguished by apostolic ruggedness and fire—elements which were indispensable in a region without roads, abounding in great bridgeless streams, and one in which the settlements were widely separated, with intervening tribes of hostile Indians. Courageous indeed was the missionary who dared to thread his way on foot following the trail of the Indian the distance of forty miles sometimes, in order to meet an appointment to preach. The most noted of the group whose names have been given was Alexander Travis, in whom were combined to a remarkable decree robustness of courage and simplicity and gentleness of spirit. To him perhaps more than to any other of the pioneer preachers are the Baptists of Alabama indebted for the fundamental basis upon which the earliest churches were planted. The library of these plain and earnest men of God was the English Bible, which was studied at night by the glare of pine-knot fires when the toils of the day were over.

FLORIDA

Early evangelistic work in Florida began in the years succeeding the close of the Indian troubles in that State. It is impossible to determine at the present time just when missionary work began in Florida. The early records of the Associations of Southern Alabama and Southern Georgia show that, so soon as they could do so, missionaries from these bodies were sent into upper and central Florida to preach the gospel. These missionaries, operating from both sides of the Chattahoochee, considered Florida an inviting field for evangelistic endeavor, and made it one with the southern sections of their respective States. Until a late period churches in Florida were members of the Associations, the territory of which embraced the southern portions of Georgia and Alabama.

Work in Florida did not assume independent formation until about 1841. The Florida Association, the first in the State, was organized about that time by the churches in the counties of Leon, Jefferson, and Madison, together with some churches in Thomas County, Georgia. This Association was followed by the organization of Alachua in 1845 or 1846, and this again by the Santa Fe in 1854.

Efforts were made at an early date by missionaries from Alabama to establish a church in Pensacola. But little headway was made in that Roman Catholic stronghold, for all the coast cities of the South fell under the dominion of the Roman Catholics at an early day, and until the Civil War nothing more than a feeble and struggling interest was maintained in that cosmopolitan town.

In 1854 the Florida Baptist Convention was organized in the home of Rev. R.J. Mays, in Madison County. It was not, however, until after the close of the Civil War that the work assumed any conspicuous proportions as distinctive State work.

WEST VIRGINIA

Baptists entered the territory of what is now West Virginia as early as 1774, at which period Simpson's Creek Church was formed. Seven years later, Rev. John Anderson, of New Jersey, organized the Greenbrier Church, and in 1807 he was instrumental in the constitution of the Greenbrier Association.

DISTRICT OF COLUMBIA

The first Baptist church in the District of Columbia was constituted in Washington City on March 7, 1802, with only six members. They were dependent for preaching upon Rev. William Parkinson, then chaplain to Congress. Five years after its organization Rev. O.B. Brown was called to the pastorate of the church.

CHAPTER II
STRUGGLE FOR FREEDOM

In seeking to discover the first traces of the Baptists in the several States of the South, we have been carried much beyond the period which now comes under review. In considering the conflicts in which the Baptist fathers were engaged in order to the establishment of religious liberty in the South, we shall have somewhat to retrace our steps to reach the source of these troubles.

The era upon which we are now entering is at once the most eventful, the most thrilling, the most prolific, and the most vital in the history of the republic. It is a period in which were laid the foundation principles upon which the union of the States was to be established and maintained throughout a revolutionary future. While the liberty-loving of the Old World had fled to America in order to escape the oppression which resulted from the union of Church and State, the advocates of this unholy alliance had also come that they might transplant the same iniquitous principles on the shores of America.

In the original occupation of the States of the South the lords proprietary's, under the direction of whom these several colonies were planted, were largely members of the Church of England. Supported by the government of Great Britain, these original founders of American colonies were defiant of opposition and most rigorous in the execution of their demands upon all dissenters. To those of other communions than that of the establishment, the outlook for religious freedom was not, for a very long period, by any means assuring. Roman Catholics formed the only exception to this remark.

Among the first who came from England to America, as we have seen, were Baptists. They were generally fugitives from the ecclesiastical tyranny of the old world. Believing that everyone should be left at liberty to worship God as he might please, or to neglect to worship altogether if he might choose, they began the propagation of these principles. In harmony with these views they contended for entire exemption from compulsory support of a system or creed of which they could not approve. This opposition they did not hesitate to express when occasion arose, though such opposition was frequently attended with extreme peril. When, therefore, taxation on the part of the establishment was resisted by dissenters, which included others besides Baptists, the persecutions against such were oftentimes violent. The specious plea of these persecutors was that while magistrates "have no power against the laws, doctrine, and religion of Christ, yet for the same, if their power be of God, they may use it lawfully and against the contrary."[1] The passage of the Act of Toleration under William and Mary, in 1689, aroused great hope among the Baptists both of America and England. But for some mysterious reason, that Act failed to become operative in America for twenty years. While, as Doctor Woolsey says, it "removed only the harshest restrictions upon Protestant religious worship and was arbitrary, unequal, and unsystematic in its provisions," still "it was the entering wedge to religious freedom." The passage of such an Act was a concession of Parliament to the dissenters both in England and America. If it did not bring the desired freedom, it had the effect of giving enlarged boldness of assertion to the Baptists. The colonies of the South, as well as those of the North, were modeled upon imitations of the mother country. The spirit of the laws, if not the laws themselves, was derived from England. In Great Britain conformity to the religion of the government was enforced by disabilities, pains, and penalties. In the charter of 1606 the Church of England was established in Virginia. It provided that "the true word and service of God and Christian faith be preached, planted, and used according to the doctrines, rights, and religion now professed and established within our realm."

This was strongly supported by subsequent legislation, which denounced all such provision as heretical and dangerous. Under the exclusive system of Episcopacy in Virginia, such oppressive laws were enacted as entailed the most cruel persecution upon all dissenters. One of these laws in 1611 required every person who settled in the colony to appear before an Episcopal minister and state his religious views. Should he refuse to do so, he should be publicly whipped. If still he refused, he was to be twice whipped. A third refusal led to his being whipped every day until he should confess. It was unlawful for dissenters to engage in religious worship except in the meeting-houses of the Episcopalians. Taxes were levied on the goods of every man, on his property, and on his crops, for the support of the Episcopal ministry or for the purchase for them of glebes or parish farms. Should a dissenter absent himself from the "service" of a church of the Establishment, he was fined fifty pounds of tobacco for one Sunday, and two hundred pounds for one month. The penalty for refusing to have a

---

[1] Doctor Cutting, in Underhill's *Struggles and Triumphs of Religious Liberty*, page 10.

child christened was two thousand pounds of tobacco. The original statute books of Virginia abound in the records of the passage of laws for building houses of worship in the parishes, the support of the clergy of the Establishment, compulsory christening, attendance on public worship, the coercive use of the book of Common Prayer, practical conformity to the order and constitution of the Church of England, and forbidding preaching, officiation at marriages, and occasions of public worship of dissenters.[1] For was there existing the disposition to abate the vigor of these unjust statutes, for when not checked by the softening influence of Christianity, or awed into inaction by adverse public sentiment, these oppressive laws were cruelly executed.[2] That the galling nature of these laws may be more fully understood, quotation is here made of one of them:

> *WHEREAS, Many schismatic persons out of their averseness to the orthodox established religion, or out of the new-fangled conceits of their own heretical inventions, refuse to have their children baptized, Be it therefore Enacted, That all persons that, in contempt of the divine sacrament of baptism, shall refuse when they may carry their child to a lawful minister in that county to have them baptized, shall be amerced two thousand pounds of tobacco; half to the informer and half to the public.*[3]

This was originally intended for Quakers, but was vigorously executed against the Baptists of the Virginia colony. This conflict against dissenters was indiscriminately waged in every possible direction. Dissenters who were members of the House of Burgesses were expelled because of their religious opinions. Men and women alike were haled before the courts and fined for failure to attend upon the services of the Episcopal Church. A striking instance of this cruel enactment, as well as of the heroism of the oppressed, occurs in the records of Middlesex Court, Virginia: "Sister Lucretia Pritchett was true pluck: she was presented at every Court and fined each time."

By far the fiercest struggle for freedom was made by the Baptists of Virginia. For the period of almost three-quarters of a century the conflict continued in that province in which the Baptists refused to de-

---

[1] Hening's *Statutes*, Vols. 1-3, 6.

[2] Semple's *A History of the Rise and Progress of the Baptists in Virginia*, pages 14-23, 294.

[3] Hening's *Statutes*, Vol. 2, page 165.

sist until the last vestige of the coalition between Church and State had been wiped out. The lofty and boastful cavalier, concerning the courtly polish of whose manners, and the gentler blood of whom so much has been said and written, was the arrogant fellow who meted out only brutal intolerance to the unoffending folk of Virginia, called Baptists. Booted and spurred and of lofty port, he looked with disdain upon the plain and simple, but honest and worthy Baptists of Virginia. The treatment which was accorded these unoffending people for the period of more than half a century was largely due to the contempt with which the cavalier importations, who were also members of the Establishment, regarded them. They were the objects of "cruel mockings and scourgings, yea, moreover of bonds and imprisonment," because they were regarded as the refuse of the earth. Indeed, these same Baptists so profoundly excited the contempt of the austere members of the Establishment in some quarters that they escaped persecution altogether. With a sneer it was said that none but the weak and wicked would join the intolerable Baptists. It was presumed that their position in the scale of social excellence was such that they would soon come to naught by reason of unseemly wrangles among themselves.

In many other localities, however, the penal code was strained to its utmost tension to suppress the Baptists, who resisted the invasion of their God-given rights. A profound contempt coupled with a bitter malice led to the perpetration upon the Baptist ministry of the most cruel treatment. The same individual held in high esteem by the Establishment so long as he was loyal thereto, became suddenly transformed into an object of ridicule and contempt so soon as he embraced the principles of the despised Baptists. Samuel Harriss, before his conversion to the Baptist faith, was a most trustworthy citizen of the Virginia colony. This is shown by the several prominent positions which he held in society. No other than a most reputable citizen could have at different times occupied the several positions of church-warden, sheriff, justice of the peace, burgess for the county, colonel of the militia, captain of Mayo Fort, and commissary for the fort and army. But at thirty-four years of age he was led to Christ, was baptized, and ordained a Baptist preacher. This was sufficient to arouse the contempt and the ire of the Episcopal clergy and to call down upon Mr. Harriss their fiery maledictions.

On one occasion he was arrested and taken into court as a disturber of the peace. He was confronted by one Captain Williams, who "vehemently accused him as a vagabond, a heretic, and a mover of sedition everywhere." Mr. Harriss made his own defense. The Court proposed to dismiss the case upon the condition that Mr. Harriss would not preach in Culpeper again for the space of a year. The persecuted preacher stated that as his home was distant two hundred miles he would possibly not disturb them for that period of time. Crossing the Blue Ridge he preached in the Shenandoah Valley, but Providence soon led him again into Culpeper where, in violation of his extorted promise, he again preached, saying: "I partly promised the devil a few days past, at the courthouse, that I would not preach in this county again during the term of a year. But the devil is a perfidious wretch, and covenants with him are not to be kept: and therefore I will preach." He was no more disturbed in Culpeper County, but on one occasion, in Orange County, he was pulled down while preaching and ruthlessly dragged about, sometimes by the hair of his head and again by the leg, but was finally rescued by his friends. On another occasion he was knocked down while preaching.[1] It was not an uncommon occurrence for sacred worship to be seriously interfered with, and sometimes broken up by representatives of the Episcopacy.

Stones and other missiles were sometimes hurled at the heads of the Baptist preachers while conducting worship in the woods, or in private dwellings. On one occasion an Episcopal minister led the tumult against a Baptist meeting.[2] Frequently Baptist preachers were insulted while performing the most sacred rites. Their persecutors would ride into the water while baptism was being administered, and make sport of the most solemn rite. When on one occasion Robert Ware was engaged in preaching he was confronted by two men who stood before him with a bottle and drank, now and then offering the bottle to the preacher and railing at him with oaths. Unable to disconcert him in this way, they drew from their pockets a pack of cards and began to play upon the platform upon which he had been preaching, just so soon as he had closed. It is said that the object of these disturbers was to provoke him into open reproof of their conduct that they might find occasion to beat him.[3]

The officers of the law transcended the limits of their authority in imprisoning men for preaching, as no law existed forbidding such ex-

---

[1] Taylor, *Virginia Baptist Ministers*, Vol. 1, page 35.

[2] Bitting, *Religious Liberty and the Baptists*.

[3] Semple, *History of the Rise and Progress of the Baptists of Virginia*, page 36.

ercise. Considering the unreasonable extremity of the penal code in many particulars, it is somewhat remarkable that there should have been the omission of a law against the preaching of dissenters. In the absence of such a law the persecutors fell back upon a statute upon which was placed a forced construction in order that they might be justified in such procedure. The statute behind which they took refuge to sustain such action was that relating to the preservation of the peace. Consequently Baptist preachers were arrested as disturbers of the peace of the community.

It is believed that the first imprisonment for preaching took place in Spottsylvania County, Virginia, on June 4, 1768. At that time John Waller, Lewis Craig, James Childs, and others, "were seized by the sheriff and hauled before three magistrates who stood in the meeting-house yard, and who bound them over in the penalty of one thousand pounds to appear at court two days after.[1] At court they were arraigned as disturbers of the peace, and on their trial were vehemently accused by a certain lawyer, who said to the court: "May it please your worships, these men are great disturbers of the peace; they cannot meet a man upon the road but they run a text of Scripture down his throat." One of the number, Walker, made an ingenious defense of himself and of his companions. Indeed, so adroit was the line of defense that the persecutors were thrown into perplexity, and finally adopted the expedient of proposing to release them upon a "promise to preach no more in the county for a year and a day." But this proposal they finally declined to accept and were consequently sent to jail. As they moved along the streets of Fredericksburg, surrounded by the guard who escorted them to prison, these inoffensive preachers sang the hymn beginning, "Broad is the road that leads to death."

Upon being liberated after the lapse of a month, Mr. Craig repaired to Williamsburg, where he appealed to the deputy-governor, Hon. John Blair, to release his comrades. Thereupon Mr. Blair addressed the king's attorney in Spottsylvania as follows:

SIR: I lately received a letter signed by a good number of worthy gentlemen, who are not here, complaining of the Baptists; the particulars of their misbehavior are not told any further than their running into private houses and making dissensions. Mr. Craig and Mr. Benjamin Waller are now with me

---

[1] Semple, page 29.

and deny the charge; they tell me that they are willing to take the oath as others have; I told them I had consulted the attorney-general, who is of opinion that the General Court only have a right to grant licenses, and therefore, I referred them to the court; but on their application to the attorney-general, they brought me this letter advising me to write to you: That their petition was a matter of right, and that you may not molest these conscientious people so long as they behave themselves in a manner becoming pious Christians and in obedience to the laws till the court, when they intend to apply for license, and when the gentlemen who complain may make their objections and be heard.

The act of toleration (it being found by experience that persecuting dissenters increases their members) has given them a right to apply, in a proper manner, for licensed houses for the worship of God, according to their consciences; and I persuade myself that the gentlemen will quietly overlook their meetings till the court. I am told they administer the sacrament of the Lord's Supper near the manner we do, and differ from our church in nothing but in that of baptism, and in their renewing the ancient discipline, by which they have reformed some sinners and brought them to be truly penitent. Nay, if a man of theirs is idle and neglects to labor and provide for his family as he ought, he incurs their censures, which have had good effects. If this be their behavior, it were to be wished we had more of it among us. But at least I hope all may remain quiet till the court.

I am with great respect,
To the gentlemen, etc.,
Your humble servant,
John Blair.
Williamsburg, July 16, 1768.

Forty-three clays elapsed after the receipt of this letter before any step whatever was taken in behalf of the imprisoned preachers; but at the expiration of that time they were released without a word. While confined in the Spotsylvania jail these men preached through prison bars to the crowds assembled without. Seeing that the multitudes were being singularly affected by the preaching done under such novel circumstances, an opposing mob gathered, and by hoots and yells sought to drown the voices of the preachers. Released from prison, these earnest men of God preached with more diligence and zeal than before. Sympathy for the liberated men was now coupled with the power of their preaching, and there was abundantly illustrated the suggestion made in the letter of Deputy-governor Blair, that persecution was only productive of richer results to the persecuted.

In December, 1770, two ardent young preachers, William Webber and Joseph Anthony, were invited by some of the inhabitants of Chesterfield County to visit that region and hold a series of meetings. The character of their preaching was such as to arouse the opposition of the magistrates, who charged Webber and Anthony with "turning the people to madness." They were promptly arrested and thrown into prison. Certain terms having been submitted, they declined to accept them for conscientious reasons and remained in prison for four months. But they were not idle. Curious and sympathizing crowds hung about the jail windows day after day, and were preached to by Webber and Anthony. The imprisonment of these young men led to results which utterly defeated the object of their incarceration, for it was the beginning of a mighty work in Chesterfield County, and led to an extensive prevalence of Baptist principles throughout that region of country. After the release of Webber and Anthony from Chesterfield jail, they repaired to Goochland County. Thence Webber proceeded to Middlesex County where we find him again thrown into prison.

While preaching he was approached by a magistrate with a drawn club, who would have felled the preacher to the ground had not the instrument been caught by someone from behind. There were several Baptist preachers present upon the last-named occasion, all of whom were arrested, the magistrate being supported by a clergyman of the Episcopacy, two sheriffs, and a posse.[1] The preachers who were seized by the officers on this occasion were William Webber, John Walker, James Greenwood, and Robert Ware. They were accompanied to the meeting by Thomas Wofford, a layman, who was severely beaten with a whip by the officers, and turned loose with a number of severe wounds. Diligent search was made through the contents of the saddlebags of these traveling ministers to ascertain if they bore treasonable papers. Failing to discover such, an attempt was made to extort from each one separately, in a room apart, a promise not to preach in the

---

[1] Semple, *History of the Rise and Progress of the Baptists of Virginia*, page 34.

county again, the magistrates promising liberation upon condition that such assurance be given. But the proposal was met by a prompt and firm refusal. The four preachers were at once thrown into a prison swarming with vermin. On the following day, which was Sunday, their friends vied with each other in seeking to contribute to the comfort of the imprisoned preachers. While these sympathizers were gathered within the precincts of the jail, the opportunity was seized upon for holding sacred worship, and services were announced to be held from the jail windows every Wednesday and Sunday thereafter. The multitudes thronged in such numbers upon their preaching that their enemies were thoroughly enraged and caused a drum to be beaten during the service, in order to drown the voice of the preacher. In all this, the preachers though imprisoned were really the victors, for these demonstrations of disorder aroused public sympathy and gained respectful audience for Baptist preachers ever afterward in that region. This sympathy on the part of the people at large was not a little enhanced when these prisoners were led forth to trial attended by armed guards, as if they had been ordinary criminals.

In the courts, personal pleas were denied them, and choice was given between abandonment of preaching in the county, and returning to jail. They quietly chose the latter alternative and being thrust into prison upon a scanty and restricted diet of bread and water. After four days' suffering for food and drink, their condition became known without, and friends really overwhelmed them with supplies of necessaries, so much so that the ministers were able for several days together to feed the poor of the town of Urbana, in which they were imprisoned.

Every incident seemed to conspire to the furtherance of the gospel. As has already been seen, public sympathy was thoroughly stirred in behalf of the prisoners and was deepened by the patience and forbearance with which they endured their wrongs. To all of this was added the sickness of Mr. Webber which, when taken in connection with the serious regard with which the public considered the unjust imprisonment of these men of God, served to invest the old jail with an air of solemnity and made it the most honored locality in all the town. The multitudes which continued to gather about the jail windows became more curious and anxious still, and, by degrees, came to regard the prison with somewhat of superstitious reverence. After remaining in jail a month and a half longer, these men were set free upon condition of giving bond for future good behavior.

In Culpeper again James Ireland was arrested and brought before magistrates who grossly maltreated him and then thrust him into jail. The harsh treatment to which he was subjected came well-nigh costing him his life. More than one attempt was made upon his life while confined in prison, but each effort failed. Gunpowder was used to blow into atoms the jail in which he was confined, and the attempt failed only because of its insufficiency. At another time suffocation was attempted by the use of brimstone, and at another still his destruction was sought by the use of poison. These repeated deliverances from death, coupled with the tokens of love from his brethren without, converted his cell into a spiritual hermitage. His vivacity of spirit led him, while writing from prison, to address his letters "From my palace in Culpeper." Like his imprisoned brethren, Ireland preached to the crowds from his iron-barred windows. In the same county of Culpeper, Sanders, Craig, Maxwell, Corbley, and Ammon were imprisoned for preaching; two private members, Maxwell and Banks, were arrested for holding a prayer meeting; and Delaney, who was not a Baptist, was arrested for allowing a meeting to be held in his home, so utterly intolerant and filled with the spirit of persecution had the authorities become.

The irony of history is illustrated in the fact that upon the identical spot where the old jail stood in Culpeper, a Baptist church is now located. A similar retributive justice has been visited upon the original location of the jail of Urbana, in the county of Middlesex, where were imprisoned Waller, Ware, Greenwood, and Webber. Numerous other instances are upon record of the struggles for conscience' sake in Virginia, extending even to the period of the dawn of the Revolution. Persecutions similar to those already enumerated were rife also in the counties of King and Queen, Lunenberg, Orange, Fauquier, Caroline, Richmond, and others.

In 1774 James Madison was so profoundly aroused by the prevailing persecutions in different portions of his native State, that he wrote to a friend in Pennsylvania:

> *That diabolical, hell-conceived principle of persecution rages among some, and to their eternal infamy be it said the clergy can furnish their quota of imps for such purposes. There are, at this time, in the adjacent county, not less than five or six well-meaning men in close jail for publishing their religious*

sentiments, which, in the main, are very orthodox.

Be it said to the honor of James Madison, that he was the inflexible friend of soul-liberty in the midst of the most stirring periods of Virginian history. He sanctioned to the utmost, the views advocated by the early Baptist fathers, and on more than one occasion, as we shall hereafter see, became the champion of Baptist petitioners in the legislature of Virginia, against the ablest advocates of the opposition.

Up to this time our attention has been fixed upon the struggles of the early Baptists of Virginia to procure freedom from ecclesiastical oppression. Great prominence has thus been given to these struggles, because of all the regions of the South, the greatest oppression was experienced by the people of that province. But ecclesiastical cruelty was not confined to Virginia, for wherever the baleful union of Church and State existed, there was oppression in some form.

In 1698 a serious blunder was committed by the Baptists of Charleston in acquiescing in a measure which was fraught with much future evil. That it would lead to such serious consequences was not, at the time, so clearly indicated by reason of the incoherent condition of society. The mistake was an agreement on the part of the entire colony, including the Baptists, of course, to suffer the passage of a bill "allowing the Episcopal minister of Charleston and his successors forever, a salary of one hundred and fifty pounds sterling, together with a house, glebe, and two servants."[1] The bill secured a passage during the administration of Joseph Blake as governor of the province. Prompted by a desire to preserve amicable relations among the different elements of the province, Governor Blake greatly favored the measure, and through his influence, as the friend of the Baptists, he succeeded in gaining their consent and co-operation. The iniquitous measure derived additional support from the amiable character and popularity of the rector of the Episcopal Church at Charleston at that time, Rev. Samuel Marshall. This last fact, coupled with the conservative policy of Governor Blake, blinded the dissenters to all apprehensions of subsequent mischief. But when, at a later period, it was discovered that the proprietors:

Concerted measures for endowing the church of the mother country, and for advancing it in South Carolina to a legal pre-

---

[1] B.R. Carroll, *History of the Colony of South Carolina*, Vol. 1, page 126.

eminence; and when it was known that in order to that end they labored to obtain a majority of Episcopalians in the provincial legislature, dissenters took alarm. It was a matter of surprise to many that the Episcopalians, by energetic maneuvering, succeeded in electing a majority of those to the provincial legislature who were friendly to their restricted views.[1]

Having the majority, these political ecclesiastics at once took steps to perpetuate the power which they had obtained. The advantage gained in the outset encouraged them to take bolder strides in the direction of a permanent establishment of churchly power in the Carolina province. The next step was the enactment of a law making it necessary for all legislators thereafter chosen "to conform to the religious worship of the Church of England and to receive the sacrament of the Lord's Supper according to the rights and usages of that church." Failure on the part of any candidate to comply with this provision, no matter how great his majority of the popular vote, rendered him ineligible to a seat in the Commons' House of Assembly. The name of such a one being dropped because of nonconformity to the provision, the candidate receiving the next highest vote was considered in the same manner, and was dropped or retained according to his compliance or noncompliance with the condition already named. It is clearly seen that such a proceeding might make one a representative, though he received the smallest number of votes. These measures were enacted under the direction of Lord Granville.

The result of this gross assumption on the part of the Establishment was great popular indignation.[2] But this did not deter the party in power from a continuance of abuses, for the measures just named were followed up by another arbitrary Act which provided for extending and maintaining the mode of worship of the Establishment. Money was provided by law for the erection and repairing of Episcopal meetinghouses; lands for parochial farms and for churchyards were provided for by donation, purchase, or grants from the proprietors at the public expense; salaries were fixed and made payable out of the provisional treasury for rectors, clerks, and sextons of the Established parishes. Episcopal clergymen were encouraged by legislative enactment to remove to the province and to exercise their clerical functions in the sev-

---

[1] Ramsey, *South Carolina*, Vol. 2, page 3
[2] Ramsey, *South Carolina*, Vol. 2, page 3.

eral parishes designated by law. To such as were disposed to accept governmental inducement, twenty-five pounds was given from the provincial treasury immediately upon their arrival, and the annual stipends, provided by law, began at once.

But another measure, equally obnoxious with those just quoted, was adopted. There was organized an arbitrary court of High Commission "for the trial of ecclesiastical causes and the preservation of religious uniformity in Carolina."

Be it said to the honor of some churchmen that because of different reasons, one or both of the last-named enactments met their strongest opposition. The creation of the ecclesiastical court awakened strenuous opposition on the part of the Society for the Propagation of the Gospel in Foreign Parts, and they declined to send out other missionaries until that act was repealed. Prompt steps were at once taken to bring to the attention of the mother country the tyranny which was prevailing in the province of Carolina. So impressed was the House of Lords with the presentation of these facts that the queen was advised to annul the offensive laws. The annulment of the proprietary charter was advised by the Board of Trade. These obnoxious laws were finally annulled, and it was manifest from this time that the charter would be revoked and that the province would pass directly under the control of the crown. The issue was at once joined, and the people were triumphant over the lords-proprietors and their representatives as early as 1720, but the change was not effected until nine years later. The utmost that was secured by this popular victory was the toleration of evangelical forms of Christianity. The Church of England, under the new charter, was established and maintained in the province at public expense, notwithstanding it is estimated that at that time at least two-thirds of the population were dissenters.

In North Carolina the condition of things was very similar to that already described as obtaining in South Carolina. As early as 1678 serious remonstrance was made, under the lead of John Culpeper, against the encroachments of provincial authority. In 1704 a partisan law was enacted by the General Assembly, "disfranchising all dissenters from any office of trust, honor, or profit."[1] A previous Assembly (1702) had enacted a law whereby each precinct should raise thirty pounds to support a minister of the Church of England. Naturally enough this pro-

---

[1] Wheeler, *History of North Carolina*, page 34.

duced much public commotion, in which all dissenters were united—Baptists, Quakers, Presbyterians, and Lutherans. A clearer view of religious intolerance in North Carolina is gained by the following extract from Williams' *History*, published in 1812:

Carolina had been settled many years, as we have seen, before bigotry or pride, under the venerable cloak of religion, began to vex the inhabitants. Provision was made near the beginning of the eighteenth century for the clergy of the Church of England. Magistrates were authorized to join people in marriage in parishes that had no minister, and dissenters from the established church were permitted to worship in public.

In the year 1741 it was enacted that the freeholders in every parish should choose twelve vestrymen on Easter Monday, who were authorized to lay a poll-tax, not exceeding five shillings per poll, for building churches, buying glebes, and maintaining the clergy, whose respective salaries was not to be less than fifty pounds proc. per annum. It was increased by a subsequent law to one hundred and thirty-three pounds six shillings and eight pence. By another law it was provided that the fee of a clergyman for marrying with license should be ten shillings, or five shillings for marrying by publication. The license was a device for increasing the perquisites of the governor. It will readily be conceived that in a parish where a great majority of the people were dissenters they would choose vestrymen who had no disposition to lay taxes for the support of a church in which they did not worship. But when it was found that the majority were not disposed to tax themselves for the convenience of other people, a law was devised for compelling them, under the sanction of an oath, to do what they accounted wrong. Every vestryman was to swear that he "would not oppose the doctrine, discipline, and liturgy of the Church of England." Every person chosen to be a vestryman and refusing to serve was to pay a fine of three pounds, and another member to be chosen by the vestry m his place. It was presumed that twelve Episcopalians, or men who were ready to take the oath, would be found in every parish, and it would follow that taxes would be laid for the Episcopal Church.

The law, unjust and artful as it was, did not serve the intended purpose, for there were parishes m which no vestrymen were chosen, except men who were called dissenters, and none of them tendered the oath to his associates. Hence it was that in many of the western parishes no provision was made for ministers of the Episcopal Church. As an Assembly had been found, during the administration of Governor Dobbs, capable of passing the shameful law to which we have referred, there were people, at a future sitting of the Assembly, ready to assist in making that law a more perfect system of ecclesiastical tyranny.

In proof of this Dr. Williamson prints a copy of an "Address to the Governor, his Majesty's Honorable Council, and the House of Burgesses of North Carolina from sundry inhabitants of the county of Rowan" praying for the enforcement of the law, or "that means be taken for compelling persons chosen vestrymen to take the oaths prescribed, or such other means as may produce a regular lawful vestry."

"There were," says Williamson, "thirty-four subscribers to the petition; six of them made their marks, and some of the other signatures are hardly legible. When thirty-four such persons could propose that six or seven hundred should be taxed for their accommodation they certainly had need of the gospel that teaches humility."[1]

The most serious expression of persecution in North Carolina occurred in Newborn, Craven County, in 1740. It seems that three Baptist preachers, Brinson, Fulshire, and Purify, upon application for license to build a church in Newbern, were confronted by certain accusers who:

Made oath to several misdemeanors committed by the s[ai]d Petitioners contrary to & in contempt of the laws now in force. Upon which it was ordered by this court the s[ai]d Petitioners be bound by Recognizance for their appearance at the next court of assize and Goale delivery to be held in this Town then and there to answer to such things as they shall be charged with and in the meantime be of Good behavior to all his Magesties Liege People.

The old record, as examined in 1883, by H.S. Nunn, editor of the

---

[1] Hugh Williams, *History of North Carolina,"* Vol. 2, pages 115-118.

Newbern Journal, disclosed the fact that these men were "publicly whipped, bound over to keep the peace, and required to give bond for their good behavior and also to take the test oath."[1]

There seems to be little doubt that the preachers already named were not only whipped, but imprisoned for the period of three months. The records of the same court bear evidence of the fact that the persecution of Baptists was quite common in that region between the years 1730 and 1745. While North Carolina was comparatively free from severe methods of persecution, still it was visited in a variety of ways upon dissenters. One of the means employed was that of the enforcement upon all dissenters of the tithe system, while another was the enforcement of the muster laws of the province against all dissenting ministers, while those of the Establishment were exempt; still another was, the prohibition of officiation in marriage by Baptist ministers. The last-named law was annulled in 1776.

Georgia Baptists were as firm in withstanding the aggressions of the State upon the prerogatives of the church as were those of any other of the Southern provinces. Their declination to pay a tax to the State for the support of the church was at once firm and positive. With equal stoutness they refused the funds offered from the public treasury for the support of their own churches. The law which prevailed in the other provinces relative to the levying of taxes for the erection and repair of churches and for the payment of the salaries of church officials obtained in the province of Georgia also.

While a dissenting congregation might apply for a grant of land whereon to build a church with some assurance that the application would not be altogether unheeded, there was an evident intention on the part of the government, both royal and colonial, to engraft the Church of England upon the province, and to contribute with partial hand to its maintenance.

When on February 21, 1785, the legislature passed an Act for the support of religion, providing that "thirty heads of families" in any

---

[1] The truthfulness of this statement has been challenged. In order to confirm it, the late Rev. C. Durham, of Raleigh, N.C., visited Newbern, but found that the old record from which the extract had been taken had "seemingly by design been mutilated —a half-page cut or torn out—a page, two pages, and at a number of places from three to six pages, have been cut or torn out. When or by whom this was done, or just what was their real object we cannot here and now discuss" (Rev. C. Durham, in *Biblical Recorder,* for March 29 and April 5, 1893).

community might choose a minister "to explain and inculcate the duties of religion," and "four pence on every hundred pounds valuation of property" should be taken from the public tax for the support of such minister, the Baptists of Georgia promptly protested. It would have been easy to avail themselves of the provisions of this Act, for they formed a large majority of the population in many portions of the province; but instead, they united in a remonstrance and sent it by the hands of Silas Mercer and Peter Smith, praying that a law so obnoxious be repealed, and it was done.[1]

The difficulties which encompassed the Baptists who first settled in Mississippi were greatly increased when they undertook to exercise the liberty of worship. As has already been seen the original Baptists of Mississippi came from South Carolina and Georgia. The headway rapidly gained in the Natchez settlements, aroused the sturdy opposition of the Romish priests. No violent demonstrations were exhibited, however, until indiscreet attacks were made by some of the Baptist ministry upon the faith of the Catholics. This uncalled-for assault furnished an occasion for the vent of Romish wrath which had been accumulating commensurately with the prevalence of Baptist principles in the new settlements on the Mississippi. Nor was the situation in the least relieved by the conversion of Roman Catholics to the Baptist faith.

After the flight of Curtis and d'Alvoy there was quiet in the Natchez settlements for a brief period, but the Baptists continued to hold their meetings with more or less secrecy, and the Romanists grew more vigilant. Owen, a Baptist preacher, was forced to secrete himself for a season, in order to escape the clutches of the watchful priests, and Bailey Chaney fled the province lest he fall into their hands. Meanwhile converts to the Baptist faith continued to multiply, and at one time a number of these remained unbaptized for a period, because all authorized administrators had fled; but in the emergency the church wisely chose Deacon William Chaney to perform the rite.

Somewhat later, a minister named Mulkey made his appearance in the Natchez district. He is said to have been a preacher of more than ordinary ability, and one possessed of excellent spirit. The former interest in Baptist meetings, which had occasioned so much concern on the part of the Catholics, was revived under the preaching of Mr. Mul-

---

[1] *Public Recs. of Ga.* MS. Vol. B, page 284, "Marshall Papers."

key. Emboldened by their late efforts in the suppression of such religions demonstrations, the Catholics sent an officer to arrest Mulkey on the occasion of one of his meetings, but the assembly, aroused by a spirit of honest indignation, boldly resisted such unwarranted interference and drove the officer and his guard away. Determining no longer to be kept upon the defensive, the infuriated people seized their arms and marched against the local fort which was under the command of Gov. Don Manuel Gayoso de Senies, at whose instigation all the previous trouble had been fomented. Alarmed by the appearance of so formidable a body of indignant people, and finding himself too weak to resist them, the governor consented to allow them to proceed unmolested with their meetings, but sent a secret agent forthwith to Baton Rouge for reinforcements, and as soon as they arrived placed himself in a hostile attitude. The Baptists were again routed, Mulkey and others left the province, and tyranny was again dominant.

About 1796 Col. Andrew Ellicott was deputed a special commissioner of the United States to confer with the Spanish authorities of the Natchez district, about which there was some dispute between Spain and America. Upon the arrival of Col. Ellicott, a Baptist minister, Rev. Mr. Hannah, applied to him for permission to preach in the camp of his escort. Deference to Governor Gayoso prompted the colonel to refer the matter to him, and Gayoso consented. The sermon by Hannah led to a subsequent discussion between himself and a batch of Irish Catholics, who had previously beaten him severely. Applying to Gayoso for protection, Hannah was summarily arrested, thrown into prison, and his feet were made fast in stocks. This led to a disturbance between the governor and Colonel Ellicott, the latter threatening to destroy the Spanish fort if matters were not speedily adjusted. After a formal negotiation of two weeks, Mr. Hannah was set at liberty. Upon the reluctant abandonment of the Natchez district by the Spaniards, the Americans promptly built a considerable arbor and appointed Rev. Bailey Chaney to "preach under the Stars and Stripes." An immense concourse of people greeted him, and great was the enjoyment of the first religious service held in the Natchez district under the government of the United States.

CHAPTER III
SOUTHERN BAPTISTS AND THE REVOLU-TION

The contest for civil liberty In America followed a long and bitter struggle for religious freedom. It would seem that the one was productive of the other, if indeed it was not the same struggle which came naturally to involve the question of civil freedom in common with that of religious emancipation in the outworking of the principle of liberty in America. Hence it is easy to see how the Baptists of the several colonies of the South would become prompt contributors to the spirit which kindled the fires of the Revolution. It was the same spirit which had animated them for almost a century in resisting the oppression of a tyrannous power. Naturally enough they would regard the impending struggle not as a political contest alone, but as one involving all that was cherished by a people seeking to be free. Great boon as political liberty is, religious freedom is a greater. In a very important sense then, the matter to be considered now is only a continuation of that which engaged our attention in the preceding chapter.

The first note of the American Revolution was sounded at Alamance, North Carolina, on May 16, 1771. To this event sufficient prominence has never been accorded, either in civil or religious history.

It was the first popular uprising of any considerable portion of the American colonists against the encroachments of the representatives of the British crown. The primary cause of this outburst of popular indignation was the passage of what is known as the "Vestry Act," referred to in the previous chapter, which was adopted by the Assembly in 1764, during the administration of Governor Dobbs. The chief provision of that measure was the support of the Episcopal clergy and the erection of Episcopal houses of worship; but the methods adopted for assessing and collecting these taxes, and for the imposition of fines and penalties, aroused at the very outset great popular opposition. The initial provision was that every freeholder who owned fifty acres of land was required by law to meet at the courthouse on Easter Monday to elect twelve vestrymen. Failure to do so subjected one to a fine of twenty shillings "to be recovered by a warrant from any justice of the peace within the limits of said county." In order to exclude all dissenters it was provided that the vestrymen be required to subscribe to an oath "not to oppose the doctrine, discipline, and liturgy of the Church of England, as by law established." To these vestrymen was given power to levy taxes, to build churches and chapels, pay ministers' salaries, purchase a glebe, erect a mansion and convenient outhouses, maintain the poor, pay clerks and readers, and defray other incidental charges of the parish; and the minister could bring suit against the vestrymen if they should fail or refuse "to lay a sufficient tax to satisfy" him. The sheriff was required under a heavy bond to collect the taxes thus imposed.

The effort to enforce such a law created widespread dissatisfaction, and meetings were soon called by the common people to confer about the opposition which was to be interposed. These were soon formed into a popular organization known as the Regulators. Instead of relenting in view of these expressions of popular disapprobation, Governor Dobbs became more exacting, and the complaints of the masses grew apace. A paper was established at Wilmington, in 1764, known as *The North Carolina Gazette and Weekly Post Boy*, which gave the current news. This pioneer enterprise greatly aided the people in their cause, as it informed them of the measures which were from time to time adopted for their oppression. Meanwhile extortions became rife in every department of government. Lossing says that "deputy surveyors, entry-takers, and other officers of inferior grade, became adepts in the chicanery of their superiors." Matters were growing rapidly worse and the situation was not in the least relieved by the receipt of the news of the passage of the Stamp Act, which information reached the province in June, 1765. Popular gatherings became general. The people were greatly agitated. After more than one popular assemblage, the people came together at Hillsboro, on April 4, 1767, and passed resolutions to pay no more taxes until they were sure of their legality; to pay officers no more fees than was rigidly required by law, unless forced to do so, and then to show open resentment; to be cautious in the selection of representatives; to petition the governor, council, king, and parliament for a redress of grievances; to maintain a continual correspondence among the members; to defray all necessary expenses; to submit all differences in judgment to the whole Regulation, the judgment of the majority to be final; and closed by a solemn affirmation "to stand true and faithful to this cause until we bring things to a true regulation."

Commenting upon this action of the Carolina patriots, Lossing says:

The resolutions passed at this meeting were almost equiva-

lent to a declaration of independence of the civil power of the State. Tryon, who became governor of the province in 1765, endeavored to crush out the Regulation movement by bringing to bear undue influence upon the North Carolina Assembly, and referred to the "Regulators as a faction of Quakers and Baptists who aimed at overturning the Church of England."

At the time of this period of agitation the Baptists were by great odds more numerous than any other religious denomination in the province, for there were twenty-two Baptist churches in seventeen of the twenty-three counties in North Carolina. Some of these churches, like the Sandy Creek Church, had a numerous membership. Even as early as 1758 its membership numbered nearly 900 members. Trifling as the numbers of the Episcopacy were, when compared with those of the Baptists, all the public offices were held by the former by reason of the failure of the Baptists to subscribe to the tenets of the Establishment. And yet the Baptists paid a large portion of the taxes by which the Establishment was maintained.

It is not difficult to see the inevitable tendency of such a condition as prevailed for many years in North Carolina. When the extreme of endurance had been reached, the people openly rebelled. The clash of arms came at Alamance. The Regulators, composed largely of Baptists, were defeated by the royal forces, and fled toward the West. The result was that this portion of North Carolina from being one of those in which Baptists were most numerous was now almost altogether abandoned by them. Fleeing westward into Kentucky, Tennessee, and Georgia, Baptist churches sprang up wherever they went. In accounting for this precipitate emigration, Morgan Edwards, a Tory Baptist,[1] said in 1775:

> *The cause of this dispersion was the abuse of power which too much prevailed in the province and caused the inhabitants at last to rise up in arms and fight for their privileges; but being routed, May 16, 1771, they despaired of seeing better times and therefore quitted the province. It is said one thousand five hundred families departed since the battle of Alamance, and, to my knowledge, a great many more are only waiting to dispose of their plantations in order to follow them. This, to my mind, is*

---

[1] "He was the only Tory in the ministry of the American Baptist churches."—Cathcart, *"Baptist Encyclopedia, page* 862.

an argument that their grievances were real, and their oppression great, notwithstanding all that has been said to the contrary.

An indication of the extent to which the thrifty Baptist communities were thinned is afforded by the fact that the membership of the Sandy Creek Church, near which the battle was fought, was reduced from 900 to a membership of 14.

Recoiling from the oppression visited upon them, the Baptists of North Carolina came to question the slightest assumption of human authority. Oppression had driven them to the extreme in the assertion of the principle of soul-liberty. This spirit was shown in the fact that the Sandy Creek Association, during a period of thirty or forty years, and the Yadkin, for a period of twelve years, refused to elect moderators to preside over them. From a position so extreme, they were dissuaded by John Gano during his missionary tour through the South.

Contemporary with these revolutionary movements in North Carolina was the activity in the same direction on the part of the Baptists of Virginia, and of other provinces of the South. Protracted oppression had made them vigilant of the discovery of the slightest opportunity to contribute to the growing complications between England and the American colonies. Promptly seizing upon these advantages, the Baptists of the South wisely and vigorously pushed them toward the desired end without halt or compromise. As citizens they struggled for civil liberty; as Christians, for religious freedom.

Of one thing the Baptists never lost sight—that of the abolition of all legal ecclesiastical distinctions. The political crisis induced by the growing exactions of the mother country impelled the Baptists to struggle more vigorously for the attainment of that much desired end, which was sought for themselves not only, but for all citizens, whether Christian, Jew, or infidel. That for which they contended was a divorcement of the Church from the State, that the former might work out its own destiny unaided by the government; in short, their ultimate object was absolute religious freedom. In this contest Baptists were aided by the Presbyterians and other members of the community. [1] That the spirit of the Baptists was entirely exempt from hostility to any other sect, and that they were actuated solely by principle, is shown by

---

[1] Semple, *A History of the Rise and Progress of the Baptists in Virginia*, pages 20, 73.

the fact that at the session of the General Association of Virginia in 1784, public fast days were set apart "in behalf of our poor blind persecutors and for the releasement of our brethren."[1]

In 1775 the General Association of Virginia memorialized the Convention of the province to make military resistance to Great Britain, setting forth at the same time in a Declaration of Principles "that the mere toleration of religion by the civil government is insufficient; that no State religious establishment ought to exist; that all religious denominations ought to stand on the same footing." Charged with a copy of the memorial, a committee was deputed by the General Association to attend the convention and to lay under tribute all legitimate means for the accomplishment of the desired end. All that was asked for was not granted, but an extraordinary concession was made when the Convention gave respectful answer, and adopted a resolution granting that "dissenting clergymen be permitted to celebrate divine worship and to preach to the soldiers." This was the entering wedge to religious equality in Virginia. Doubtless on the part of the Convention this was intended so to conciliate the Baptists that they would desist from further effort. So far from that being true, however, it only served to stimulate them to greater energy and more vehement protests. If it gave hope and encouragement to Baptists, it must have indicated to the clergy of the Establishment that their power was already beginning to decline. But a supremacy so long and profitably enjoyed was not to be easily surrendered. Accordingly the clergy of the Establishment began at once an active canvass, circulating petitions to be signed in behalf of the retention of the Episcopacy as a permanent legal establishment, which in turn provoked the Baptists to procure counter petitions. The efforts of the Baptists resulted in procuring the names of ten thousand persons who were chiefly freeholders.

The year 1776 marks the era of the adoption of the Constitution of Virginia, which instrument enjoys the distinction of being "the first written constitution for a free, sovereign, and independent State which the history of the world has called forth." The constitution was prefaced by the Bill of Rights, the sixteenth section of which, as written by George Mason, provided for the "fullest toleration." But through the instrumentality of James Madison, the term "toleration" was stricken

---

[1] Semple, *A History of the Rise and Progress of the Baptists in Virginia,* page 56.

out and all men were declared equally entitled to the free exercise of religion. The famous section as amended by Madison reads as follows:

> *That religion, or the duty which we owe to our Creator and the manner of discharging it, can be directed only by reason and conviction, not by force or violence, and therefore all men are equally entitled to the free exercise of religion according to the dictates of conscience; and that it is the mutual duty of all to practice Christian forbearance, love, and charity toward each other.*

It will be remembered that Mr. Madison had been a witness to the wrongs perpetrated upon Baptists under the guise of toleration, and was therefore the better prepared to give heed to the formal application of that people to expunge a "term intrinsically fallacious and fraught with dangerous implications."

Animated by the victories already achieved, the Baptists now took fresh courage throughout the State of Virginia. Their work had just begun. They became more aggressive. Endurance of protracted wrong deepened their determination to break off the yoke of English tyranny. They stimulated every possible agency of opposition and set in motion a strong popular current which was pressing with increasing force against the Establishment, already quaking to its foundation. Others besides Baptists, who had previously held themselves somewhat aloof and had regarded the long and trying struggle with an air of conventional propriety, now joined the aggressive party against the Establishment. This was notably true of the Presbyterians, whose privileges had greatly exceeded those of the Baptists. The Hanover Presbytery for 1776, while entreating equal protection for all sects, asked to be exempt from the payment of taxes for the support of any church further than might be agreeable to their choice as individuals or because of voluntary obligations.[1]

The year 1776 being that during which the first session of the independent legislative assembly convened, was one of the most notable periods of our denominational history. Anticipating the assembly of the legislature, the Baptists were active for months throughout Virginia circulating petitions for the enrollment of the names of those who favored the extension of the benefits of religious liberty to every class of

---

[1] Foote, *Sketches of Virginia*, page 324.

citizens. When the General Assembly met in its initial session during this year, it found itself overwhelmed with such a flood of petitions as to compel the most serious consideration. This strong array of petitioners from every portion of Virginia, clearly forecast the approaching conflict. The "crowding" petitioners were referred to a committee of seventeen, of which Jefferson and Madison were members. A long and bitter contest followed, which is described by Jefferson in his autobiography as "the severest in which he had ever engaged." He further says: "After desperate contests in that committee almost daily from the eleventh of October to the fifth of December, a bill was brought in repealing the laws which restrained freedom of religious opinion or worship, exempting dissenters from all levies, taxes, and impositions whatever for the support of the Established Church." This was an overwhelming victory—a long stride toward absolute freedom.

But gigantic as had been the struggle, and well won as was the victory, the end of the contest was not yet reached. Seeing that the foundations of the Establishment were being gradually sapped, its friends became desperate in their efforts to arrest the tottering fabric. Consequently they succeeded in securing the passage of a declaration to the effect that provision ought to be made for continuing the succession of the clergy and for superintending their conduct.[1] There was in the bill passed an "express reservation whether a general assessment should not be established by law, on every one, for the support of the pastor of his choice; or whether all should be left to voluntary contributions."

Having gained so much, through legislative measures, the Baptists were willing to bide their time for a season, persuaded that their ultimate object would eventually be attained. But they were not idle as patriots and in the expression of loyalty to the cause of the colonies. Elder McClanahan, a Baptist minister from Culpeper County, raised a company of soldiers for the Continental service mainly from the members of Baptist churches. While he led them to battle as their captain, he ministered to their spiritual wants as their chaplain.[2] In commenting upon the preaching of Elder McClanahan, in connection with his service as captain of a company of volunteers, Howe takes occasion to remark that "the Baptists were the most strenuous supporters of liberty."[3] The valuable service rendered by our ministry to the cause

---

[1] Jefferson, *Works*, Vol. 1, page 39.
[2] Howe, *Virginia Historical Collections*, page 238.
[3] *Ibid.*, page 238.

evoked from Washington the declaration that "Baptist chaplains were among the most prominent and useful in the army."[1] Among those who shouldered their muskets and entered the ranks of the American army was Rev. David Barrow, one of the most eminent, as well as one of the most useful, of the Baptist ministry of that period. On the field of carnage he was as efficient as he had been in his peaceful ministrations at home.[2] Rev. Daniel Marshall, though an old man, was unremitting in his patriotic appeals in behalf of the struggle for independence, notwithstanding he was several times warned and threatened by the British soldiery. So persistent was he in denunciation of the mother country, that he was at last arrested and placed under strong guard; but having obtained leave to speak, he so overwhelmed his enemies with his exhortations and prayers, that they promptly set him free.

The influence by the Baptists against the crown was not restricted to any particular portion of the country. They were actuated by the same spirit throughout the entire South. The province of South Carolina was among the first to give expression of her loyalty to the provincial congress. She organized the "Council of Safety," as the executive power was called, composed of a body of thirteen eminent citizens. One of the chief concerns of this Council was, by public speaking, to bring the people into sympathy with the revolutionary movement, by conciliating them to the newly formed government, enlisting their support of it, and removing their prejudice and misapprehension. From the beginning of the Revolution, Rev. Oliver Hart and his church, at Charleston warmly espoused the cause of the country. By reason of his acquaintance and influence in the back country, Mr. Hart was chosen, together with Rev. William Tennent, another Baptist, and Hon. William H. Drayton, to arouse the patriotism of the Carolinians in behalf of the American cause.[3] Not less conspicuous for his influence and patriotism was Rev. Richard Furman Sr., D.D. Indeed he is said to have incurred the wrath of Lord Cornwallis so seriously that the British commander offered a considerable sum for his apprehension. According to Thomas Jefferson, two-thirds of the inhabitants of Virginia were dissenters when the Revolution began;[4] these were composed almost entirely of Baptists and Presbyterians. While the latter had a

---

[1] *Manning and Brown University*, page 136.
[2] Semple, page 359.
[3] Sprague, *Annals of the American Baptist Pulpit*, pages 48-49.
[4] Jefferson, *On the State of Virginia*, page 169.

number of eminent men, the number of their communicants was small when compared with those of the Baptists. This furnishes an indirect indication of the patriotism of Baptists during the great struggle for freedom.

With 1777 came a renewal of the determination on the part of the Baptists of Virginia to separate Church and State. Having that end in view, the General Association of Virginia at its session in 1777 appointed a committee to ascertain and report to that body whether there were existing in the Commonwealth any oppressive or ecclesiastical laws. The result of this action was an elaborate report setting forth the fact that quite a number of laws which seriously interfered with the exercise of religious liberty were still prevailing. This report gave rise to a formal and respectful address to the legislature by the General Association, calling attention to these oppressive and obnoxious laws, and with the transmission of the address was another inundation of petitions from the Baptists and Presbyterians protesting most vehemently against the maintenance of a State Church. Against these were arrayed the petitions from the Episcopalians and Methodists, as the latter at that period cooperated with the Establishment. The presentation of these conflicting documents before the lawmakers of Virginia occasioned no little interest. Out of this came a law suspending the collection of taxes for the support of religious teachers.[1] While this gave additional elation to the Baptists, it served to embolden them for future aggression.

Two meetings of the General Association were held during the year 1778. Encouraged by what had been accomplished at previous sessions, a committee on "civil grievances" was again raised, resulting in the submission of a report remonstrating most stoutly against a general assessment for the support of all denominations—a conciliatory measure which had been set on foot by the supporters of the Establishment to prevent the total wreck of that fated institution. The report also strongly inveighed against the law granting to Episcopal clergymen the exclusive right, under the penalty of illegitimacy of issue, to perform the marriage ceremony. These solemn protests took the same course as those of the year before—they were transmitted to the legislature by means of a most competent committee. It seems that the most that was accomplished by this Baptist delegation was favorable pro-

---

[1] Hawks, Vol 1, page 139.

spective action on the part of the legislature; for at the session of the General Association the following year, the draft of a bill establishing religious freedom was placed before the members of the General Association and it was generally approved. Here as before commissioners were appointed to visit the legislature, urging that body to legalize the marriages which, under the advice of Patrick Henry, dissenting ministers had celebrated. The result of this persistent activity of the Baptists was the enactment of a law repealing all laws authorizing the collection of taxes for the support of the clergy. Jefferson's estimate of this action was that "the Establishment of the Anglican Church was entirely put down." This was the result of an intense struggle on the part of the Baptists, which was prolonged through three years.

Some of those who entered into cooperation with the Baptists when the issue was first joined, forsook them when the matter of general assessment was forced into the struggle. Dr. Hawks, the Episcopal church historian, sums up the struggle thus:

> *In each successive meeting of the Legislature from 1776 to 1779, this quxstio vexata[1] was brought up for discussion. . . In 1779, all things being ready for a final vote, the question was settled against the system of a general assessment, and the Establishment was finally put down. The Baptists were the principal promoters of this work and, in truth, aided more than any other denomination in its accomplishment. Their historian boasts that they alone were uniform in their efforts to destroy the system of an assessment and to introduce the plan of a voluntary contribution. Whether this be so or not, it is very certain that in the Associations of that sect, held from year to year, a prominent subject of discussion always was as to the best modes of carrying on war against the Establishment.*

The year following that of the overthrow of the Establishment, the enactment of a law legalizing marriage by dissenting ministers was procured. As has been suggested, Patrick Henry urged Baptist ministers to disregard the law in the celebration of the marriage ceremony with the expressed opinion that this was the speediest method of sweeping it from the statute books—and it proved true. It is a remarkable fact, however, that four years after the Declaration of Independ-

---

[1] Latin for "Vexing Question"—Editor.

ence, oppressive laws were existing upon the pages of the colonial, or State, statute books.

We have now reached a period (1780-81) when the South was overrun by British troops. The theatre of war in the Southern provinces was Virginia and South Carolina. The well-known loyalty of Baptist preachers to the cause of freedom made them conspicuous objects of vengeance to the British commanders, and for some of these ministers handsome rewards were offered by the royal generals. Baptist church-es too were desecrated by being transformed into storage houses, temporary magazines, and field hospitals. Special delight seems to have characterized the seizure of these temples of worship and the reduction of them to hostile service. However, this ceases to be a matter of surprise when it is borne in mind that Baptists were the most ardent of dissenters and the most belligerent of patriots. In Virginia and the Carolinas, during the two years, 1780-81, the greatest demoralization prevailed among Baptist churches. Pastors were driven from their stations, flying sometimes for their lives, while many of them entered the army as chaplains or commanders; and congregations were broken up and scattered in every possible direction. The Revolution was the occasion of the early occupation by Baptists of regions westward. This movement preceded the opening of the Revolution, because of the exactions of the crown officers, and continued throughout the years of the gigantic struggle.

As we have seen, the utmost consistency was maintained by the Baptists of the South during the Revolutionary War. The struggle itself was only a more emphatic and sanguinary expression of the protests which had been made for a long period prior to the clash of arms. Throughout the years of the war Baptists were equally conspicuous in pressing the claims of liberty before legislative assemblies and in resisting the invasions of the royal armies. Speaking of the aggressive spirit of the Baptists in Virginia during this stormy period, Dr. Hawks, the learned Episcopal historian, says of them:

> *After their final success in the matter of voluntary contribution, their next efforts were to procure a sale of the church lands, and their efforts never ceased until the glebe lands were sold.*[1]

---

[1] Hawks, Vol. 1, page 53.

The Baptist General Association of Virginia was most unremitting in its efforts to snap the last bond that united Church and State. During both sessions, held in the years 1782 and 1783, committees on "Civil Grievances" were appointed and the two items, still dear to the Establishment—the retention of glebe lands and the popular assessment for the support of ministers of all denominations—were made themes of firm remonstrance. The usual committee was appointed to wait upon the legislature, but these measures were, for the time being, disregarded in view of the pressing demands of the political necessities of the time. In 1783 the General Association entrusted the matter of the direction of grievances to a General Committee composed of not more than four delegates from each district Association. This committee in 1784 renewed with vigor its protests before the legislature, arraigning before that body the proposed laws for general assessment, and the incorporation of religious societies, the vestry, and the marriage laws. A commissioner was deputed to bear the memorials of this committee to the legislature. This year, the General Assembly went so far as to pass a law authorizing all ministers to officiate at marriages.[1]

At the preceding session of the General Assembly, in 1783, action upon the general assessment bill was postponed in order that an expression from the people might be had. This served to elicit the full strength and influence of the Baptist denomination in Virginia. It was fully realized what was involved in this popular expression and Baptist influence was strained to its utmost tension. Under the direction and management of the General Committee, the people in the different counties were urged to prepare petitions against the proposed assessment as being repugnant to the spirit of the gospel and the freedom of religion. The text of the resolution upon which such action was based, in Virginia, read as follows:

> *Resolved, That it be recommended to those counties which have not yet prepared petitions to be presented to the General Assembly against the engrossed bill for a general assessment for the support of the teachers of the Christian religion to proceed thereon as soon as possible; that it is believed to be repugnant to the spirit of the gospel for the legislature thus to proceed in matters of religion; that the holy author of our religion needs no such compulsive measures for the promotion of*

---

[1] Semple, pages 34, 69-70.

his cause; that the gospel wants not the feeble arm of man for its support; that it has made, and will again, through divine power, make its way against all opposition; that should the legislature assume the right of taxing the people for the support of the gospel, it will be destructive of religious liberty.

The contest had been so ingeniously narrowed down by the opponents of the dissenters as to restrict the aggression almost entirely to the Baptists, who never stood more alone than now while they strove to defeat these adroit measures. Up to this time, the Baptists had been able to rely upon the friendly cooperation of the Presbyterians, but that communion was now divided. There were then arrayed against the Baptists: both the Episcopalians, the Methodists, and a goodly portion of the Presbyterians. The specious and insidious pretext of the opposition was that an assessment of the people should be made to provide a remedy for the alleged decay of morals and the general decline of religion.

The issue was squarely joined when a petition from the Isle of Wight County appeared before the legislature praying that everyone be compelled to contribute of his substance for the support of religion. Fortunately for the Baptists, they enjoyed the cooperation of such eminent representatives as James Madison, George Mason, and Thomas Jefferson. But they were in turn opposed by such patriots as Patrick Henry, George Washington, Richard Henry Lee, and John Marshall. The general assessment bill was championed by Patrick Henry, who was pitted against James Madison, who appeared as the leader of the opposition to that obnoxious measure. It was a struggle of giants. The discussion was vigorous and vehement. For a time, it seemed that the battle was lost to the Baptists. When the bill was ordered read the third time, that it might be put upon its passage, its advocates were confident. There was no hope left save in delay. Rallying the opposition to the measure, its managers succeeded in having action postponed to another session. This led to a representation of the matter to the masses of the people. Mr. Madison was foremost in calling popular attention to the subject in an admirable paper which was known as the *Memorial and Remonstrance,* which was extensively circulated and read by thousands. Meanwhile the advocates of assessment were by no means idle, for they circulated twenty-four copies of the bill in each county in the commonwealth. Upon the reassembling of the legislature in October, 1785, the great table in the Assembly hall almost sank under the weight of the petitions and remonstrance against the general assessment measure. Public protests were so overwhelming that the advocates of the measure surrendered without further struggle. Baptists had finally won.

As the friend of soul-liberty, Jefferson seized upon the opportunity which was now presented for the submission of the following bill looking to the establishment of religious freedom. This was adopted December 16, 1785, and is still the fundamental law of Virginia:

> *AN ACT TO ESTABLISH RELIGIOUS FREEDOM.*
>
> *Be it enacted by the General Assembly, That no man shall be compelled to frequent or support any religious worship, place, or ministry whatsoever, nor shall he be enforced, restrained, molested, or burthened in his body or goods, nor shall otherwise suffer on account of his religious opinions or belief; but that all men shall be free to profess, and by argument to maintain, their opinions in matters of religion, and that the same shall, in no wise, diminish, enlarge, or affect their civil capacities.*

There was not the slightest relaxation of effort on the part of the Baptists to wipe out the remaining traces of oppression and to thwart their enemies in efforts to procure such legislation as would entrench them in ecclesiastical supremacy. The General Committee now turned its attention to the opposition of the measure looking to the incorporation of the Episcopal society. At the meeting of this committee held in 1786, it was resolved,

> *That petitions ought to be drawn and circulated in the different counties and presented to the next General Assembly, praying for a repeal of the Incorporating Act, and that the public property which is by that act vested in the Protestant Episcopal Church be sold, and the money applied to public use, and that Reuben Ford and John Leland attend the next Assembly as agents in behalf of the General Committee.*

In this step the Presbyterians rejoined the Baptists, insisting that the act be repealed and the property distributed. In opposition to this pronounced expression, the Episcopal Convention recommended to the parishes throughout the State that petitions be prepared and presented offsetting the memorials of the Baptists and Presbyterians, but to no purpose; for on January 9, 1787, the law was repealed. The work to which the Baptists had applied themselves so assiduously for a long period was now almost completed, there being but one remaining element of the original Establishment which demanded their attention, and that was the settlement of the glebe land question. Passing judgment upon this, the General Committee decided that the glebe lands were the property of the people—rightly belonged to the public—because bought with money collected by taxes from the people generally. With this was coupled a solemn protest against its exclusive use by the minister of the parish in which the lands were located. This question had to be brought to the attention of the public in such way as to enable intelligent action to be taken.

Baptists were as industrious in the urgent prosecution of the claims of this question as they had been with every other. In 1799 their efforts were rewarded by the passage of an act recognizing the principle that all property belonging to the Episcopal Church devolved on the good people of the commonwealth. This was followed by an act in 1802 ordering the sale of the glebes. In a summary of these events, Dr. Hawks says:

> *Persecution had taught the Baptists not to love the Establishment. In their Association they had calmly discussed the matter, and resolved on their course. In this course, they were consistent to the end; and the war which they waged against the church was a war of extermination. They seem to have known no relentings, and their hostility never ceased for twenty-seven years.*[1]

When the struggle began, there was little or no encouragement to prosecute the work dear to the Baptists of the South. Almost hoping against hope because of the formidable odds opposing them, the Baptists steadfastly pursued their claims, holding every inch of ground gained, and gathering new boldness with each advantage, until there was a complete severance of Church and State. They were equally active in the field and in the legislative chamber for the consummation of the single purpose of securing to the new republic the fullest freedom. The ratification of the Federal Constitution by the Virginia Convention was largely due to the exertion and self-sacrifice of a Baptist minister,

---

[1] Hawks, Vol. I., pages 137-138.

John Leland. Mr. Madison being absent from the State on public business at the time when a representative was to be chosen, Leland was agreed upon as a candidate for the position which would have been occupied by Madison in the Convention of 1788, which convention was to ratify or reject the national constitution. Upon his return to Virginia, Madison visited Leland and spent some time with him, which resulted in the withdrawal of the latter from the race in favor of the former. Mr. Madison's presence in the convention was most opportune, as it is quite sure that the ratification of the constitution was due to that fact. The new constitution encountered the opposition of Patrick Henry who thought it "squinted toward monarchy." By reason of his personal popularity and splendid oratory he carried the people with him, and would have defeated ratification but for the influence of Madison. Commenting upon this, Senator John S. Barbour, of Virginia, asserts:

> *That the credit of adopting the Constitution of the United States, properly belongs to a Baptist clergyman, formerly of Virginia, named Leland. If Madison had not been in the Virginia Convention, the constitution would not have been ratified, and as the approval of nine States was necessary to give effect to this instrument, and as Virginia was the ninth State, if it had been rejected by her, the constitution would have failed (the remaining States following her example), and it was through Elder Leland's influence that Mr. Madison was elected to that Convention. It is unquestionable that Mr. Madison was elected through the efforts and resignation of John Leland, and it is all but certain that that act gave our country its famous constitution.*[1]

The national Constitution, while generally acceptable, was not faultless. Naturally enough it was most rigidly examined by those who had struggled so long and sacrificed so much for the young nation just now in its swaddling clothes. At the session of the General Association of Virginia in 1788, the General Committee had submitted for consideration the question, "Whether the new Federal Constitution, which had now lately made its appearance in public, made sufficient provision for the secure enjoyment of religious liberty?"

---

[1] Sprague, *Annals of the American Baptist Pulpit*, page 179.

A unanimous opinion was reached by the committee that it did not. This occurred three months previously to its ratification by the State Convention, in doing which that body made certain reservations among which was that the liberty or right of no denomination can be abridged by the government. Certain essential rights, among which was that of liberty of conscience, cannot be abridged, restrained, or modified. That there might be no doubt attendant upon the action of the Virginia Convention, the General Committee held a consultation with Mr. Madison as to future action, and afterward addressed a communication to President Washington on the same subject. After reference to their struggles for religious freedom, and after respectful allusion to the part taken by Washington in the contest, the Committee said:

> *The want of efficacy in the confederation, the redundancy of laws and their partial administration in the States, called aloud for a new arrangement of our systems. The wisdom of the States for that purpose was collected in a grand convention, over which you, sir, had the honor to preside. A national government in all its parts was recommended as the only preservation of the Union, which plan of government is now in actual operation.*
>
> *When the Constitution first made its appearance in Virginia we, as a Society, had unusual strugglings of mind, fearing that the liberty of conscience (dearer to us than property and life) was not sufficiently secured; perhaps our jealousies were heightened on account of the usage we received in Virginia under the British government when mobs, bonds, fines, and prisons were our frequent repast.*
>
> *Convinced on the one hand that without an effective national government the States would fall into disunion and all the consequent evils; on the other hand, it was feared we might be accessory to some religious oppression should any one Society in the union preponderate all the rest. But amidst all the inquietudes of mind our consolation arose from this consideration, the plan must be good, for it bears the signature of a tried, trusty friend; and if religious liberty is rather insecure in the Constitution, "the administration will prevent all oppression, for a Washington will preside." According to our wishes the unanimus voice of the Union has called you, sir, from your be-*

loved retreat to launch forth again into the faithless seas of human affairs to guide the helm of the States. Should the horrid evils that have been so pestiferous in Asia and Europe— faction, ambition, war, perfidy, fraud, and persecutions for conscience' sake—ever approach the borders of our happy nation, may the name and administration of our beloved President, like the radiant source of day, scatter all those dark clouds from the American hemisphere.

This letter to Washington was the wise and timely product of John Leland, a man of fertile resource, calm judgment, courageous disposition, and of ripe piety.

In reply to the letter, of which the foregoing is an extract, President Washington wrote:

If I could have entertained the slightest apprehension that the Constitution framed by the convention where I had the honor to preside might possibly endanger the religious rights of any ecclesiastical society, certainly I would never have placed my signature to it; and if I could now conceive that the general government might ever be so administered as to render the liberty of conscience insecure, I beg you will be persuaded that no one would be more zealous than myself to establish effectual barriers against the horrors of spiritual tyranny and every species of religious persecution. For you doubtless remember I have often expressed my sentiments that any man conducting himself as a good citizen, and being accountable to God alone for his religious opinions, ought to be protected in worshiping the Deity according to the dictates of his own conscience.

While I recollect with satisfaction that the religious Society of which you are members have been throughout America uniformly and almost unanimously the firm friends to civil liberty and the persevering promoters of our glorious revolution, I cannot hesitate to believe that they will be faithful supporters of a free yet efficient general government. Under this pleasing expectation I rejoice to assure them that they may rely upon my best wishes and endeavors to advance their prosperity. In the meantime be assured, gentlemen, that I entertain a proper sense of your fervent supplication to God for my temporal and eternal happiness.

> *I am, gentlemen,*
> *Your most obedient servant,*
> *George Washington.*

The outcome of this correspondence was the submission by James Madison, in the House of Representatives, of the first amendment to the Constitution of the United States. Although it encountered strong opposition at first, it was finally passed by the House and afterward approved by two-thirds of the States and became a law. The Baptists have all along insisted that the credit of this amendment belongs to them. It was for this that the appeal was made to Washington, who promptly recognized the wisdom of it. The request commended itself to the judgment of Madison also, and gave to him an additional opportunity to endear himself to the Baptists of the South by submitting the amendment and securing its passage.

The adoption of the first amendment to the Constitution should have ended the struggle; but it was not until 1798 that all the barriers were swept away and dissenters were admitted to equal privileges with the Episcopalians of America.

CHAPTER IV
DENOMINATIONAL EXPANSION

IN 1770 the Baptists of the South were, in point of numbers, quite a weak folk. At that period there were but few church organizations in the States now covered by the territory of the South. While a few of these were strong, relatively speaking, the most of them were feeble. Of the seventy Baptist churches reported for 1770, according to a recent author, only seven were accounted as existing in the South.[1] There were, however, known to be more than that. Still there were perhaps not so many as 10,000 Baptists in the United States when the Revolution began. The effect of that great struggle was to disperse the Baptist churches of the Southern provinces. Baptists were intensely enlisted in the cause of freedom, and almost none of the churches observed stated seasons of worship. For the most part, the pastors were enlisted as chaplains, or as soldiers in the ranks.

After the close of the war, however, there was a speedy reaction. Differences were forgotten in the single aim to unify the denomination in order to give a lasting effect to the achievements wrought. The sufferings and struggles which all had undergone in common, served to weld them the more easily after the gigantic contest had closed. This was illustrated by the easy fusion of the "Separate" and "Regular" Baptists of Virginia in 1787. This was the signal for union throughout the provinces, so that within a few years after the fusion in Virginia the denomination presented a united front. This spirit of unity which, in turn, was the result of that singleness of aim for the principle for which the Baptists of the South in common suffered and contended, was the fountain source of the denominational expansion with which the period following the Revolution was signalized. A grateful sentiment everywhere prevailed because of the achievement of liberty. Places of worship which had long been desecrated by the vile uses to which they were subjected by the enemy, were venerated more than ever before. Meeting-houses were rebuilt where they had been demolished, repaired where they had been damaged; and congregations gathered again with alacrity and gratitude, and resumed, without fear of interruption, the worship of God. Only the sufferers from persecution could realize how precious was the boon of freedom, and it is but natural that these people should be frequently found at their places of worship.

The beneficent reaction from the turbulent period of the Revolu-

---

[1] H.K. Carroll, LL.D. in *The Religious Forces of the United States*, page 25.

tion was favorable to the production of the grateful feelings which prevailed universally among the Baptists of the South. This spontaneous spirit which dictated an equally spontaneous worship, was the starting point of the phenomenal growth which characterized the denomination during the subsequent periods throughout the Southern States.

From this prevalent condition of the Baptist churches inevitably sprang a revival which not only greatly augmented the membership of the churches already existing, but rapidly multiplied the number of churches themselves. It seems that as early as 1784 there were in Virginia alone 151 churches and 14,960 members, and eight years later the number of churches had increased to 218, with a membership of 24,443. The revival wave swept into the opening years of the nineteenth century, so that in 1810-12 we find Virginia with 292 churches and 35,665 members. These numbers are furnished as to the resident membership of Virginia Baptist churches, although Semple estimates that between 1791 and 1810 fully one-fourth of the Baptists of Virginia removed to Kentucky. Notwithstanding that the Revolutionary period found the Baptists of the North far outnumbering those of the South, in 1814 there were nearly twice as many members in the Baptist churches of Virginia as in those of New York, and there were many more in Virginia than there were in all the New England States together.

The same spirit of revivalism extended into North Carolina; but it was not until 1800 that the most memorable revival in the annals of that State occurred. James McGready, a Scotch-Irish Presbyterian preacher, began a revival in North Carolina in the first years of the nineteenth century, which shook the State to its center, and which was soon felt in Kentucky, Tennessee, and Ohio. The return of peace had brought to most of the Carolina churches many demoralizing practices which required sturdy heroism to attack and expose. From the labors of this wonderful man, the Baptists derived immense increase to the membership of their churches throughout North Carolina.

Attention has already been called to the organization of the earliest churches in North Carolina, among which there were many struggling interests. In 1784 we find in the State 42 churches, with a membership of 3,276; eight years later, in 1792, the number of churches had increased to 94 and the membership to 7,503. The results of the McGready revival are manifest in the figures furnished for 1812, for then we find 204 churches in the State, with a membership of 12,567. As the churches of Kentucky were recruited from those of Virginia, so the churches of Tennessee derived their strength from those of North Carolina.

Some of the churches of South Carolina were almost extinguished by the Revolution. The part borne in the great struggle by the leader of the South Carolina Baptists, Oliver Hart, in arousing the patriotism of the colonists and in inciting them against the royal forces, so aroused the wrath of the British commanders that on the approach of their armies to Charleston, Pastor Hart was advised by his friends to seek a safe retreat. He made his way northward to Hopewell, New Jersey, and never again returned South. His church, which had so long been a center of evangelistic influence in southern South Carolina, was almost destroyed. With the restoration of peace, Mr. Hart was recalled to the pastorate of the church, but declined. Dr. Richard Furman was then called from the high hills of the Santee to Charleston, where he entered upon a career of marvelous usefulness on October 18, 1787. The membership was easily rallied and Charleston again became a controlling center of influence to the Baptist denomination in the South. The churches throughout South Carolina shared in the revival spirit which was now prevailing throughout all the Southern settlements. McGready, the noted revivalist, visited the State in 1802 and followed up the work which had been accomplished in North Carolina. Immense audiences thronged upon his preaching, variously estimated from four to eight thousand, drawn together from a group of districts, and even from many counties in Georgia. As was true in the West, here were the remarkable physical demonstrations attendant upon the revival meetings of the period. Sudden loss of strength, swoons, outcries, groans, involuntary but violent spasmodic jerkings of the body—all these manifestations were witnessed during these remarkable meetings in the Carolinas.

The growth of the denomination in South Carolina is indicated by the fact that in 1784 there were in the State 27 churches, with a membership of 1,620; by 1782, or within a period of eight years, the number of churches was almost tripled, there being then 70 churches, with a membership of 4,167; in 1812 the churches numbered 154, and the total membership was 11,325.

Only a passing notice has been given to Dr. Richard Furman, who became pastor at Charleston in 1787. Nothing could have been more fortunate than his settlement in the Charleston pastorate just at the time that he assumed the care of the church. Just rallying from the ill effects of the war, and realizing again its strength, for a long period the center of denominational influence in the State, with its opportunities and possibilities greatly increased by the changed conditions induced by the return of peace, the church at Charleston needed a master-hand, directed by consummate prudence, to grasp the situation and wield effectively the agencies within reach. These elements were combined in Richard Furman, who readily became the leader of Southern Baptists, and was the peer of any man in the denomination of the entire country. He was without university training, but was endowed with a high order of intellect, which was studiously cultivated by self-application until he became one of the most cultured men of the period. His tastes led him to retain the dress of the colonial gentleman long after it had been generally abandoned. He never failed to appear in his pulpit with the gown and bands. Favored with fortune, he made a liberal and judicious use of his means and wielded a commanding influence throughout the State. The subsequent prosperity of the churches of South Carolina is, in large measure, due to the influence of Richard Furman Sr., D.D.

The first churches constituted in Kentucky were, for a considerable period, in a sluggish condition. Though the population had increased to twenty or thirty thousand, and though eight Baptist churches had been in existence for years, still up to 1784 no one had been baptized in Kentucky. Assiduous missionary labors and earnest preaching seem to have availed nothing in the way of quickening spirituality in the churches or of arousing anxiety among the masses. But a revival was experienced in 1785 which drew the Baptist churches of that State into closer union, for no community of interest had up to this time bound them together. Two years later John Gano removed from New York to Kentucky, and contributed greatly to the efficient organization of the Baptists of the State. He was readily accorded the position of leadership in the denomination and was profoundly venerated to the close of his life.

Again, in 1789, a revival of profound and wide-reaching power prevailed throughout Kentucky. This revival was not restricted, however, to that State, but was prevalent throughout the upper States of the South, especially in Virginia. In some portions of Kentucky it lasted through a period of three years, and had the happy effect of blending the denomination into greater unity and of giving it greater efficiency.

During the period of this remarkable spiritual demonstration thousands were baptized and many new churches were constituted. This revival was followed by what is known as "The Great Revival" of 1800, in which nearly all the States of the South and West largely shared. This was the revival which began under James McGready in North Carolina, and which swept over the Southern and Western States and Territories and shortly changed the aspect of religious society. All opposition seemed to yield to the advancing tide of spirituality. Haunts of evil were closed, and the obscenity and profanity so characteristic then of the wayside inns and other places of popular resort gave place to prayer and praise. The multitudes of a given region would concentrate at the same point, spread their tents, and establish a "camp meeting." Persons rode on horseback and in wagons a distance of a hundred miles sometimes to attend these extraordinary gatherings. At a point near Paris it was believed that there were concentrated at one time as many as twenty thousand people. One of the occasions of worship is thus described by an eye-witness:

Here were collected all elements calculated to affect the imagination. The spectacle presented at night was one of the wildest grandeur. The glare of the blazing campfires falling on a dense assemblage of heads simultaneously bowed in adoration and reflected back from long ranges of tents upon every side; hundreds of candles and lamps suspended among the trees, together with numerous torches flashing to and fro, throwing an uncertain light upon the tremulous foliage and giving an appearance of dim and indefinite extent to the depth of the forest; the solemn chanting of hymns swelling and falling on the night wind; the impassioned exhortations; the earnest prayers, the sobs, shrieks, or shouts, bursting from persons under intense agitation of mind; the sudden spasms which seized upon scores and unexpectedly dashed them to the ground, all conspired to invest the scene with terrific interest and to work up the feelings to the highest pitch of excitement.[1]

Here were the most marvelous manifestations of physical excitement connected with that great movement. It is said that during a given service three thousand persons were known to have been prostrated at one time upon the ground in an apparently lifeless condition. Others were thrown into violent convulsions which were popularly called "the

---

[1] *History of the Presbyterian Church*, page 137.

jerks," while others rolled upon the ground or ran frantically here and there; others still, danced and sang; while still others barked like so many dogs. While the revival was largely directed by the Presbyterian ministry during its earlier stages, the Baptists were equally the recipients of its advantages. In 1790 we find in Kentucky 42 churches, with an aggregate membership of 3,105; in 1800, at the beginning of "The Great Revival," there were 106 churches, with a membership of 5,119; in 1803 there were 219 churches, with a membership of 15,495. One of the most salutary results of the series of revivals in Kentucky was the obliteration of the trifling differences which existed between the Separate and Regular Baptists. Several attempts had been made to bring about this fusion in Kentucky, but it was not consummated until 1801.

The Baptists of East Tennessee retained their associational connection with the Sandy Creek Association of North Carolina until 1786, when they entered into the constitution of the Holston Association, which at first embraced only seven churches. This region shared in the gracious results of the revival of 1800-1803, so that six years after its constitution the Holston Association included 36 churches, with a total membership of 2,500. From this, in consequence of its overgrown condition, was set off the Tennessee Association. Baptists did not become permanent in Middle Tennessee until during the Revolution, and about the year 1780. In 1791, Ambrose Dudley and John Taylor rode on horseback from Kentucky, a distance of two hundred miles, through an uninhabited region, to assist in the constitution of the Tennessee Church at the mouth of Sulphur Fork River. For three years this church stood a solitary outpost of evangelization, with no other nearer than one hundred miles. But when in 1794 White's Creek Church was planted in Middle Tennessee, this was the signal for an advance in the Baptist cause. The last-named church emigrated bodily from North Carolina under the lead of Elder Dorris and settled at the source of Sulphur Fork River. It appears that the removal of Mr. Dorris to Middle Tennessee proved to be a misfortune to the struggling cause in that region, for his presence was a source of disturbance alike to his church and to the Association of which it became a member. It was in this portion of Tennessee that the remnants of a disorganized church, which had been formed in 1765, were found. This original organization had been forced to disband in 1774 because of the atrocities of the Indians in that region. In 1797 there were five churches in Middle

Tennessee in such proximity as to enable them to constitute the Mero Association. Subsequent to this the Cumberland Association was formed, which had in 1806 a membership of 39 churches. The Elk River Association was created in 1806. In 1808 a sufficient number of churches withdrew from the Cumberland to form the Red River Association, and again, in 1810, another instalment severed their membership with the Cumberland and constituted the Concord Association. The expansion of the denomination in Tennessee is indicated by the following statistics:

In 1784 there were in the Territory of Tennessee six churches, with a membership of less than 400; in 1792 there were 21 churches, with a membership of 900; in 1812 the churches had increased to 156 with a total membership of 11,325.

About 1807 Baptists had extended southward into the Alabama Territory, where in the settlements, both in the northern and southern ends of the Territory, there was steady development. The denomination in Alabama did not begin to grow rapidly until after the battle of New Orleans and the consequent peace with Great Britain. With the close of that struggle and the attendant cessation of Indian hostilities in the South, immigration flowed rapidly into Alabama from the older States toward the east as well as from Tennessee.

But little progress was made by the Baptists of Georgia until after the Revolution. From Tuckaseeking, as a common center of his labors, Botsford extended his evangelistic efforts up and down the Savannah River, sometimes preaching in Georgia and again in South Carolina. On the Georgia side his labors extended as far north as the Kiokee settlement, and as far south as Ebenezer. Mr. Botsford was ordained to the full work of the ministry in 1773, by Oliver Hart and Francis Pelot. For years he was a most zealous and efficient missionary in the populous settlements of Georgia and South Carolina. When in 1780 Mr. Hart fled before the advancing British, Mr. Botsford accompanied him as far north as Virginia, but returned after the restoration of peace. The four or five struggling churches of Georgia might have become extinct during the stormy period of the war but for the heroism of Daniel Marshall. He seems to have been left alone by Abraham Marshall, his son, Silas Mercer, and Edward Botsford, all of whom sought safety in retreat during the hottest period of the Revolution. But defying all danger, Daniel Marshall labored on as indefatigably and serenely as if universal peace prevailed. To the three churches of Kiokee, Botsford, and Red Creek, which were constituted previous to the war, were added those of Little Brier Creek and Fishing Creek, which were formed by Daniel Marshall during the Revolution. There was still one other church, the name of which is not now known, which was situated on Buckhead Creek, the pastor of which, Matthew Moore, was a loyalist. During the Revolution the membership was scattered and the church became practically extinct. In 1787 it was revived through the efforts of Revs. James Matthews and Benjamin Davis, who gave it the name of Buckhead Creek Church.

With these few organizations as a nucleus, extending in a line up and down the Savannah River, the denomination began its marvelous development in Georgia after the declaration of peace with England. To Daniel Marshall more than to any other, are Georgia Baptists indebted for the successful planting of churches of our faith in the first period of their history. He was an ideal organizer, and was unremitting in his efforts to develop the churches of which he had the oversight. Wisely calling into exercise the gifts of the membership of a church, he developed them as fully as the prevailing conditions allowed. Embryonic indications were quickly observed by the wise pastor, and gifts were nourished into the fullest usefulness possible. From such spiritual tutelage came some of the brightest names of Georgia Baptist history—Alexander Scott, Sanders Walker, Samuel Cartledge, Silas Mercer, Abraham Marshall, Loveless Savidge, Samuel Newton, William Davis, Jeremiah Reeves, Joseph Baker, and others. Through the active missionary labors of such men, the denomination entered upon its new career in the years which followed the Revolution.[1]

The organization of churches into Associations was a fruitful means of expansion. This was notably true with the early churches of Georgia. In 1784 a meeting preliminary to the constitution of the Georgia Association was held, though the body was not formally organized until the following year. The stimulation resulting from the annual gathering of such bodies in these early times was shown in the multiplication of churches within their territory. For instance, in Wilkes County alone, within the territory of the Georgia Association,

---

[1] Beginning with one Baptist church in 1772, there were in Georgia two in 1773; three, in 1771; four, in 1777; seven, in 1780; eight, in 1782; nine, in 1781; eleven, in 1785: fifteen, in 1786; twenty, in 1787; thirty-three, in 1788; thirty-five, in 1789; forty-two, in 1790, and fifty-three, with a membership of nearly four thousand five hundred, in 1791.

there were organized twenty-two churches during the brief period of six years. By the year 1794, ten years after its constitution, the Georgia Association contained fifty-six churches, several of which were in South Carolina. The overgrowth of this body suggested the formation of the Hephzibah Association, and later still of the Sarepta, both of which were created from churches drawn from the parent organization. This was a period of enthusiastic progress to Georgia Baptists. The State was fortunate in having superior leaders from the beginning. Daniel Marshall, a man of rare powers with the masses, having died in 1784, his mantle of leadership fell upon Silas Mercer, a man of sterner qualities than his predecessor, but a preacher of great power and influence with the people. Mercer had removed from North Carolina to Georgia in 1775, and was trained for his life-work through the silent agency of Daniel Marshall. Mercer was cordially and ably sustained by Abraham Marshall.

In 1786 Rev. Jeremiah Walker made his appearance in Georgia after his deposition from the ministry in Virginia for unbecoming conduct. Just before leaving Virginia, however, he had been restored to the ministry. He was accompanied to Georgia by Mr. Tinsley, who had been his fellow-sufferer of persecution by imprisonment in Virginia. The early churches of Georgia had been singularly free from the taint of heterodoxy and had entered upon a career of great promise when Walker and Tinsley appeared upon the scene as the ardent advocates of Arminianism. They found ready sympathizers in two Baptist preachers, Matthew Talbot and Nathaniel Hall. Walker was a man of much popular dash, was able, and possessed of a fascinating oratory. With the assistance of those already named in this connection, he undertook to promulgate Arminian views in Georgia. In the very outset these men encountered the most obstinate resistance, accompanied by affectionate remonstrance on the part of the leaders of the denomination, with the hope of recovering the Arminian advocates from their error. For a period this was the occasion of much disturbance. Finally, when the disorderly elements refused to yield, they were finally expelled and order restored. Walker soon after died and his associates passed from public notice. Less toleration was accorded the presentation of Arminian views, perhaps, because the Methodists were contesting every inch of territory with the Baptists in pressing their claims upon public attention.

Among those who were becoming conspicuous for denominational leadership at that period was Sanders Walker, who was perhaps the first Baptist preacher ever ordained in Georgia. He was a Virginian by birth, but was attracted westward by the alluring reports prevalent in the other States of the advantages enjoyed in the newer territory of the West. He became a tower of strength in his adopted State.

Still farther westward, in Mississippi, the territory was rapidly occupied after the close of the war of 1812. But little denominational progress was made before that time. The conglomerate character of the population, coupled with the hostility of the Indians, forbade rapid headway until order was established. In the earlier years of the present century New Hope Church was constituted in Adams County; Bethel Church, in Bayou Sara; and New Providence and Ebenezer, in Amite.

In briefly reviewing the causes which produced this phenomenal growth of the Baptists, we may name as a prime factor the reaction from the persecution to which they were subjected during a large portion of the preceding century. This strain of long-continued persecution made the reaction one of great force and energy. Such harsh treatment not only gave a tremendous rebound to the persecuted, but it elicited a popular sympathy, to which was added an eager interest aroused by the uncurbed fervor of the preaching of the Baptist ministry. The conjunction of two such genial elements largely accounts for the rapidity of denominational expansion after the return of peace.

Another factor which operated to bring about this great spiritual upheaval was the missionary zeal of the early Baptist ministry of the South. The world never witnessed more consecrated earnestness than was displayed by these rude preachers of the early days of the denomination in the Southern States. Most of them came from the walks of common life, and were, for the most part, tillers of the soil. They would labor upon their farms until near the close of the week, studying their plain English Bibles at night, and at the proper time would start to their appointments, often more than forty miles away. Not infrequently in pioneer regions, where the trail of the Indian was the only means of uniting the different settlements, these hardy men would encounter streams swollen and bridgeless, but undaunted would swim to the opposite side and prosecute their journeys with alacrity. Their familiarity with the needs of the masses would enable them readily to meet the demands of every occasion. The popular esteem excited by their disinterested zeal made the utterances of these plain, unlettered men almost oracular. Disturbances of whatever character in the new settlements were often submitted to the calm decision of the pious Baptist missionaries, and the conclusions to which they were led by their rugged sense of right, not only enabled them to adjust difficulties, but gave to them a wonderful hold upon the popular mind and heart.

The strength and compass of this influence were increased by the fact that the labors of these men were uncompensated. Under the stress of existing conditions this was unavoidable. Through self-abnegation alone could the gospel be given to the rude settlers upon the frontier, as they were frequently subjected, for the first few years, to great privation. This unrequited labor gave to the early preacher unusual liberty and plainness of speech which he exercised without stint. Though advantageous at this time, this failure to exact compensation from the early churches proved a barrier in after years to church development in the South. When, as the result of such unflagging zeal and unremitting labor, churches began to multiply throughout the early settlements of the South and Associations began to be organized, evangelization became more systematic and effective. A Baptist organization, whether it was a church or a district Association, became at once an evangelistic center, and so surely as an unevangelized district lay within reach, just so surely did it fall under the influence of the progressive home missionary of the Baptists.

Following up their success by preaching Sunday after Sunday under the difficulties and embarrassments already named, these men of fiery zeal would quit their homes for weeks together, when their crops would no longer demand rigid attention, and preach day after day to assembled hundreds.

More rapid headway was gained by the Baptists of the South in the periods immediately succeeding the Revolution, by reason of the thorough accord of the polity of Baptist churches with the genius of the government and the republican spirit of the masses. If Baptists did much toward achieving American independence, the consummation of that event in turn did much for their denominational expansion. The reaction from royal dominion and from everything that pertained to the crown was terrible, and out of this condition sprang the revivals which swept in succession over the South for more than twenty-five years after the close of the Revolutionary War.

The unremitting endeavors of the Baptist ministry of this early period were not a little stimulated by the presence of Methodist circuit riders in all the settlements of the South. Bold, active, enterprising, and aggressive, these early Methodist ministers ardently disputed every inch of ground with the Baptist missionary. During the Revolution the Methodists had not proved steadfast as dissenters, and in the efforts of the Baptists to undermine the Establishment, they were oftener than otherwise in sympathy with the supporters of the crown. This operated with no little effect against the Methodists after the close of hostilities, but they were unchecked in sturdy effort. Baptists were more than a match for them in the rural districts, but in the centers of population the Methodists, for a period, gained a firmer footing. Popularity of method, coupled with an accommodation of requirement for church membership, did much to favor the progress of the Methodists in the growing towns of the South. There is little doubt that the aggressive front of this Revolutionary rival in the field of evangelism contributed in no small measure to the welding together of the two divisions of the Baptists of the South.

CHAPTER V
EDUCATIONAL WORK

The phenomenal growth of the Baptist denomination in the South in the early periods of its history suggested to a few of the most prominent among them the importance of providing for a better equipped ministry with which to organize and direct this great host which had enlisted under the denominational banner. With rare exceptions the ministry of the Baptists of the South at this period was composed of illiterate, but earnest and devout men. Among them were a few educated leaders who were the first to formulate methods by which the intellectual standard of the Baptist pulpit might be elevated. On account of several particulars this was a most formidable undertaking, which was assumed by a few courageous spirits, for it was manifest from the outset that such a praiseworthy enterprise would be resisted by the unlearned ministry. Some among the illiterate ministers seemed to regard such a suggestion as a reflection upon their ability to preach; others considered it as an impious hint that the divine call to the ministry was not complete without the patchwork of men; while others still looked upon such a proposal as a disposition to pander to individual and public pride. Thus it came to pass that a suggestion which was capable of the greatest good became, in the hands of the unenlightened and prejudiced ministry, a cudgel to be used against pious and progressive leaders.

Themselves illiterate, these very preachers, many of them in their opposition, found hearty support in the great uneducated masses which had been brought into the churches.

The Baptist denomination in the South, after the close of the extraordinary revival periods which distinguished the early years of the century, was a great unorganized, undisciplined mass, the dominating purpose of which seemed to be to do just as they might wish. If they were to accomplish the results for which, as a denomination, they seemed providentially destined, then efficient organization was necessary. But such organization was not possible without intelligent direction, and intelligent direction must necessarily begin with the local pastoral leaders. Thus the more progressive of the Baptist ministry thought in the beginning of the present century. But how was such a project to become operative when it was resisted largely by the class of men whom it sought to benefit? These men, sustained by the rank and file of the denomination, placed almost insuperable barriers in the way of this disinterested plan of denominational progress.

There was nothing of malice in the opposition shown by an unschooled ministry against intellectual development. Men were never sincerer than they. Herein lay the greatest factor of strength on the part of the opposition. Ignorance is the parent of prejudice, and prejudice is the foe of progress. United with religion this combination, in which religion usually forms a subordinate part, is generally resolved into a sublimated superstition. These honest, though unlettered men, ignorant of the laws of mental development and regardless of the total absence of divine promise to support their views, insisted that if called of God to preach there would be supernatural provision for the duty as occasion might require. This they honestly believed and earnestly advocated in the presence of assembled multitudes as ignorant as their reputed leaders themselves, if not more so. Undaunted by these grave odds and realizing the immensity of their undertaking, such men as Furman and Pelot, of South Carolina, and Holcombe and Mercer, of Georgia, together with a few others throughout the South, resolved upon the creation of means for the better equipment of the Baptist ministry. Without concert of action these men, in widely separated States, were moved by the same impulse because the conditions were everywhere the same throughout the States of the South. As a beginning, means were raised with which to purchase books, and wherever practicable ministers were gathered into classes and taught. In the course of time these small beginnings were suggestive of ampler provisions and finally of schools for the better training of the Baptist ministry. From these crude original plans grew the denominational colleges now to be found in all the Southern States.

The earliest associational and conventional organizations in the South were founded upon a dual idea, denominational extension and the education of the ministry. This work began as far back as the pastoral administration of Oliver Hart in Charleston prior to the Revolution, for it was he who first moved in the matter of constituting a distinct Association. Into this original organization three churches entered—the First Church of Charleston, Ashley River, and Welsh Neck. This action took place as early as 1751. The chief agents in this progressive movement were the pastors of the churches named—Oliver Hart, John Stevens, and Philip James. Early the following year they were greatly reinforced by Francis Pelot, pastor of Euhaw Church, who was a man of ample means, for according to Morgan Edwards, he "owned three islands and about three thousand seven hundred and eighty-five acres on the continent, with slaves and stock in abundance."

In 1775 John Gano became an evangelist of the Charleston Association. One of the chief cares with which he was charged was that of seeking out gifted young men called of God to preach and to recommend them to the Charleston Association. In 1756 an educational fund was raised by the Charleston Association amounting to one hundred and thirty-three pounds. Among those who became the beneficiaries of this fund were Evan Pugh, Samuel Stillman, and Edmund Botsford. These early South Carolina pastors were liberal contributors to Rhode Island College during the presidency of Dr. Manning, with whom Mr. Hart was intimately acquainted.

These incipient efforts in education were cut short by the Revolution. Manifestly the least possible in educational matters had been done in the South when the period of hostile agitation came. Considering that which had been accomplished, it is remarkable that denominational progress in the Southern States up to the close of the Revolution was due to the work of an uneducated ministry. The success achieved during these trying times by men untrained in the schools remained for a long period a barrier to enlarged ministerial and pastoral development.

In 1788 President Manning addressed a letter to the Virginia Baptists through the general committee, urging them to take steps to establish a seminary of learning. The only action taken, in consequence of this communication, was the adoption of a resolution to appoint a committee "to forward the business respecting a seminary of learning." The matter dragged its slow length along until 1793, when it was revived and committed to the hands of Rev. John Williams and Mr. Thomas, who submitted a plan which was at the time deemed practicable, but was subsequently dropped, the question being dismissed. The subject was revived in 1809, when it seems that the only two subjects before the General Meeting of Correspondence of the Virginia Baptists were "the religious education of children and the establishment of some seminary or public school to assist young preachers to acquire a literary knowledge." The question which related to the establishment of an institution of learning was referred to a committee of two "to acquire information and digest a plan for such a seminary." But nothing came of all this until many years later. The utmost that was accomplished by such action was to keep the subject before the mind of the denomination. In order to meet the deficiency, every kind of makeshift was resorted to. The general plan in a given section of country was to establish a ministerial library by means of a common fund and lend the books to such young ministers as might be desirous of improvement. In not a few instances the most learned of the ministry would assume the task of the voluntary instruction of such as were willing to accept it.

Among those who rendered valuable help to young ministers should be named Dr. John M. Roberts, pastor of the High Hills of Santee Church, South Carolina. For a number of years this scholarly preacher gave gratuitous instruction to the beneficiaries of the Education Fund of the Charleston Association.

During the first quarter of the present century much time and thought was devoted by Southern Baptists to the matter of education. To the need of the times, growing more imperatively manifest every year, were added the fervid injunctions of Luther Rice, whose devotion to the sacred cause was equally divided between missions and education. Nothing was more manifest than an increasing need of preachers of ability and influence to occupy the pulpits of the growing centers of population; but there was not sufficient unanimity of sentiment in any of the States of the South to devise a plan for denominational instruction. Resolutions abounded, committees were appointed, and reports were adopted without number; but no practical shape was given to the matter. Added to the difficulties already named was another which was a silent barrier to the general plan of creating institutions of learning, that of the rapid development of the virgin resources of the new States of the South. This brought general prosperity to the entire region, and individual fortunes to thousands. Among the favored ones were many Baptist preachers who would come into the possession of lands and slaves which gave to them both means and leisure to prosecute their studies privately. The most active and wide-awake in the management of temporal affairs, they were, as a class, the most progressive, ambitious, and talented of the ministry. Their interest in the matter was largely neutralized by their failure to appreciate the emphatic necessity of an institution for the betterment of the ministry generally.[1]

In the revival of the spirit of denominational education in the South near the close of the first quarter of the present century, we find South

---

[1] Semple, pages 116-117.

Carolina again in the lead. The same cause which led to the constitution of Associations after the multiplication of churches, now operated to induce the organization of State Conventions when Associations had been greatly increased—that of giving stability, regularity, and uniformity to denominational enterprise. Foremost in this work was Dr. Richard Furman, who was instrumental in procuring an assembly of delegates from the Charleston, Savannah River, and Edgefield Associations, in the city of Columbia in 1821. The result of this meeting was the formal organization of the Baptist State Convention of South Carolina, with Dr. Furman as president. An address was prepared by the distinguished president to be submitted to the Baptists of the State, in which address great emphasis was laid upon the importance of an educated ministry. Anticipating objections that might be raised against this suggestion, Dr. Furman disposed of them, one by one, in a most masterly way. Time was needed for this sentiment to take root. The year following, Dr. W.B. Johnson, who succeeded Furman as president of the body, took up the same subject and discussed it more fully still.

In order to ultimate success, and for reasons of economy, the Baptists of South Carolina were desirous of cooperating with those of Georgia in the establishment of an institution of learning in common, for the denomination in both these States was agitating the question of providing means for the better equipment of the ministry. The question of ministerial education was that which underlay all the denominational male colleges founded by the Baptists in the South and to every one was there a theological department attached until the institution of theological seminaries in the country. The plan for establishing a cooperative institution between the Baptists of Georgia and South Carolina was settled upon and negotiations entered into with every indication of success; but the obstruction of State lines could not be overcome and the undertaking fell through.

Consequently, in 1826 the Convention of South Carolina established a school at Edgefield Courthouse and called it the Furman Academy and Theological Institution, and Prof. J.A. Warne was placed in charge of it. The books which had been gathered for the use of ministerial students by the General Committee of the Charleston Association formed the nucleus of a library for the new institution. But the enterprise was short-lived, perishing after the second year. Still the better training of the ministry remained a burning question. What should be done under the stress of circumstances? A practical answer to this question was undertaken by the retention of the theological department of the extinct institution, over which was placed Rev. Jesse Hartwell, after its removal to High Hills. In 1829 Mr. Hartwell was formally elected principal of the Furman Theological Institution. During the following year, Samuel Furman, a son of the late Charleston pastor, was associated with Mr. Hartwell as co-principal. After a struggle for life extending through two or three years, the institution perished. Still the urgent necessity of such an institution remained. In 1835 another effort was made in Fairfield district, where there was associated with scholastic training the idea of manual labor. For a period of years this was a favorite scheme in the South—this union of mental and manual labor—and yet no theory ever failed more signally to eventuate in practical result. Under the principalship of Prof. W.E. Bailey, late of Charleston College, the mongrel institution, manual, classical, and theological, was begun. It was not without tokens of success. New buildings, a well-equipped faculty, and encouraging patronage gave to the young enterprise much assurance of success; but the buildings were burned in 1837, Professor Bailey resigned a year later, and the school suspended in 1840. Subsequent enterprises were undertaken with varying fortunes during the next decade, with which, at different times, were conspicuously connected Dr. Hooper, late of the University of North Carolina; Professor Maginnis, who was afterward connected with the institutions at Hamilton and Rochester, N.Y.; and Rev. J.L. Reynolds and Prof. Jeremiah Chaplin Jr. From these efforts and struggles was finally developed Furman University which was established in 1851.

The Baptists of no State have made a better record in matters educational than those of Georgia, nor have the Baptists of any State been more highly favored with gifted leadership. One of the foremost promoters of education in Georgia was Dr. Henry Holcombe, who was originally a Revolutionary officer. Born in Virginia and reared in South Carolina, he entered the American army while quite a young man and rose to distinction. Being led to a study of the New Testament he was convinced of his duty, and promptly mounted his horse and rode twenty miles from camp in order to be baptized. Returning he delivered a sermon to his command while still sitting astride his horse. In 1785 he was ordained to the ministry, and at once took a conspicuous place in the denomination of his adopted State, Georgia. He was chosen a delegate to the State Convention which adopted the national constitution. Afterward he became pastor of the Euhaw Church, South Carolina, and later became pastor at Savannah. It seems that the Baptist meeting-house at Savannah was being rented by the Presbyterians at the time of Mr. Holcombe's call. The few Baptists of the city had suggested that a call be made to Dr. Holcombe to serve jointly the Presbyterians and the Baptists. Under these peculiar conditions he accepted the call upon a salary of two thousand dollars, which was perhaps the largest that had ever been received by a Baptist pastor up to that time. In 1800 he organized a Baptist church with a membership of ten, which ran up to sixty within two years more. He was a true yoke-fellow with Furman in devising and prosecuting methods for denominational expansion. Like the pastor at Charleston, Holcombe was magnificent in his physical proportions, being six feet two inches high, and weighing three hundred pounds. Among his public services may be mentioned his origination of the Georgia penitentiary system and the part borne by him in founding the Savannah Female Orphan Asylum.

But the most signal services rendered by him were in conjunction with the efforts of Jesse Mercer to procure concert of action in the denomination along the lines of missions and education. Holcombe was the first to give distinct expression to denominational education in Georgia by founding the Mt. Enon Academy for the education of Baptist youth. Public interest in denominational education did not begin to manifest itself in Georgia until 1825. Among the items contributed that year by the Baptists of Georgia was the sum of seventeen dollars and fifty cents for ministerial education. Under the inspiration of a sermon preached the following year by Dr. W.B. Johnson, of South Carolina, the sum of one hundred and eight dollars was collected "for the education of pious young men." A beneficiary was adopted in consequence, and the executive committee was instructed "to prepare some plan by which a fund for bestowing a theological education upon beneficiaries might be provided." This was the first step in the direction of denominational education taken by the Baptists of Georgia. The same conditions prevailed in Georgia which existed elsewhere throughout the South—the majority of the Baptist ministers were unlearned but consecrated men, while some of them were very ignorant. Exceptional instances were found in such men as W.T. Brantley Sr., Jesse Mercer, Adiel Sherwood, Henry J. Ripley, Iverson L. Brooks, J.P. Marshall, B.M. Sanders, and J.H.T. Kilpatrick. These led in the first movement to establish an institution of learning of high grade. While many supported such a project, many more opposed it.

The retirement of Holcombe from Georgia to accept a call from Philadelphia left Jesse Mercer the acknowledged leader of the Baptists of the State. Henceforth he became the zealous apostle of denominational progress, stoutly resisting the opposition which arose formidably from many quarters. While those whose names have been furnished gave him substantial aid and sympathy, his truest yokefellow was perhaps Adiel Sherwood, who was both a preacher and an educator. "While pastor at Eatonton he was principal of the academy at that place and did excellent service in a variety of ways for the denomination. He was an enthusiastic assistant of young men looking to the ministry, and was instrumental in the preparation of a number for their work, among whom was Jesse H. Campbell.

The Baptists of Georgia manifested their interest in general educational matters during the twenties by liberally contributing to Columbian College in response to the appeals of Luther Rice, through whom and Jesse Mercer they contributed not less than $20,000 to that institution. This liberality was in large measure due to the fact that Jesse Mercer was a trustee of Columbian College. Among the means employed with marked success by Mr. Mercer to further denominational interests was *The Christian Index*, the columns of which he employed with powerful effect in parrying the blows of the opponents of education and missions, and making possible at that time those interests among Georgia Baptists.

The Georgia Baptist Convention was organized in 1822. The suggestion of the constitution of such a body came first from the Sarepta Association, but the year following it rescinded its action. The Georgia Association, together with the Ocmulgee, met at Powelton in June, 1822, and formally organized the body. By degrees other Associations fell into line and evangelistic and colportage work[1] was pressed with all the vigor possible. A turn in the tide of affairs came a little later, however, and it seemed, from the great opposition encountered by the supporters of the Convention, that it would go to pieces. But a most propitious period of the Convention was just ahead, for in 1829 Josiah Penfield bequeathed to the Convention $2,500 as the basis of a permanent fund for the purposes of theological education, to be paid on con-

---

[1] A distribution of Bibles and other religious materials.—Editor.

dition that an equal sum be raised by the Convention. The sum was speedily raised, Jesse Mercer heading the list with $250, Dr. Cullen Battle following with $200, and others still following with similar amounts. At the session of the Convention for 1831 it was resolved, "That as soon as the funds will justify it this Convention will establish in some central part of the State a classical and theological school." It was further provided that this was to be connected with a manual labor department, and that only those preparing for the ministry should be admitted. Adiel Sherwood promptly pledged himself to raise by subscription $1,500 for the purchase of needed lands. In 1832 an eligible site for the location of Mercer Institute was purchased in Greene County, and in honor of Josiah Penfield the village was named for him.

The rapid progress of the denomination and the preparations of the Presbyterians to establish a college of high rank, prompted Jesse Mercer to undertake greater achievements. He aroused much popular enthusiasm by proposing the erection on a magnificent scale of a great institution of learning at his home at Washington, Georgia, to be known as "The Southern Baptist College." A charter was promptly obtained and agents went to work to raise an endowment fund. $100,000 was soon subscribed, and no doubt the plan would have been realized had a financial crash not come at that time. As a result the value of the subscriptions was depreciated, the charter had to be surrendered, popular enthusiasm cooled, and before the financial crisis had spent its force the possibility of reviving the suspended interest had passed. Such of the subscriptions as could be transferred to the institution at Penfield were diverted to that purpose, and thus began Mercer University.

B.M. Sanders became the president, S.P. Sanford one of the professors, and Adiel Sherwood was elected professor of theology. Mercer gave to the institution, including his bequest, about $43,000. Several efforts were made to remove the institution from Penfield; but no change of location was effected until 1870, when it was removed to Macon. The presidents of the institution have been: Sanders, Smith, Dagg, Crawford, Tucker, Battle, Nunnelly, and Gambrell.

The avowed purpose of the formation of the Baptist State Convention of North Carolina was the creation of means for denominational education. At the meeting of the Convention in 1832 it was definitely recommended by the committee on education and unanimously adopted by the Convention "to purchase a suitable farm, and to adopt other preliminary measures for the establishment of a Baptist literary institution in this State upon the manual labor principle." During the same year 615 acres of land were purchased in Wake County, but the school was not opened until 1834. It was called Wake Forest Institute, and Samuel Wail, of New York, was elected principal. Beginning with an enrollment of twenty-five students, the number was soon increased to seventy.

At first the students were required to perform three hours of manual labor daily; this, however, was soon reduced to one hour each day. The hoe and the plow were, however, made the concomitants of the desk and the blackboard throughout the year. During the second year the school was blessed with a revival which planted it deeply and permanently in the hearts of the denomination. In 1838, by an amendment of the original charter, the name of the school was changed to that of Wake Forest College. Ten years later the college was overwhelmed with a debt of $20,000 and seemed ready to sink. The outlook was sufficiently despairing to induce both the president of the Board of Trustees and of the college to resign. At this juncture Elder James S. Purefoy undertook a voluntary agency to lift the burden, which he valiantly succeeded in doing the first year. With this the institution took a fresh bound forward, so that by 1861 it had an endowment of $46,000, the raising of which was mainly due to the indefatigable efforts of President Wingate. Wake Forest College emerged from the wreck of war with an available endowment of only $14,000. By being wisely administered the endowment steadily increased, and by the close of 1883 the college had an endowment of $100,000, one tenth of which had been a gift of Mr. J.A. Bostwick, of New York. In 1886 he added the princely gift of $50,000, and yet again in 1890, being desirous of aiding the college and at the same time of stimulating the Baptists of North Carolina to self-help, Mr. Bostwick offered to add one-half to whatever amount up to fifty thousand dollars might be raised for the endowment by March 1, 1891. When the time expired there had been raised $26,000. The institution is at present in a most flourishing condition. The presidents of the college have been Waite, Hooper, Wingate, Pritchard, Boyall, and Taylor.

The proximity of Columbian College to Virginia, and the interest shared in that institution by the Baptists of that State, doubtless had much to do with the delay of the establishment of a denominational school in the State. But by the year 1830 it was seen that Columbian College was inadequate to the growing demands in Virginia for a better qualified ministry. This consideration led to the founding of the Virginia Baptist Education Society, with a view of "devising and proposing some plan for the improvement of young men who, in the judgment of their churches, are called to the work of the ministry." Of this Society John Kerr became the president and James B. Taylor the secretary. A committee, composed of W.F. Broadus, J.B. Taylor, J.B. Jeter, and H. Keeling, was appointed to draw up a plan and report upon the expediency of distinct action relative to providing means for the more efficient qualification of the ministry. In its report the committee made declaration of the fact that it recognized the importance as well as the obligation of continued loyalty to Columbian College. It further stated that in its judgment it was not deemed expedient to undertake the immediate establishment of an institution of learning under the auspices of Virginia Baptists. As far as the committee would venture was the suggestion of placing the ministerial beneficiaries "in the families of experienced ministering brethren whose education, libraries, and opportunities to give useful instruction may enable them to render essential service to their younger brethren." With this was coupled the idea of enabling ministerial students to become self-supporting by laboring in the surrounding regions of country. But this crude arrangement was necessarily short-lived. Other States were pressing forward in educational work and their young ministers were being fitted for future labor under the most encouraging conditions possible. It was soon discovered that if Virginia Baptists were to maintain the position which they had held for a half-century, something more was needed to be done than to adopt a haphazard plan like the one set forth, and none were more ready to abandon it than the eminent men who recommended it. That abandoned, the inevitable plan of a manual labor school was adopted. A site was bought in the neighborhood of Richmond; Robert Ryland, a graduate from Columbian College, was elected to preside over it; and the school was duly named the Virginia Baptist Seminary. Mr. Ryland discouraged the attempt to organize a school at once, but the popular current in favor of the prompt opening of such an institution was too strong to be stemmed. Failing in this objection he sought to have eliminated from it the manual labor feature; but he failed in this also. While he detected in the existing plan elements of failure, he wisely surrendered his convictions and awaited practical demonstrations for a vindication of his views. Mr. Ryland soon illustrated his practical knowledge of the science of agriculture by seeking to enrich a field of corn with salt, placing a handful at the root of each stalk and—killing it! He was not without the greatest diligence in seeking to make the enterprise successful, but he soon found himself almost alone in his efforts, as the denomination left the institution largely to shift for itself. After an experiment of two years the manual labor feature was shown to be unpractical, as usual, the farm was sold, and an attractive property was bought within the city limits of Richmond. It was not until 1840 that a college was established by the Baptists of Virginia. Perhaps, after all, there was advantage in the delay, as the denomination came to have a loftier conception of a college at a later period than it evidently had fifteen years before Richmond College was founded. Additional advantage was gained by the unsurpassed instruction given at the University of Virginia, the influence of which was most stimulating and elevating throughout the State. The leading denomination of Virginia with its splendid record could not afford to establish an institution of inferior character within so short a distance of the famous university.

The Civil War found Richmond College with an endowment of $100,000, the most of which was lost in consequence of that great struggle. Prostrated as the people were by the war, they rallied anew to the support of Richmond College, and in 1866 it was enabled to open its doors again to students. Like other denominational colleges in the South, Richmond College has been the recipient of Northern benefactions, without which it could not have so speedily rallied; but with such assistance, it has been placed upon a solid basis and is perhaps the most advanced, in its standard of instruction, of all the Baptist colleges of the South.

The Baptists of Kentucky were among the first of the States of the South to take steps to found a denominational school. A charter for Georgetown College, then known as Georgetown Literary and Theological Institution, was procured as early as 1829. Dr. William Staughton, a minister and educator of distinction, who had been president of Columbian College, was called to the president's chair, but died in Washington while on his way to Kentucky to assume the office to which he had been elected. In 1830 Dr. Joel S. Bacon was elected to succeed him. Dr. Bacon at once found himself involved in serious complications with the Disciples, who were at that time breaking with the Baptists throughout the State, and whose claims against the school were such as to plunge it into litigation. After struggling against adverse conditions for two years, he resigned. The institution dropped to the level of a high school, in which condition it remained until 1838. Rockwood Giddings having now become president, he addressed himself to the work of procuring subscriptions for an endowment, and raised $80,000. In 1840 Dr. Malcom succeeded Giddings as president, and raised the standard of the college above that which it had ever enjoyed. Then followed the presidencies of Drs. Reynolds, Campbell, Crawford, Manly, and Dudley—the last named being a descendant of the famous pioneer preacher, Ambrose Dudley. Georgetown College is at present presided over by Dr. A.C. Davidson and is in a most prosperous condition.

Bethel College, in the same State, was projected by Bethel Association in 1849. Begun as a high school, it was elevated to the standard of a college in 1856, when Mr. Blewett became its first president. With the exception of two years during the war, the school has been in successful operation ever since it began. Its presidents have been George Hunt, Professor Rust, Noah K. Davis, LL.D., at present professor of Moral Philosophy in the University of Virginia; Leslie Waggoner, sometime president of the University of Texas; and Dr. W.S. Ryland, who is the present incumbent of the presidential chair. The college enjoys an endowment of $100,000.

In 1845 the Western Baptist Theological Institute was located at Covington, Kentucky, and had the misfortune to be an object of contention as long as it existed. Located on the border at a time when sectional passion was highest, it was destined to be short-lived. It ran a troublous course of ten years, when the valuable property was sold and the proceeds were divided between the irreconcilable elements. The Ministerial Education Society of Kentucky was constituted in 1844, and as is indicated by its name, its object was "to aid in acquiring a suitable education, such indigent, pious young men of the Baptist denomination as shall give satisfactory evidences to the churches of which they are members that they are called of God to the gospel ministry." Meagerness of resources limited the operations of this society, yet in a quiet way it rendered much valuable aid to young men fitting themselves for the ministry. The final success of Georgetown College obviated the necessity of the continued existence of the society.

Like Kentucky, Tennessee had two institutions of learning belonging to the Baptists—Union University, at Murfreesboro, and Carson College, in Jefferson County. After the accomplishment of some excellent work under President J.H. Eaton, and Dr. J.M. Pendleton as theological professor, Union University became extinct. Its career was doubtless shortened by the Civil War. In 1873 another institution was founded at Jackson, known as the Southwestern University,[1] which is now under the successful management of President M.C. Savage.

Carson-Newman College, formerly Carson, was founded near the town of Mossy Creek in 1850. It was chartered under the patronage of the General Association of the State and derived its name from its chief benefactor, Hon. James H. Carson, who bequeathed to the institution $15,000, the interest of which was to be used in the education of young ministers. The institution has of late years come into the possession of a partial endowment, and is at present presided over by President J.T. Henderson.

Early in the thirties, the Baptists of Alabama began the agitation of the question of establishing a denominational school, suggested, as in other States, by the growth of the Baptists and the inefficiency of their ministry. In resolving to establish such a school the Baptists of Alabama adopted the manual labor plan, in spite of its failures in other States. At this time the leaders of the denomination were D.P. Bestor, Hosea Holcombe, Alex. Travis, J.H. DeVotie, and A.G. McGraw. In 1834 provision was made for the contemplated school to go into operation as soon as practicable with two departments, literary and theological. W.L. Williford became the first principal, and D.P. Bestor was elected to deliver lectures upon theology. After a brief career the enterprise failed, and in consequence, the Baptists of Alabama found themselves loaded with debt, after wrestling with which for a period, the denomination sold the property and for a number of years abandoned the matter of education altogether. Meanwhile the deficiency was met as far as was practicable by supplying young ministers with theological works. Driven by sheer necessity to establish a school to meet the urgent demands of the denomination, Howard College was organized in 1842. Under the able management of S.S. Sherman, it was gradually developed into a respectable collegiate institution. From the period of its establishment to the outbreak of the Civil War it was ardently fostered by the Baptists of Alabama. After an eventful history

---

[1] Now known as Union University.—Editor.

of almost fifty years, the college was removed from Marion, its original location, to East Lake, near Birmingham, where it now is. At the outbreak of hostilities in 1861, the college was in the enjoyment of a handsome endowment, which was entirely wrecked by the war. Efforts to endow the institution within the last twenty-five years have been unavailing. In spite of its vicissitudes the college has continued to do excellent work. Its presidents have been S.S. Sherman, H. Talbird, S.R. Freeman, J.L.M. Curry, J.T. Murfee, B.F. Riley, and A.W. MeGaha.

Not unlike that of the other States, the educational work of the Mississippi Baptists was at first fragmentary and unsatisfactory. The State Convention was founded upon the dual idea of education and missions. The school which ultimately came into the possession of the Baptists had rather a checkered career. Chartered in 1826 as Hempstead Academy, its name was changed by legislative enactment the following year to that of Mississippi Academy, for the endowment of which the Board of Trustees was authorized to raise by lottery $25,000. For four years the rents arising from thirty-six sections of the school fund donated by the national government to the State was given to the academy. In 1830 the name of Mississippi College was given to the institution, and in 1842 it was transferred to the Presbyterians, who retained it just eight years. Having been surrendered to the State at a time when the Baptist Convention of Mississippi was assembled at the capital, the college was tendered to that body and accepted. Once in their possession, the Baptists promptly placed an agent in the field, who raised for its endowment within ten years $100,000 in cash, and $30,000 in subscriptions. With the war came a suspension of operations and the destruction of the endowment. In 1867 Dr. Hillman became president, and found the institution encumbered with a debt of $10,000, which he promptly liquidated, placed the buildings in repair, and by 1873 raised an endowment of $40,000. The college is located at Clinton and is a largely attended and popular institution.

Until a comparatively late period the Baptists of Louisiana were dependent upon institutions in other States for the education of their youth. In the pioneer movement of the denomination in this State in the matter of education, there was an attempt made to place an institution upon a higher plane than had been made in most of the other States of the South. A full-fledged university, at least in name, was at first contemplated at Mount Lebanon, to be known as the Mount Lebanon University. This enterprise was projected by Dr. B. Egan, who was warmly supported by Rev. George W. Bains, the pastor of the church at Mount Lebanon. For five years, beginning with 1847, the subject was agitated. Nor was anything done as late as 1852, save to determine the establishment of a school of high grade "with a theological department connected therewith...and as auxiliary to the object, a female seminary."[1]

Rev. W.H. Bayless was chosen financial agent by a newly organized Board of Trustees, and soon raised $107,068.12. A lot was procured and a building of sufficient capacity to accommodate two hundred students was arranged for. William E. Paxton, A.M., was chosen to institute the new enterprise by opening the school for the preparatory department. This he did in March, 1853, with an attendance of about twenty-five students. At a subsequent meeting of the State Convention in July the sum of $5,280 was subscribed to the theological endowment fund.

In 1856 the collegiate department was organized and Dr. Bartholomew Egan was chosen as president with a corps of four professors. Both the president and the professor of theology agreed to serve gratuitously, while the other instructors served in the preparatory department. Commendable zeal was manifested by all engaged in the struggling enterprise, and by the close of 1857 a fund equal to $25,000 had been raised. The services of Rev. Jesse Hartwell, D.D., as president, were procured in 1858. Strangely enough, in 1859 the Baptist State Convention of Louisiana memorialized the legislature for aid, and received as a donation from the State treasury $10,000.[2]

President Hartwell dying about this time, Rev. W. Carey Crane was secured to succeed him at the head of the college. The collegiate year of 1861 closed with 127 students enrolled. The Civil War checked the growth of the enterprise, and finally the school was suspended. The building was impressed by the Confederate authorities into service as a hospital and was thus used until the close of the war. Ineffectual efforts were made to revive the school after the close of the struggle, under the less pretentious title of a high school, but in the chaotic condition of the country it collapsed and was finally abandoned.

In avoiding the Scylla[3] of a manual labor school, which was for

---

[1] Paxton's *History of Louisiana Baptists*, page 446.
[2] Paxton's *History of Louisiana Baptists*, page 480
[3] A sea monster in Greek mythology.—Editor.

many years a favorite project in so many of the States of the South, the Baptists of Louisiana had foundered in the Charybdis[1] of a university enterprise.

With less success and far less business sagacity was another university undertaken by the Baptists, at Shreveport, in 1870. The Helm School property, embracing seventy acres of land, was purchased in the suburbs of Shreveport, with a view of establishing a university. Unfortunately, alike for the projectors and the Southern Life Insurance Company, policies were taken in that corporation in favor of the university, and the insurance company advanced the money with which to erect a college building. The school opened in 1871. Three years later no building had been erected, the railway which was to connect the school with the city was yet unbuilt, business depression came, the yellow fever ravaged the city, the money panic of 1874 swept on apace, the insurance company by whose generous aid the institution was to be set upon its feet failed, all of which was succeeded by the mechanics' liens and the foreclosure of the mortgage created for the money already borrowed. Thus ended the short but eventful career of Shreveport University.

The chief institution of the Baptists of Louisiana at present is Keachi College, a co-educational school. The Keachi Female College and the Keachi Academy for boys were united in 1879, with Rev. J.H. Tucker as president. Dying in 1881, President Tucker was succeeded by Rev. T.N. Coleman, who was followed by Rev. C.P. Fountain, and he in turn by Rev. C.W. Tomkies, the present incumbent of the administrative chair.

The Baptists of Florida were reduced to divers makeshifts for education until 1887, when Mr. John B. Stetson, of Philadelphia, founded at Deland "The John B. Stetson University." Though the youngest of the denominational schools of the States of the South, it has made a most honorable record since it was founded. John F. Forbes, A.M., PH.D., is the gifted and progressive president of Stetson University.

Columbian University, Washington, D.C., has had a unique history. It was conceived by Luther Rice as a National Baptist institution, which should derive great importance from its surroundings in the nation's capital. The chief purpose of the devoted founder was to link into closest intimacy the great interests of education and missions in

---

[1] A whirlpool at the entrance of Scylla's cave in Greek mythology.—Editor.

such a way that they might mutually aid and supplement each other. The original conception of such a plan was doubtless due, in part, to the missionary enthusiasm aroused by the enlistment of American Baptists in foreign mission work in Burma and partly to the vast advantages arising from the availability of educational appliances at Washington. With consuming zeal Rice undertook to press the claims of these great interests in conjunction, but the public mind failed to grasp them in their dual capacity. Such enthusiasm was aroused in behalf of the national Baptist university that it became a rival of foreign missions rather than a twin sister. For three years the denomination, North and South, was stirred by appeals in behalf of Columbian University. Local societies were organized throughout the country in the interest of the national university, and large sums of money were raised before the meeting of the Triennial Convention for 1820. At the session of that body the matter of a practical union of education and missions was maturely considered, and it was decided that education in America and missions in Burma lay so far apart that they could never be associated in a practical plan for the furtherance of both, and a disjunction of these interests promptly followed. Financial embarrassments soon menaced the college and led to the suspension of its work in 1827, only to be revived, however, the following year under the new administration of Dr. Stephen Chapin as president, who was its presiding officer for fifteen years, and who not only cancelled the indebtedness, but revived the institution.

Upon the retirement of Dr. Chapin from the presidential office, Professor William Ruggles was placed at the head of the institution temporarily, for in 1843 Dr. Joel S. Bacon became president. He found the institution without debt, and equally without endowment. Dr. Bacon remained president until 1854, when Professor Ruggles was again called, for a season, to the head of the college. During the administration of Dr. Bacon the work of endowment was prosecuted at different times by Drs. A.M. Poindexter and William F. Broadus, of Virginia, the latter procuring subscriptions to the amount of $20,000, and by that means secured the fulfillment of a conditional promise of John Withers, of Alexandria, Virginia, for an equal amount. Rev. G.W. Samson, D.D., became president in 1859, and maintained the college with signal ability during the troublous period of the war. In spite of the difficulties of the peculiarly trying period during which he was president, both the efficiency and the material value of the institution were greatly enhanced. Dr. Samson resigning in 1871, J.C. Welling, LL.D., became president. In 1873, Hon. W.W. Corcoran agreed to give to the university $200,000 provided its friends would raise an additional $100,000. This condition was complied with and the institution entered upon a new career of prosperity. Rev. B.L. Whitman, D.D., is now (1898) the president of the University, and all indications point to an unprecedented prosperity on the part of the institution.

The institutions for the education of girls and young women conducted under the auspices, either directly or indirectly, of the Baptists of the South, are somewhat numerous.

Some of these schools sustain organic connection with the State Conventions, while others are the result of private or local enterprise. The latter class are Baptist only by virtue of the fact that their founders, or owners, are Baptists. It is impossible, for obvious reasons, to give to these schools equal prominence with those which have been established directly by the denomination for the other sex. The schools to which attention has been given in the present chapter have been founded primarily for the purpose of affording scholastic advantages to the young ministry of each State, while the schools for young women have come in response to a demonstration of public sentiment for womanly culture, and usually irrespective of denominational lines.

It is not practicable in a work of restricted compass like this to enlarge upon the histories of these valuable schools for young women, but in an appendix, attention is called to such as come practically or entirely under the direction of the denomination in the several States of the South.

CHAPTER VI
DIVERGENT VIEWS

While essentially one, the Baptists of the States of the South have never been in sentiment a unit. There have been differences of views among them from the beginning. Already occasions have arisen for calling attention to the divergent views of the early Baptists of Virginia, the Carolinas, and Georgia. The original divergence of views came between the General and the Particular Baptists, the former advocating the doctrine of the possibility of universal redemption in contradistinction to the doctrine of a limited redemption, or the salvation of the elect as held by the Particulars.

Adherents to both of these views came among the earliest Baptists from beyond the Atlantic. The principles and practices of the General Baptists were characterized by more or less laxness. Requiring no experience of grace, nor statement of doctrine, the General Baptists were reckless in the administration of the ordinances. They were Immersionists, and this was about the only point upon which they and the Particular Baptists were agreed. The easy-going requirements of the General Baptists, involving little or no renunciation of one's former life, made them popular. Their most noted representative in the South, in its earliest history, was Paul Palmer. Unfortunately but little is known of this remarkable man, but the indications are that he came direct from England to North Carolina. While to him is usually accorded the honor of being the pioneer Baptist preacher of North Carolina, the strong probability is that he was attracted to that province by the Baptist churches already existing, of which we have no definite record. The remarkable exemption of the Baptists of North Carolina from persecution possibly served as an inducement to the liberty-loving Palmer, whose greatest delight was found in preaching. The views held by Palmer were in entire accord with those held by the Arminian Baptists of England. Wielding an immense influence over the colonists of North Carolina, Palmer sowed broadcast the seeds of Arminianism in the early churches of the province. But after the advent of Whitefield the tide was turned toward Calvinism. Alike from two centers of influence, Philadelphia and Charleston, there went forth Calvinistic missionaries, and the result was a rapid and radical change to the standard of the Particulars.

The next division of sentiment was that which existed between the Separate and the Regular Baptists, the former being really Calvinistic Methodists, and composed chiefly of Whitefield's followers. They sprang up in 1750, and were first called New Lights. Subsequently, however, they were organized into separate societies by Shubal Stearns, and because of this independency of organization came to be called Separates. A year after he originated this new sect Stearns became a Baptist, as we have already seen, and most of the Separates followed him into that denomination. When this great leader adopted the views of the Baptists, the Separates as a sect became extinct. They, however, carried their distinctive views with them into the Baptist fold, which views were that believers are guided by the immediate teachings of the Holy Spirit, such supernatural indications being regarded by them as partaking of the nature of inspiration, and above, though not contrary to, reason. The Separate Baptists were by far the most conspicuous opponents of the establishment during the period of persecution in Virginia. It was the representatives of the Separate Baptists who were imprisoned in the jails of Virginia, who were whipped, and who, in spite of these dire persecutions, preached from their prison windows. In 1787 a union was effected between the Separate and Regular Baptists upon a basis mutually satisfactory, and both designations, as independent branches, were discontinued.

But the denomination was destined to still greater distractions and fiercer internal dissensions than were produced by original divisions. As has already been shown there was much local evangelization accomplished by the Baptists during the pioneer period of Southern history. In the upper and older regions of the South the Separate Baptists carried with fervid zeal the gospel in the most remote settlements. With increase of numbers, especially in the populous centers, came a desire for improvement in ministerial qualifications, partial compensation, and enlarged ideas of missionary operation. The advocacy of such views aroused opposition which manifested itself in a general anti-missionary spirit which did much to impede the progress of the Baptists in the South. This class of opponents threw themselves directly in the way of all efforts to develop the denomination along educational lines. It required a hard and protracted struggle to establish a school of learning of any character in the South. While ministerial education was regarded by the most prominent among the Baptists as being imperative, it was this which excited the most strenuous opposition on the part of the ignorant.

It is not difficult to see that the logical consequence of all this was the factious and fiery opposition subsequently raised against all agencies for the spread of the gospel. If human agency was objectionable in the equipment of the sacred ministry, it was equally so in the creation of means for disseminating the sacred gospel. Hence Sunday-schools, Bible societies, and Mission Boards were ranked in the same objectionable category with ministerial education. It was at this point that the fiercest struggle began on the part of the Baptists of the South, and it may be said that it has been continued to the present time. As local missionaries the Baptists have never been surpassed by any other people in the South. Their ministry has been the most active and self-sacrificing in giving the gospel to the destitute regions; but if the effort were made by the most progressive to urge the claims of the remoter portions of the world, firm opposition would ensue. Planting themselves steadfastly in this position, those of more restricted views waged a steady and relentless war throughout the States of the South against foreign missions.

The strength of this opposition was increased by the appearance of two journals upon the scene, *The Signs of the Times* and *The Primitive Baptist*. These factious organs came from States outside the South, and their wild statements were accepted by the gullible multitude as if they were oracles. The anti-missionary element of the denomination insisted upon being called "Old Side" or Primitive Baptists," the obvious purpose being to assimilate to themselves the original principles of the denomination, and to cast aspersion upon such as had departed from the faith and practice of the original standards by the introduction of new-fangled practices.

The most ridiculous assumptions were entertained by these anti-effort Baptists, and fostered by the organs already named, which found their way as stated intervals into the South. One of these sheets insisted that the money collected by pastors, mission agents, and others, was never applied to the objects for which it was claimed to be raised, but was devoted to schemes of speculation in the cities of the North. That was equaled only by the following piece of vaporing which is a literal quotation from the Minutes of the Pilgrim's Rest Association of Alabama:

> *We view theological schools unwarranted in the word of God and dangerous to religious liberty. And wherever they have been organized, whether Jewish, Pagan, Heathen, Roman Catholic, or Christian, they have been a source of persecution and bloodshed on the church of Christ.*

And this effusion was the product of one of their leaders. Another of their ministers wrote:

> *Do not forget the enemy (the missionaries); bear them in mind; the howling, destructive wolves, the ravenous dogs, and the filthy and their numerous whelps. By a minute observation and the consultation of the sacred, never-failing, descriptive chart, even their physiognomy in dress, mien, and carriage, and many other indented, indelible, descriptive marks, too tedious at present to write. The wolfish smell is enough to alarm, to create suspicion, and to ascertain; the dogs' teeth are noted, and the wolves for their peculiar and distinct howl, etc.*

Whatever there may or may not be in this jargon, there can be no doubt of its bitterness and violence against mission agents. One of their number asserted on one occasion that if an angel should come from heaven and declare the missionary cause was of God he would not believe it. Where ignorance, prejudice, and blasphemy were dominant in such a host as had been gathered into the Baptist churches throughout the South it is not a matter of wonder that the development of the missionary spirit had been slow.

But un-awed by these demonstrations, the advocates of missions were firm and pronounced in the enunciation of their principles. The two wings became more separated as the intensity of sentiment grew. There was, however, a perceptible growth of the missionary spirit and a corresponding decline in that of the opponents of missions. If the increase encouraged and emboldened, the one the decrease made the other more obdurate and reckless. An occasional break would occur in the ranks of the opponents and result in new accessions to the missionary Baptists. The change of sentiment, when it came, was favorable to missions. There was, however, one extraordinary exception to this rule in Tennessee, where there was a decided reaction against missions. It seems that Luther Rice, during his tours of the South, had succeeded in arousing much zeal in missions among the churches of Tennessee. But about 1820 the current of sentiment changed and the reaction assumed a most malignant form. Indeed, so serious did the opposition become that it is said, "not a man ventured to open his mouth in favor of any benevolent enterprise or action." The result was that the work of organization effected by Rice went to pieces, a deplorably chaotic condition in the churches followed, the friends of the opposition rallied, and the cause of missions was for a long time paralyzed. The influence of this reaction spread into adjoining regions. Largely in consequence of this the churches of North Alabama almost without exception became anti-missionary.

The lack of interest in missions has been accounted for in various ways.

It has been alleged that the illiteracy of the masses of the people was a serious barrier, which was enhanced by the fact that their time was so absorbed in clearing the land and bringing it into cultivation. Further, that the emphasis given to hyper-Calvinism, which was pushed to such ridiculous conclusions as to disparage all human effort, was a serious obstruction to the progress of missions. Under such an influence as that exerted by a strong-willed and illiterate ministry, it is easy to see how the hyper-Calvinists would come to prevail.

Again, the aggressive movements of the Methodists, the Cumberland Presbyterians, and the Disciples, with their Arminian teaching stiffened the resistance of the hyper-Calvinistic Baptists, and thus impaired the possibility of commanding the necessary means for missionary enterprise. Lastly, the activity of Daniel Parker, the apostle of opposition to missions was a most formidable obstruction to the development of the spirit of missions.

To these may be aptly added that of worldliness, which grew apace with the development of the country and the accumulation of wealth. Any pretext was welcomed which served to lessen the outflow of money from private coffers.

Disorder and dissension reigned among the churches and Associations of the South until about 1836 or 1838, which time is generally regarded as the period of "the great split." By this time the anti-mission forces had become very hostile, and insisted upon a withdrawal from all churches and Associations which favored missions. This cleavage was most fortunate. The separation was the dawn of a better day to the missionary Baptist churches of the South. The difference between the histories of the two branches of the Baptist family is most instructive. The one has grown with enlightenment and development, has founded and maintained its schools of learning, has established a most reputable denominational press, has produced a type of scholarship which is equal to that of the most advanced, has planted its churches in the most commanding centers, and has sent its missionaries to the farthest regions of the globe. The other has steadily kept itself in the remote rural regions, beyond the confines of enlightenment and progress.

Another most fruitful source of disturbance among the churches of the South was the promulgation of the views of Alexander Campbell, who made his advent as the founder of a new sect during the anti-missionary agitation. Indeed, as far as he could, Mr. Campbell appropriated the disturbance to the furtherance of his own views. He coincided with the anti-mission elements, both in their opposition to missions and to pastoral support. Through his organ, *The Christian Baptist*, a small religious monthly which appeared first in 1823, Mr. Campbell, with an exceedingly pretentious regard for literal conformity to Bible standards, put himself into direct alliance with the opponents of missions, Bible societies, education societies, Boards, and, indeed, of all evangelical agencies. Possessed of a voluble tongue and disputatious spirit, he soon won his way to local renown as a debater. Making a preaching tour through the States of Kentucky and Tennessee as far South as Nashville, Mr. Campbell created an ovation, and won for himself considerable distinction.[1] This was the beginning of a notable career. Adroit in argument, incisive in sarcasm and caricature, shrewd in repartee, and possessed of an overweening confidence in his ability, Mr. Campbell was a polemic Ajax in the region where he began the propagation of his tenets. Abandoning the beaten tracks of discussion, he invested his views with a charm and novelty that never failed to catch the ear of the multitude.

No season could have been more opportune for the advent of such a reformer as Mr. Campbell than the one in which he appeared. The churches were ripe for a change. Hyper-Calvinistic or antinomian views had been thundered from the pulpits for many years together. The constant discussion of so contracted views around the fireside and in the home circle, as well as from the pulpit, had worn away the patience of thousands of auditors. The presentation of dry, dull speculations which sprang from hyper-Calvinistic views, palled upon the intellectual taste. The people hungered for bread and were given a stone.

At this juncture Alexander Campbell flashed into sudden prominence. To him the prevailing conditions furnished a golden opportunity, and right well did he improve it. Hundreds flocked to the standard of "the Reformer," a designation in which he delighted. Under his di-

---

[1] Dr. A.H. Newman, *American Church History* (Baptist), Vol. 2, pages 438-439.

rection a sect was gradually formed which assumed the self-styled name of "Reformers," but opprobrious called by their opponents "Campbellites." The appearance of Mr. Campbell was the signal for strife, divisions, alienation, and irritation. His disputatious supporters were most active in proselyting. With more of zeal than of propriety they were constantly thrusting their views upon all with whom they met. This movement came as a great shock to the churches of Virginia and Kentucky. It rapidly spread into the adjacent States. In some instances entire churches were caught in its toils. This was notably true of the First Church of Nashville, Tennessee, which for a season fell completely under the domination of the Disciples. Doubtless the division between the followers of Campbell and the Baptists would have occurred in Kentucky earlier by three years, but it was stayed by the great revival which began in 1827. By the severance of fellowship on the part of Baptist churches from the adherents of Campbell, the way to an independent organization was made easy.

Professing to return to the original principles of Christianity, the new sect assumed the name of "Disciples." Accessions were gained to the ranks of the new organization alike from the Baptists, Methodists, and Presbyterians; but the Baptists furnished the greater number. For a period of years the sect was very popular. It swept like a prairie fire over the new West and far into the States of the South. For a time it seemed that it would overwhelm every other denomination. Adherents continued to flock to it by the thousand. In the acquisition of converts the utmost scrupulousness was not always observed. Every means was laid under tribute to arouse prejudice, engender discord in churches and communities, and to produce confusion in the minds of the wavering. Boisterous in declamation, and brazen in the assertion of their views, the followers of Mr. Campbell made rapid headway with the excited multitudes which thronged upon their preaching. Whatever else may be said of this agitation, there is little doubt that antipedobaptism and immersion were greatly helped by it. The stress vehemently laid upon immersion by the Disciples emphasized to the minds of thousands of Pedobaptists the importance of a thorough examination of the subject. The result was the conversion of very many to the doctrine of immersion.

An additional cause of distraction in the Baptist churches of the South is what is known as "Old Landmarkism," a term the honor of the authorship of which is divided between Drs. J.M. Pendleton and J.R.

Graves. They were the first to give expression to the views which characterized a party of Baptists who came well-nigh going sufficiently far in the extremity of their views to form a distinct sect. This party prevailed mostly in the Southwest. The movement under Doctors Pendleton and Graves was an attempted reaction from the growth of conservatism in the Baptist denomination South. The principal features of "Old Landmarkism" were an insistence of Baptist apostolic succession; a declaration of the absolute necessity of properly authorized administrators of baptism in order to the validity of the ordinance; the refusal to accept as valid baptism that which is administered by a Pedobaptist; a denial that Pedobaptist organizations are churches, and that their ministers are properly authorized preachers of the gospel. At a later period Doctor Graves sought to graft upon these views that of non-intercommunion, in which he denied the scriptural right of a member of a Baptist church to commune with any other than that of which he is a member.

These views were urged with great energy in the valley of the Mississippi, finding an expression, for the most part, through *The Tennessee Baptist*, of which Doctor Graves had been the editor since 1846. Doctor Graves was a polemicist of no ordinary ability, and a speaker of much charming magnetism. In him were equally blended the facile writer and eloquent speaker, so that through word of mouth as well as through the columns of *The Tennessee Baptist*, he was able to sway multitudes of those whose eyes and ears he was enabled to reach. For many years his paper was an engine of power among the Baptists of the Southwest. Nor was he without some following throughout the States of the South. His views boldly urged furnished a fruitful source of discussion, not altogether unattended at times by bitter dissension.

For about a quarter of a century this spirit held sway chiefly in the region of the great basin of the Mississippi but after that time a reaction set in and enlightened conservatism reasserted itself. While there are still to be found in different portions of the South and Southwest some who cling to the views of the original "Land markers," they are few in comparison with those of a quarter of a century ago.

CHAPTER VII
INTEREST IN MISSIONS
PRIOR TO THE SEPARATION

The early Baptists of the South were noted for their zeal in home missions. To this fact, more than to any other, is due the marvelous expansion of the denomination during the first half century of its history. The early Baptist ministry of the South has never been excelled in its unquenchable zeal in providing the destitute with the gospel. Hardy and heroic, these primitive preachers of the South were in the advance guard of Southern civilization, lured partly by the unexplored but inviting region which lay toward the setting sun, and in part by a desire to extend the limits of Christian evangelization. Along with the redemption of the wilderness and the waste places was the reclamation of the multitudes from vice.

These heroic men braved all dangers and endured every hardship in their determination to preach. Rarer exhibitions of missionary zeal were not illustrated even during the apostolic age. Already occasions have arisen several times for reference to this spirit of early evangelization.

Resistance to the work of home missions was never made; but when the matter of foreign missions was suggested to the early churches, opposition was at once aroused. Objections to such a movement became vehement, as it was deemed a clear infringement of the divine prerogative thus to undertake the evangelization of the peoples of the remoter portions of the earth.

It seems never to have occurred to these matter-of-fact, but necessarily contracted, people that the objections against foreign missions would admit of equal application to home missions. The effort to lead the great mass of Baptists in the States of the South to view the matter of missions as indivisible and worldwide has been a protracted one; indeed, in not a few localities the attempt up to this time has been utterly without avail. There are thousands of Baptists in the churches of the South who are misnamed missionary Baptists.

The first organized effort in the South looking to evangelization began in the Charleston Association when John Gano was sent first to the Yadkin district of North Carolina as a missionary. The precedence of South Carolina Baptists in evangelistic enterprise has been perpetuated to the present. From the beginning they enjoyed the pre-eminence of a distinguished leadership—a leadership as devoted as it was able.

The churches of South Carolina have never receded from the high plane of beneficence to which they were led by Screven, Hart, and Furman. Even in advance of the great interest awakened in foreign missions by the conversion of Judson and Rice, Dr. Furman had shown commendable zeal in raising funds for the publication of the Bible translations of Carey and Marshman. The wisdom of Richard Furman was conspicuous in coupling with this praiseworthy labor that of seeking to stimulate, on the part of the pastors of that early period, a desire for better preparation for their work. His sagacity prompted him to look beyond immediate results in connection with this missionary movement—he desired to see the spirit becoming an abiding one. In order to that end, he sought to elevate the ministry while he strove to gather in contributions. The masterly manipulation of existing agencies which resulted in the constitution of the South Carolina Baptist State Convention in 1821 is an evidence of the splendid leadership of Richard Furman. The Convention was founded upon the two-fold idea of ministerial education and missionary expansion. To the mind of Dr. Furman they were as inseparable as shadow and substance. When Luther Rice visited the South, urging with equal fervor education and missions, he found that he had been preceded in the advocacy of those associated ideas in at least one locality.

Together, as yoke-fellows, Rice and Furman stood upon the floor of the Triennial Convention in Philadelphia, in 1817, in advocacy of these inseparable interests. No one familiar with the Baptist denomination can fail to see the wisdom of these men of God in the equal urgency of the two claims.

Following close upon the organized efforts of the South Carolina Baptists were those of the denomination in Georgia. Scarcely any organization was undertaken before the advent of Jesse Mercer. Like Furman, in the adjoining State, Mr. Mercer associated with the evangelization of the world an enlightened ministry. He was the prime mover in the formation of the famous Powelton Conferences, out of which grew the missionary and educational organizations of the Baptists of Georgia. These conferences were developed into the General Committee, which was composed of members from each district Association in Georgia, with the distinct object in view of promoting State missions by organized itinerant preaching, and to establish a school among the Creek Indians, who occupied the territory stretching along the western confines of the State. These movements gradually led to the constitution of the State Convention and the founding of Mercer University.

Abraham Marshall was made the chairman of the General Committee of Georgia, and Henry Holcombe, secretary. A general address was issued directed, in part, to the Baptists of the State and partly to "all gospel ministers not of their order within this State [who] wish the unity of the spirit in the bonds of peace." The first portion of the address related to the Baptist denomination, and was intended to explain the nature of the movement, and to invite cooperation in its furtherance. The second portion, addressed to the ministry of other denominations said: "With the greatest respect and affection, we invite you, Reverend Brethren, to an investigation in order to a scriptural adjustment of the comparatively small points in which we differ." Praiseworthy as this movement was, and sincere as were its promoters, it was impaired in the outset by the attempt at denominational union. It failed equally in commanding the approbation of the Baptists and the members of other denominations. It really did not represent the prevailing sentiment of Baptists, and was repelled by the Pedobaptists. The invitation was responded to at the next meeting of the committee by two ministers of other denominations, one a Methodist and the other an Episcopalian; but the subject of denominational unity was never once referred to. Attention was henceforth devoted to missions and ministerial education.

But the serious blunder committed in the outset in the attempted fusion of Baptists with other denominations alienated the rank and file of the Baptists throughout the State. Associations passed over the matter with ominous silence which indicated the grave suspicion that the Baptist denomination was being betrayed into the rankest open communionism. The members of the General Committee were never able to repair the blunder to the satisfaction of the denomination. This was followed by a period of inaction in the churches. But in 1813 there was a revival of interest in missions, originating in the Savannah River Association. Under the lead of Dr. William B. Johnson advanced steps were taken in home evangelization, and it was also resolved, "That the churches be exhorted to use their best endeavors toward the support of foreign missions." This was immediately followed by the organization of a Baptist Foreign Mission Society in Savannah, of which Dr. William T. Brantley became the corresponding secretary. A circular letter addressed to the Baptist Associations throughout Georgia succeeded in arousing much missionary enthusiasm. It at once became manifest that if anything was to be accomplished there must be a more compact organization. This necessity was so universally recognized that the General Association of Georgia was constituted in 1822, and this led, five years later, to the formation of "The Baptist Convention for the State of Georgia."

Repeated efforts had been made by the Baptists of Georgia to institute means to Christianize the Indians whose tribes lay along both the eastern and western banks of the Chattahoochee River. At last, in 1823, an Indian Reform mission and school were established in the Creek nation at Withingtoil station, about thirty miles south of the present site of Montgomery, Alabama. These interests were assigned to the care of Rev. Lee Compere.

These struggling efforts, however, do not represent all that was being accomplished by the Baptists of Georgia for during this entire period, extending from the opening years of the century to 1827, and much later, they were generous contributors to the missionary enterprises of the denomination at large. Much skill was needed to generate a disposition to aid in the causes fostered by the denomination, but this was not wanting on the part of such leaders as Holcombe, Brantley, Mercer, Sherwood, Marshall, Sanders, and Kilpatrick.

During the earlier years of the century, and within the period which followed immediately upon the great McGready revival, the condition of affairs was peculiar in North Carolina. From about 1812 to 1832 there was a stagnant spirit among the churches of that State. They were possessed of sufficient energy and vitality, however, to resist the progress of missions, either local or foreign. During the period named, embracing not less than twenty years, there were not more than six thousand members added to the Baptist churches of North Carolina. An attempt was made about 1815 to arouse the churches from their stupor, and to effect an organization for systematic missionary effort, but without avail. Josiah Crudup and Robert T. Daniel, the recognized leaders of that time, were unable to arouse the slightest interest in missionary endeavor.

Again, in 1826, an effort was made to create zeal in behalf of missions, which effort culminated in the constitution of a struggling organization known as the Baptist Benevolent Society, which in turn led to the formation of the North Carolina Baptist State Convention. This organization was effected in a large barn, near the town of Greenville, on March 20, 1830. The enterprise was the result of the wise direction and untiring zeal of Rev. Thomas Meredith, who prepared the constitution in advance of the meeting, and who had the satisfaction of seeing it adopted substantially as it came from his pen.

The purpose of the young organization was plainly but forcibly presented in the second article of the constitution:

> *The primary objects of this Convention shall be the education of young men called of God to the ministry and approved of by the churches to which they respectively belong, the employment of the missionaries within the limits of the State, and cooperation with the Baptist General Convention of the United States in the promotion of missions in general.*

A mere handful constituted this original body with full knowledge that such action would encounter stout opposition. The means, with which the proposed work was to be accomplished, had yet to be created. Within the State there were at that date about 15,000 Baptists of all shades of belief. They received the announcement of the formation of the Convention with an indifference well-nigh appalling. But the courage which had nerved to the constitution of the body impelled to the establishment of plans for the consummation of the purposes proposed. With the utmost deliberation twelve men were appointed to canvass the State in the interest of the proposed objects of the Convention. Without compensation these men were to traverse the State in every direction and urge the claims of the Convention in the face of a most determined opposition. Mr. Meredith prepared an address which was to be sent to the Baptist churches throughout North Carolina, setting forth the object of the Convention and appealing for cooperation. The struggle was a severe one and the progress made not at all encouraging. But the promoters of the movement were prepared for the worst, and hence were not daunted by the resistance encountered. The step proved the starting-point of the development of the denomination in North Carolina, which development has continued until the State has become the third in numerical strength of the States composing the Southern Baptist Convention. From the churches of North Carolina have come many of the wisest and ablest of Baptist leaders, among whom may be named the Mercers, the elder Brantley, the elder Basil Manly, John Kerr, R.B.C. Howell, and A.M. Poindexter.

The struggles of the Virginia Baptists both before and after the

Revolution served to sink out of view their minor differences and to make them more cohesive. But the progress of the missionary spirit of that State was not unchecked by those opposed to missions.

After the subversion of the Establishment under the auspices of the General Committee, another body was organized in 1800, known as the Committee of Correspondence. This last-named organization served somewhat as a Board in arousing interest in the matter of missions and the general direction of denominational affairs. The Committee of Correspondence lasted until 1823, when the General Association of Virginia was organized. While the fewness of numbers entering into this organization must not be altogether attributed to opposition to organized effort in evangelistic enterprise, yet it was significant. Only fifteen delegates coming from a few Associations entered into the constitution of the General Association. At the period of this organization there were not less than 40,000 Baptists and twenty district Associations in Virginia. R.B. Semple was chosen as the first president of the General Association, and J.B. Jeter and Daniel Witt were appointed the first missionaries. These devoted men sought to accomplish two ends, that of converting the masses in destitute regions and that of educating the churches in the matter of missions.

It was about this time that Alexander Campbell came into prominence as a doughty disputant arrayed against salaried ministers and organized missionary effort. The public mind was greatly distracted by the utterances and conduct of Mr. Campbell, who was withstood by Taylor, Jeter, Witt, and Semple. While Mr. Campbell succeeded in urging some to the adoption of his views, and in alienating others, the bulk of the denomination was brought into sympathy with the general work of the Baptists of the entire country. The Baptists of Virginia shared largely in the enthusiasm aroused by Luther Rice in behalf of Columbian College and the Burmese mission, and their leaders were conspicuous members of the Triennial Convention.

As has been shown, the Baptists of Maryland have never been numerically strong, but they were among the first in the States of the South to exhibit a missionary spirit. As early as 1793 the Baltimore Baptist Association was constituted and soon put itself upon record as a missionary body. Eventually, however, there grew up an anti-missionary spirit which continued to gain ground until 1836, when by a majority of seven the anti-missionary Baptists came into control of the Baltimore Association. By a vote of sixteen to nine, the Association, in 1836, adopted resolutions against "uniting with worldly socie-ties," coupled with a declaration of non-fellowship with such as had done so. This meant a severance from all such agencies as missionary organizations, Sunday-schools, and Bible, tract, and temperance socie-ties. This action brought about a rupture and terminated the missionary zeal of the Association. The organization through which the Baptists have expressed their interest in missions is the Maryland Baptist Union Association, which was organized as a distinctively missionary body in 1836. Into this body were gathered those who resisted the en-croachments of the anti-missionary Baptists, and since its inception the Maryland Baptist Union Association has been an enthusiastic mission-ary body.

At an early period Baptists recognized the necessity of planting churches in the national capital. As early as 1802 a church was orga-nized in Washington, then a town struggling into life, with all the rude evidences of a frontier settlement, and with a scattered population of 4,000. Only six members entered into the constitution of the First Bap-tist Church, founded in Washington on March 7, 1802. For pastoral service and pulpit supply the infant church was forced to rely upon Rev. William Parkinson, who was then chaplain of Congress.

Near the close of the year, an unpretentious meeting-house was built on the corner of I and Nineteenth Streets. For five years this struggling interest was forced to depend upon the chaplain to Congress for whatever of preaching or pastoral oversight it enjoyed. But in 1807 Rev. O.B. Brown assumed pastoral charge of the church and served it during the remarkable term of forty-three years. It was into this church that Spencer H. Cone entered as a member after his conversion and abandonment of the stage. From this church Mr. Cone received his li-cense as a preacher. In 1814, Hon. O.C. Comstock, a member of Con-gress, joined the church, was baptized, and licensed to preach. The lo-cation of the church was changed in 1833 to Tenth Street, where a new meeting-house was built. In 1859 the First and Fourth churches were united. Its pastors have been Messrs. Brown, Hill, Cole, Samson, Gil-lette, Cuthbert, and Stakely.

The Second Church, sometimes called the Navy Yard Church, was constituted on June 10, 1810, beginning with a membership of only five. The first place of meeting of this small body was a diminutive frame building. It was in this little house that Spencer H. Cone began his career as a preacher. At that time Mr. Cone was a clerk in the

Treasury Department, from which station he rose to the position of chaplain to Congress. The names of Lynd, Neale, Chapin, Maginnis, Poindexter, Bacon, Adams, Sydnor, Boston, and Cole, appear in the roll of the pastors of this church.

These enterprises represent the interests founded in the national capital during the period now under review. It was with great difficulty that the Baptists were enabled to gain a permanent footing in Washington, and but for the loyalty and devotion of a few zealous men and women, Baptist settlement in the national capital would have been greatly delayed.

Other interests than those already named have come into existence since the period now under consideration, but of these this is not the place to make mention. In their associational connection and missionary work, the Baptist churches of the District of Columbia are divided in membership between the Columbia Association and the Potomac Association, of Virginia.

In the early periods of their history, the Baptists of Kentucky were a most enterprising folk, especially in domestic missions. Their interest in general missionary work dates from the great revival of 1800. Prior to that time but little was attempted by the itinerant Baptist preachers of Kentucky beyond the borders of that State. Fired with the enthusiasm of the great revival of 1800 which shook the State to its center, Baptist missionaries extended their labors beyond the Ohio and into the States of Ohio, Indiana, and Illinois on the north, and Tennessee on the south.

According to Dr. J.M. Peck, Kentucky Baptists were the first Protestants to enter the State of Illinois. Rev. James Smith was the heroic missionary who essayed to cross the border into the wilderness which was afterward developed into that great State. "While thus engaged, he fell into the hands of the Indians, from whom he was ransomed by his brethren for the sum of $175. In 1801 the South Elkhorn Church sent a request to the Elkhorn Association "to send missionaries to the Indian nations." The matter received prompt attention by the appointment of a committee

of five members to hear and to determine on the call of any of our ministers, and if satisfied therewith, to give them credentials for that purpose; to set subscriptions on foot, to receive collections for the use of said mission; and it is recommended to the church so to encourage subscriptions for said purpose,

> *and have the money lodged with the deacons to be applied for*
> *that purpose whenever called for by the committee. The follow-*
> *ing brethren are appointed: David Barrow, Ambrose Dudley,*
> *John Price, Augustine Eastine, and George Smith.*

The result was that John Young was sent from the Elkhorn Association as a missionary to the Indians.

As early as 1816, when the subject of foreign missions was being pressed upon the attention of the churches throughout the South, we find in Kentucky six missionary societies which were liberal contributors to the treasury of the Board at Philadelphia.

The churches of Kentucky having been blessed again with a remarkable revival in 1817, their attention seems to have been turned afresh to the matter of missions, for it was immediately followed by the creation of a school for Indian children near Georgetown. This was the work of the Kentucky Missionary Society, which gave to the new school the name of Choctaw Academy. This new interest prospered through a period of years, and sent out to the Indians of the far West two missionaries, Samson Birch and Robert Jones.

Then came the period of distraction attendant upon the advent of Alexander Campbell. In close connection with Mr. Campbell was the appearance in that region of Daniel Parker, an illiterate but remarkable man, whose chief purpose seems to have been the destruction of the missionary spirit among the churches. With all the confidence of ignorance he boldly asserted the unscripturalness of missions, and challenged to disputatious combat any who dared controvert his position. While Daniel Parker was thus engaged he was diligent also in the inculcation of the two-seed doctrine in the State. The combination of two such agencies as those of Campbell and Parker came well-nigh destroying the spirit of missions in the churches of Kentucky. In 1832 the Baptist State Convention of Kentucky was organized, but it was soon rent in pieces by internal dissension, and in 1836 was driven to dissolution. The following year, however, an effort was made to revive the suspended interest under the designation of the General Association of Kentucky Baptists, the organization being distinctively founded upon the idea of State evangelization. This cautious proceeding indicates that it was no longer prudent or possible to press the claims of foreign missions upon the churches. From being one of the most progressive of the States of the South in the prosecution of missionary work, Kentucky became, for a period, one of the most actively aggressive States against it, so strong was the influence of Campbell and Parker.

Tennessee shared largely in the same spirit. The Baptist churches of that State were among the first warmly to espouse the cause of missions in foreign parts, but this was followed by a most violent reaction. During the visit of Luther Rice to the State, the churches were greatly aroused upon missions, and for a season their zeal was ardent; but there came a sudden turn, and the transformation was complete, the rankest opposition possible to missions coming to prevail. The churches suffered from this spiritual paralysis for a long period of years, even up to the outbreak of the war between the States. True, there were churches here and there throughout the State engaged in contributing to missions, but they were the exception and not the rule. Repeated efforts were made to overcome this depression, but they were unavailing.

In Alabama, as in Tennessee, there was a struggle long and bitter between the missionary and anti-missionary Baptists, for the ascendency. The contest was fiercest in the northern and eastern portions of the State, but no section was exempt from strife. The annual meeting of every district Association was the occasion of intense struggle between those who favored and those who opposed missions. Still, the more progressive elements of the denomination were active in local missionary work, and untiring in their efforts to cultivate benevolence, on the part of the churches. The period of organized evangelistic effort in Alabama dates from 1816, when associational missionaries began work.

In 1823 the State Convention was organized solely upon the basis of missions, and at once fifteen evangelists were sent into different portions of the State. They were everywhere met by hostile demonstrations, but were resolute in the prosecution of their work. The leaders conspicuous at this period were Travis, Bestor, and Holcombe, the residence of each of whom was respectively in the southern, central, and northern portions of the State. By concert of action they succeeded in maintaining sufficient organization to hold in check the opposition, and at the same time prosecute their work.

Mississippi Baptists were among the last to constitute a general State organization. Previous to such organization, which took place in 1839, just a few years before the constitution of the Southern Baptist Convention, missionary work had been prosecuted throughout the State by local Associations. Considering the rapid growth of the population after the battle of New Orleans and the subsequent peace with Great Britain, and the difficulties encountered in a new region, a most praiseworthy work was accomplished by the Baptists of Mississippi in the cultivation of the home field.

The planting of the Baptist cause in Louisiana was so entirely due to missionary effort in the midst of the most forbidding obstructions that it was natural for those brought into the churches under such conditions themselves to imbibe the missionary spirit. For many years identified with the Baptist organizations of Mississippi, the denomination in Louisiana at last began to become distinctive in its own local work.

The constitution of Associations began as early as 1818 when the Louisiana Association was organized. This was followed by the constitution of similar bodies on both sides of the Mississippi as the denomination expanded. The Louisiana State Convention was not organized until 1847—two years after the constitution of the Southern Baptist Convention.

Thus it will be seen that during the long period extending from the Revolution to the organization of the Southern Baptist Convention the denomination in the South was especially active in the work of local missions, and along the lines of advanced missionary effort. The rapid increase of population in the South made it necessary for much local effort to be expended. So important, emphatic, and long continued was this necessary work in the midst of a raw and incoherent population, that it became more difficult to divert attention to the equally important matter of world evangelization. Then it cannot be denied that the commercialism of the times acted as a serious hindrance to the fostering of missions. It is not easy to enlist the devotion of men in sacred work, the necessity of which is not visibly manifest, when these men are engrossed in subduing the harsher forces of nature, allured meanwhile by the prospect of great gain. To such the injunctions and admonitions of the pulpit respecting benevolence are regarded as being merely functional. These conditions may favor a spirit of worldliness and do, but proportionately they hinder the spirit of benevolence.

CHAPTER VIII
FORMATION OF THE SOUTHERN BAPTIST CONVENTION

The Southern Baptist Convention was one of the direct effects of the agitation of the question of African slavery. Many years before the separation took place between Northern and Southern Baptists, the question of slavery bad been warmly discussed in Baptist circles and councils. Many of the largest owners of slaves in the South were Baptists who were eminent in denominational ranks. They were as pronounced and sincere in the defense of the institution of slavery as were the Baptists of the North in its denunciation. The counter-sentiment of the two sections grew commensurately during the last quarter preceding the outbreak of the Civil War. The agitation of the question in the columns of the journals both of the secular and religious press, on the platform, in the pulpit, and upon the floor of Congress, necessarily widened the breach between the North and South. As an institution in the South, slavery assumed three phases— social, economic, and political. It had spent its force as a social institution by the year 1835, while to the end of its existence it continued to affect the South economically. It was as a political agency that it was to effect the direst consequences. As such, it split in twain great ecclesiastical bodies and finally involved the country in bloody strife.[1]

The sway of wisdom and moderation in the councils of the Triennial Convention held in abeyance for many years the passions of the less discreet. Except that now and then friction was produced by some injudicious utterance or production, nothing occurred to mar the general harmony of the Baptist denomination of the United States until 1844. This was due to the influence of wise and cool spirits who studiously suppressed all initial manifestations of bitterness. The purpose was clearly deliberate on the part of the denominational leaders, both of the North and South, to keep out of sight as far as possible this impending trouble. Up to 1844, Southern churches vied with those of the North in their contributions to the treasuries of the societies maintained by the Triennial Convention.

To some, however, it seemed clear that dissolution was inevitable; to others, it was equally clear that disruption could be averted. To the latter class belonged that princely leader, Richard Fuller, who in 1844

---

[1] Edward Ingle, *Southern Side Lights*, page 262.

offered in the Triennial Convention the following:

> *WHEREAS, Some misapprehension exists in certain parts of the country as to the design or character of this Convention, and it is most desirable that such misapprehension should be removed; therefore,*
>
> *Resolved, That this Convention is a corporation with limited powers for a specific purpose defined in its constitution; and therefore that its members are delegated to meet solely for the transaction of business prescribed by the said constitution; and that cooperation in this body does not involve nor imply any concert or sympathy as to any matters foreign from the object designated as aforesaid.*

The resolution was promptly seconded by Spencer H. Cone, of New York, and sustained by William Hayne, of Massachusetts, and J.B. Jeter, of Virginia. But it was stubbornly resisted by Nathaniel Colver, of Massachusetts, who expressed the desire that he be not handicapped respecting any matter that might come for consideration before the body.

After some discussion, the resolution was withdrawn and the following was offered and adopted:

> *WHEREAS, There exists in various sections of our country an impression that our present organization involves the fellowship of the institution of domestic slavery, or of certain associations which are designed to oppose this institution;*
>
> *Resolved, That in cooperating together as members of this Convention in the work of foreign missions, we disclaim all sanction, either expressed or implied, whether of slavery or of antislavery; but as individuals we are perfectly free both to express and to promote our own views on these subjects in a Christian manner and spirit.*

This evoked from Dr. Fuller upon the floor of the Convention the expression that he was perfectly calm and dispassionate respecting slavery. While he was unconvinced that slavery was a sin, personally he considered it a great evil. He further said that in this opinion his brethren in the South did not share. He hoped and prayed that the institution might be abolished.[1]

---

[1] A.H. Newman, *American Church History*, Baptist, Vol. 2, page 445.

It was claimed by the pro-slavery advocates in the Baptist denomination in the South that just subsequent to the Triennial Convention for 1844, the Board of Foreign Missions procured the retirement from its service of Rev. John Bushyhead, a highly respected Indian Baptist preacher, because he was an owner of slaves. This created an impression throughout the South that slaveholders would not henceforth be admitted to appointment under the Board. During the same year, 1844, the famous controversy on slavery occurred between Wayland and Fuller. The latter replied to certain abolition expressions which appeared in the columns of *The Christian Reflector*, and in doing so quoted from Wayland's *Elements of Moral Science* to sustain the Southern view of the question against that expressed by the journal named. This called for a reply from Dr. Wayland, and thus the controversy began. The champions were the recognized leaders of thought in the denomination North and South. Both the ethical and scriptural grounds of the great question were passed under review, and opposite conclusions were of course reached. The only good, perhaps, flowing from the controversy was an exhibition of a courteous and Christian spirit which distinguished it throughout.

The discussion of the most serious features of the institution in so calm and courteous a manner served, for a season, to allay bitterness of feeling. But this was of brief duration. The secular press fed the flame of public excitement. The halls of Congress rang with oratory in the discussion of the many-sided subject. Occasions for division, though slight, were often magnified by the advocates of both sides of this burning question. Arguments flew to and fro like shots in battle. Any pronounced action on either side repelled at a greater distance the other. This was shown by the attribution of certain utterances to Dr. R.E. Pattison, the Home Secretary of the Boston Board, which utterances intimated that the Acting Board of the Triennial Convention would no longer tolerate the matter of slavery. It was these utterances which called forth the famous Alabama Resolutions. The matter was brought to the attention of the Alabama Baptist State Convention by a query from the Tuscaloosa Church, the authorship of which was attributed to Dr. Basil Manly Sr. The query was presented thus: "Is it proper for us, at the South, to send any more money to our brethren at the North, for missionary and other benevolent purposes, before the subject of slavery be rightly understood by both parties?" This was productive of sharp and decisive action. This query, together with a communication addressed to the Alabama Baptist Convention from the Georgia Baptist Convention, was referred to a committee of which Dr. Basil Manly Sr. was chairman. The result of the committee's action was embodied in the following resolutions:

> *WHEREAS, The holding of property in African Negro slaves has, for some years, excited discussion as a question of morals, between different portions of the Baptist denomination united in benevolent enterprise; and by a large portion of our brethren is now imputed to the slaveholders in these Southern and Southwestern States as a sin at once grievous, palpable, and disqualifying;*
>
> *1. Resolved,... that when one party to a voluntary compact among Christian brethren is not willing to acknowledge the entire social equality with the other, as to all the privileges and benefits of the union, nor even to refrain from impeachment and annoyance, united efforts between such parties, even in the sacred cause of Christian benevolence cease to be agreeable, useful, or proper.*
>
> *2. Resolved, That our duty at this crisis requires us to demand from the proper authorities in all those bodies to whose funds we have contributed or with whom we have in any way been connected, the distinct, explicit avowal that slaveholders are eligible, and entitled equally with non-slaveholders, to all the privileges and immunities of their several unions; and especially to receive any agency, mission, or other appointment which may run within the scope of their operations or duties.*

It was further insisted that in the event of the moral character of an applicant being challenged, such question should be referred for settlement to the church of which he is a member. The transmission of future contributions to these societies was made contingent upon the satisfactoriness of the answer given to these questions.

The reply of the Foreign Mission Board was made in a similar strain. It says:

> *In the thirty years in which the Board has existed, no slaveholder, to our knowledge, has applied to be a missionary. And as we send out no domestics or servants, such an event as a missionary taking slaves with him, were it morally right, could not, in accordance with all our past arrangements or present*

plans, possibly occur. If, however, any one should offer himself as a missionary, having slaves, and should insist on retaining them as his property, we should not appoint him. One thing is certain, we can never be a party to any arrangement which would imply approbation of slavery.

The critical reader cannot fail to discover certain caution and reservation in the deliverances from both quarters. The language is charged with a reserved force, and beneath the conventional courtesy there slumber the fires of determination. The deliverance of the Alabama Baptist State Convention was the most decisive utterance that had up to this time emanated from either side. It is believed that the incisive character of the challenge did much to precipitate final separation.

Very soon practical emphasis was given to the position taken by the Home Mission Society by its refusal to appoint James E. Reeves, a missionary within the Tallapoosa Association, of Georgia. This refusal was made directly to the Executive Committee of the Georgia Baptist Convention and was based upon the ground that Mr. Reeves was a slaveholder. The Executive Committee, composed of J.L. Dagg, V.R. Thornton, J.B. Walker, Thomas Stocks, and B.M. Sanders, promptly instructed the treasurer of the Convention to withhold all funds from Northern societies until further instruction. This was followed by an address to the people of the United States, reciting in detail the action of the Home Mission Society.

The hour for dissolution had come. One by one the Conventions of the Southern States began to withdraw. Along with them went the missionary auxiliary societies which had been such copious contributors to the Boards of the Triennial Convention. The Board of the Foreign Missionary Society of Virginia, suggested that the Baptists of the South be invited to meet in Augusta, Georgia, in May, 1845, to indicate a course of action for the future. Meanwhile the national anniversaries of the denomination met at Providence, Rhode Island. The report of the committee appointed the year before by the American Baptist Home Mission Society to consider the subject of an amicable dissolution of said Society, was submitted. It was as follows:

WHEREAS, The American Baptist Home Mission Society is composed of contributors residing in slaveholding States; and,
WHEREAS, The constitution recognizes no distinction among

the members of the Society as to the eligibility of all the offices and appointments in the gift both of the Society and the Board; and,

Whereas, it has been found that the basis on which the Society was organized is one upon which all the members and friends of the Society are now willing to act; therefore,

Resolved, That it is expedient that the members now forming the Society should hereafter act in separate organizations at the South and at the North, in promoting the objects which were originally contemplated by the Society.

Resolved, That a committee be appointed to report a plan by which the object contemplated in the preceding resolution may be accomplished in the best way and at the earliest period of time consistently with the preservation of the constitutional rights of all the members and with the least possible interruption of the missionary work of the Society.

The submission of this report gave rise to a prolonged discussion. Prominent in the lead of this discussion was the able and conservative President Wayland. He threw the weight of his powerful influence against precipitate action in the matter of dissolution; but extreme abolition sentiments on the part of Northern members and exacting demands on the part of members from the South proved more than a match even for Francis Wayland. The report was adopted and the hour for final severance had struck. The Alabama resolutions, to which answer had been made by the Executive Committee of the Foreign Mission Board, were taken up and considered and the action taken by the committee was endorsed. This was the result of a report of a committee of which President Wayland was chairman. The report was one that breathed conciliation throughout. It said:

1. The spirit of the constitution of the General Convention, as well as the history of its proceedings from the beginning, renders it apparent that all the members of the Baptist denomination, in good standing, whether at the North or South, are constitutionally eligible to all appointments emanating either from the Convention or the Board.

2. While this is the case, it is possible that contingencies may arise in which the carrying out of this principle might create the necessity of making appointments by which the brethren of the North would either in fact, or in the opinion of the Christian community, become responsible for institutions which they could not, with a good conscience, sanction.

3. Were such a case to occur, we should not desire our brethren to violate their convictions of duty by making such appointments, but should consider it incumbent on them to refer the case to the Convention for its decision.

In the discussion of this vital question, involving in great measure the benevolence of a large, influential, and wealthy body of Christians, the ablest men of the denomination were engaged. It was not a time for heated or precipitate action. The utmost prudence and caution were needed. Much as dissolution was deplored, it seemed unavoidable.

Conservatism was to be found in the ranks of the representatives of both sections. Could their counsel have prevailed, the rupture might not have come quite so early. But as it was, no continued cooperation could be had without a serious impairment of the necessary enthusiasm as well as of the copiousness of the benevolence on the part both of the North and of the South. Between the two sections slavery had become a question of great irritation. Bitterness was engendered with advancing time. The disturbing influence of slavery was felt in every sphere. It was next to impossible, with the country agitated as it was, for Northern abolitionists and Southern slaveholders to dwell together in unity. The quietness and wisdom with which these matters were dealt, and the type of Christian character displayed during these stormy times, reflect the ability and nobility of the men engaged.

Inevitable as the separation was between Northern and Southern Baptists, it was, for some reasons, unfortunate. Had it not come, as it came, in 1844, it must needs have occurred in 1861. Though if it could have been delayed until 1861, the probability is that the dissolution would have been only a temporary one. While both sections have sustained loss by the severance, it can scarcely be denied that the South has suffered more. Considered from a calm and dispassionate point of view, it is clear that the South has suffered greatly by the loss of the conservatism which has attended the councils of Northern Baptists. Not that the South has been without conservatism, for it has measurably prevailed in spite of the tension to which Baptist liberty in the South has been at times subjected. That which else might have verged upon denominational dogma in some instances, has been counterbalanced by the conservative sentiment of such States as Maryland, Virginia, Georgia, and the Carolinas. These Atlantic States have, since the formation of the Southern Baptist Convention, represented the cool conservatism in the Baptist councils of the South, and have saved the denomination from the very extreme from which it theoretically recoils.

May 8, 1845, marks a memorable epoch in the history of Southern Baptists. In response to the call made for the assemblage of Baptist representatives from the South, 377 delegates met at the time named, in the city of Augusta, Georgia, for the purpose of forming the Southern Baptist Convention. These delegates were representatives from eight Southern States, Maryland, Virginia, North Carolina, South Carolina, Georgia, Alabama, Louisiana, Kentucky, and the District of Columbia.

It was an occasion of great enthusiasm. Dr. W.B. Johnson, who had won distinction as a parliamentary officer in the Triennial Convention, was chosen president, Hon. W. Lumpkin, of Georgia, and Dr. J.B. Taylor, of Virginia, were elected vice-presidents, and Rev. Jesse Hartwell and James C. Crane were made secretaries of the new organization.

The genius of the body was voiced in a resolution which was the result of the work of a committee of two from each State. That resolution was as follows:

> *That for peace and harmony, and in order to accomplish the greatest amount of good, and for the maintenance of those scriptural principles on which the General Missionary Convention of the Baptist denomination of the United States was originally formed, it is proper that this Convention at once proceed to organize for the propagation of the gospel.*

This was unanimously adopted.

An elaborate address was prepared, and appealed "to the brethren of the United States; to the congregations connected with the respective churches; and to all candid men." The address opens with the frank statement:

> *A painful division has taken place in the missionary operations of the American Baptists. We would explain the origin, the principles, and the objects of that division, or the peculiar circumstances in which the organization of the Southern Baptist Convention became necessary. Let not the extent of this*

*disunion be exaggerated. At the present time it involves only the Foreign and Domestic Missions of the denomination. Northern and Southern Baptists are still brethren. They differ in no article of the faith. They are guided by the same principles of gospel order. Fanatical attempts have indeed been made, in some quarters, to exclude us of the South from Christian fellowship. We do not retort these attempts, and believe their extent to be comparatively limited. Our Christian fellowship is not, as we feel, a matter to be obtruded upon any one. We abide by that of our God, his dear Son, and all his baptized followers. The few ultra Northern brethren to whom we allude must take what course they please. **Their** conduct has not influenced us in this movement. We do not regard the rupture as extending to foundation principles, nor can we think that the great body of our Northern brethren will so regard it. Disunion, however, has proceeded deplorably far. The first part of our duty is to show that its entire **origin** is with others.*

Then follows a statement of the successive events which gradually contributed to the formation of the Southern Baptist Convention. In this was set forth the charge that the Triennial Convention had broken with the principles upon which it was founded. The address declares concerning the original document which was the basis upon which the Convention was established: "Its constitution knows no difference between slaveholders and non-slaveholders." The address further declares that the members of the Southern Baptist Convention had not severed from the constitution "of the original union." It further claims that the founders of the Southern Baptist Convention had "acted in the premises with liberality" toward "the brethren of the North." Says the same document, "Thrust from the platform of equal rights between the Northern and Southern churches, we have but reconstructed that platform."

A little further on the emphatic declaration is made:

We will not practically leave it on any account**, much less in obedience to such usurped authority, or in deference to such a manifest breach of trust as is here involved; a breach of covenant that looks various ways, heavenward and earthward. **FOR WE REPEAT, THEY WOULD FORBID US TO SPEAK UNTO THE GENTILES.

Then follows a declaration which involves a firm purpose to preach the gospel everywhere. Thus is presented in analytical detail, the causes of the separation, the principles of the Southern Baptist Convention, and its objects. The elaborate address concludes:

> *In parting with our beloved brethren and coadjutors in this cause we could weep, and have wept, for ourselves and for them; but the season as well of weeping as of vain jangling is, we are constrained to believe, just now past. For years the pressure of men's hands have been upon us far too heavily. Our brethren have pressed upon every inch of our privileges and our sacred rights, but this shall only urge our gushing souls to yield proportionately of their renewed efforts to the Lord, to the church universal, and to a dying world; even as water pressed from without rises but the more within. Above all, the mountain pressure of our obligations to our God, even our own God; to Christ, and to him crucified; and to the personal and social blessings of the Holy Spirit and his influences, shall urge our little streams of the water of life to flow forth; until every wilderness and desolate place within our reach (and what extent of the world's wilderness, wisely considered, is not within our reach?) shall be glad, even as this passing calamity of division; and the deserts of unconverted human nature rejoice and blossom as the rose.*

Two general Boards called the Domestic Mission Board and the Foreign Mission Board were formed and located respectively at Marion, Alabama, and Richmond, Virginia. A vice-president for each of the two Boards was appointed from each State represented in the Convention. The meetings were appointed to be held triennially after the manner of the original convention of the United States. Richmond, Virginia, was named as the next place of meeting, and June 10, 1846, as the date. This done and the first session of the Southern Baptist Convention adjourned.

Although these devoted men had counted the cost of such an immense undertaking, the contemplation of their grave responsibilities weighed upon their spirits like the burden of the Lord upon the prophets of olden time.

CHAPTER IX
WORK UNDER CHANGED CONDITIONS

When they set themselves to organize the work of the new Convention, the founders were embarrassed with unavoidable complications. It was not an easy task for the churches, Associations, and State Conventions to sever at one blow the ties which bound them to the Triennial Convention, and at once adjust themselves to new conditions.

It was clear, from the beginning, that the peculiar circumstances which invested the newly constituted body would forbid a speedy entrance upon the proposed work. One of the peculiar features was that connected with the missionaries already upon the field. Some of these were Southerners, but they had been laboring under the auspices of the Triennial Convention. Would they be invited to sever their connection with the parent body, and place themselves under the care of the new Convention? Even should they do so, would the Southern Convention assume the work thus begun by the parent body? Would this not be an additional occasion for friction and prolonged disturbance?

All these suggestions came to the sober-minded leaders who recognized the necessity of an organization distinct from the Triennial Convention. These difficulties had been considered in advance, and were not discovered after the bridges had been burned. Relief was sought, so far as the Southern-born missionaries were concerned, by a proposal to the Northern Board to enter into partnership in the work on foreign fields; but the Northern Board wisely declined any such possibility of future complication. Finally the settlement of the question was left to the foreign missionaries themselves. If they should desire to remain under the old Board, well; if not, they would be cordially received by the Southern Board.

But slight extrication from prevailing difficulties was found by the close of the first year of the Convention. At the appointed time the delegates met in Richmond. The meeting was one of dignity and decorousness. About one hundred and fifty delegates responded to their names. Representatives were present from the American and Foreign Bible Society, The American Sunday-school Union, The American Baptist Publication Society, and the General Association of Kentucky, all of which indicated a willingness to fraternize the members of the new Convention, and as far as practicable to cooperate with them.

The delegates addressed themselves to work with a solemnity befitting the occasion. This is indicated by a series of solemn resolutions offered early in the session, from which the following is an extract:

> *Resolved, That before the final vote upon questions of vital importance (and at such other times as may be deemed suitable by the body), the business of the Convention shall be suspended, and prayer offered up to Almighty God for the guidance of his Spirit.*

No little enthusiasm was awakened by the presence of Rev. J.L. Shuck, missionary to China, and Yong Seen Sang, a native Chinaman, who had been converted and had accompanied Mr. Shuck to America. Mr. Shuck had been in the employment of the Northern Board, but now accepted appointment under the Foreign Board of the Southern Baptist Convention. Thomas Simmons, recently returned missionary from Burma, was also present during the session. The China mission was reinforced by the appointment of the additional missionaries, S.C. Clopton and George Pearcy.

In consideration of the difficulties which invested them, the members of the Convention found occasion for gratitude in that they had been able to accomplish so much during the preceding year. The provisional Boards, both foreign and domestic, had done well. The Foreign Board reported collections to the amount of $17,735, while the Domestic Board closed the year with $13,193, some of which amount consisted of pledges. In order to facilitate its work among the churches, the Foreign Board had instituted an organ of communication known as *The Southern Missionary Journal*, which afterward became *The Foreign Mission Journal*. In its first report the Domestic Mission Board showed a commendable spirit of enterprise by proposing to plant mission stations along the Pacific coast, the shores of California, and southward into Mexico. That portion of the report was not adopted, however, for fear of arousing suspicion of political combinations.

One of the distinctive features of the proceedings of this session was the proposal to increase the facilities for Christianizing the Southern slaves. The belief being prevalent that a white man would not be able to endure the climate of Western Africa, it was deemed wise to send thither at least ten colored missionaries from the South, and to maintain such a force all the while. The attitude of the Baptists of the slave States to the Negro in 1846 may be judged by the following, which was earnestly adopted:

> *Resolved, That in view of the present condition of the Afri-*

can race, and in view of the indications of Divine Providence toward that portion of the great family of fallen men, we feel that a solemn obligation rests not only upon the Convention, but upon all Christians, to furnish them with the gospel and a suitable Christian ministry.

The Convention adjourned in the midst of hopefulness and enthusiasm, and yet with a profound sense of the grave responsibility assumed. The evangelization of a large portion of the American Union had been undertaken. A full share of the work in foreign fields would have to be assumed by the new body. Vast sums of money would have to be raised and wisely disbursed in the accomplishment of these purposes. But the spirit of the Richmond Convention afforded a guarantee of ultimate success. A basis was laid for extensive work. A Foreign Board, duly equipped, was permanently located at Richmond, Virginia, and a Board of Domestic Missions was fixed at Marion, Alabama. A committee was appointed "to consider and report upon the expediency of organizing Boards of managers for Bible and publication operations."

Steps were at once taken to occupy the destitute territory of the home field as early as practicable. Florida and Texas were, at this time, most inviting fields for missionary endeavor. Into the former of these States a few Baptists entered as early as the first quarter of the century, and a Baptist church was established, the first in the State, as early as 1825, in the county of Jackson. Governmental liberality and protection gained for these new States large accessions of population, which were scattered in widely separated settlements over broad areas. Toward such regions as these the Domestic Mission Board directed its energies and resources, leaving local destitution to be cared for by the district Associations and State Conventions. As rapidly as it could the Board followed in the wake of the advancing rank of population as it pressed westward. Even as early as 1846, Mexico, as a missionary field, was challenging the attention of Southern Baptists.

The defined work of the new Convention was the evangelization of the frontier regions of the South, giving the gospel to the slaves, Christianizing the Indians of the Territories, colportage operations, and the extension of missionary work in foreign fields. Vigorous activity in the new regions of the South, which were thickening with a frontier population, was not begun too early by the Southern Baptist Convention. As the Domestic Mission Board sought to draw to its allegiance the interior churches of the South, it encountered much difficulty. Church independency was asserted even in the district Associations, and more vehemently in regard to the State Conventions, and when it came to an invited acquiescence with the general Boards it seemed the nethermost of centralization, and many openly protested. Indeed, that spirit has not altogether departed from many interior churches in the South to this day. The expanding strength of the Boards of the Southern Baptist Convention is due to the increasing acquiescence of the churches of the South, and it is proper to state that this acquiescence has been proportionate to the growing efficiency of the Southern Baptist ministry.

Through the years, from the formation of the Southern Baptist Convention to the present, there has been in progress in the South what is known in modern political phraseology as an "educational campaign." In the presentation of the respective claims of the two Boards the advantage has been on the side of the Domestic Board, the visible achievements of which in the new settlements of the South have been all along strikingly manifest. The Foreign Board was forced to await a fuller development of missionary sentiment for the cultivation of which it is in no small measure indebted to its twin sister—the Domestic Mission Board.

In the early history of the Convention there was a great demand for patience, energy, sagacity, and spiritual devotion. The territory covered by the Convention was vast, embracing fourteen large States, with an aggregate area of 955,664 square miles, and with a population of eight million, a large portion of which was rural in character, and thoroughly unevangelized. To reach this mass there were at the period of the formation of the Convention about two thousand Baptist preachers of all grades and classes in the States of the South. Only a few of this number were thoroughly educated, while many could barely read. Others were superannuated, and hundreds of them were partly or altogether secularized, and were employed as teachers, physicians, merchants, farmers, mechanics, and lawyers. These were unevenly distributed throughout the South. In the older States they were more efficient; in the newer, they were altogether unequal to the demands of the prevailing conditions.

Up to the period under discussion, Baptists were almost entirely confined to the country. Not until a later period in Southern history, when towns and cities began to spring up and to grow, did many of the most select elements of the rural population begin to resort to these thriving centers. Baptists being generally the dominant folk in the rural regions, many representatives of that denomination removed to the centers to improve their fortunes. These of course were formed into churches. In the selection of pastors they sought for those who were the peers of the occupants of the pulpits of other denominations. This gave increased emphasis to the matter of ministerial education, and made necessary the establishment of a theological seminary. Inasmuch as the Baptists of the South were almost altogether restricted to the country districts, it was fortunate that many of their ablest ministers insisted upon remaining in the country, though often tempted by city churches, to become their pastors. Some of these cultured gentlemen were owners of plantations and large bodies of slaves, and they preferred the independence of country life to the most inviting city pulpits. Some, like Andrew Broaddus, of Virginia, persistently declined the most urgent and tempting calls to the city, preferring the easy conventionalities of rural life and worship. One such man, here and there, was a tower of strength in an educational process such as the Southern churches were at that time passing through. The circle of the influence of such a man was immense, and at a time like the one under consideration, most salutary.

When the detached work of evangelization was undertaken, it was found that, in some regions of the South, white inhabitants of matured age had never heard the gospel preached. Colporters found white adults of both sexes who had never heard a sermon nor seen a minister of Christ.

The work of the organization of the incoherent elements, especially of the new States of the South, was slow and tedious. The Convention was most deliberate in its choice of officials for its Boards. The corresponding secretaryship of the Domestic Board was first tendered to J.L. Reynolds, but he declined to accept it. D.P. Bestor was next invited to the charge of the interest, but he frankly declined because he did not regard himself suited to such a position. R. Holman was then called upon and accepted the position. Upon his retirement from the service of the Board, Joseph Walker was chosen to succeed him. When Mr. Walker resigned, Mr. Holman was recalled to the office of the secretaryship, and successfully conducted the affairs of the Board to the beginning of the Civil War. M.T. Sumner was the next secretary, and for almost a score of years gave successful direction to the affairs of the Domestic Mission Board. Having resigned, W.H. McIntosh was elected secretary, which position he held until the removal of the Board to Atlanta, Georgia, in 1882, when I.T. Tichenor became secretary.

The zeal and ability with which the affairs of the Southern Baptist Convention were conducted from the beginning are seen in the results of the work of its agencies. For instance, during the first thirteen years of the career of the Domestic Mission Board, the contributions were seven times greater than those contributed to the American Baptist Home Mission Society by the same States during the thirteen years just preceding the organization of the Southern Baptist Convention. The Board served to give an impulse to every department of denominational work by impressing the churches with a sense of enlarged responsibility, and by arousing greater confidence in the possibility of an early evangelization of the South. Active agencies kept the matter fresh before the churches, and in proportion to the excitement of interest, the anti-missionary barriers gave way. Harmonious cooperation between the Domestic Board and the churches opened the way to a fair consideration of the claims of the Foreign Board.

Keeping pace with the tide of population which moved steadily westward, the Domestic Board was enabled to establish churches in the inception of such centers as Houston and Galveston, Texas, while older cities, like New Orleans, were entered and interests were planted. Likewise in Arkansas and Missouri successful work was accomplished by the Domestic Board. Southward also, into Florida, the attention of the Board was directed. Seizing such commercial points as Key West and Tampa in that State of growing importance, the interior of the State was more easily reached. The evangelization of Florida was largely procured through the agency of the Domestic Board. In occupying the State, the Board was fortunate in finding a few organizations, such as the Florida Association, which was constituted in 1841, as these furnished a vantage-ground for aggressive action. Eventually the Indians came under the fostering care of the Domestic Board, which still supplies them with missionaries. A summary of the work accomplished by the Domestic Board from 1845 until 1861, the period of the outbreak of civil strife, was, the appointment of 750 missionaries, the adding of 15,000 members to the churches, the erection of 200 meetinghouses, the constitution of 200 new churches, and the collection and disbursement of $300,000.[1]

The activity of the Board was, of course, crippled during the Civil War, during which time it directed its attention to the evangelization of the Southern armies. Here its success was as signal has it had been upon the fields of peace. Among those whom the Board employed as army evangelists were such distinguished men as I.T. Tichenor, E.W. Warren, J.B. Hawthorne, R. Holman, W.C. Buck, A.D. Sears, J.J.D. Renfroe, A.E. Dickinson, and J.L. Reynolds.

The Board shared in the general depression which immediately succeeded the Civil War, and in its gradual resuscitation had to rely chiefly upon the border States of Maryland, Kentucky, and Missouri. New vigor was given it upon its removal to Atlanta. Dr. I.T. Tichenor was induced to leave the presidency of the Agricultural and Mechanical College of Alabama to assume the secretaryship of the Board. As an indication of the fresh vitality infused into the Board there were thirty-six missionaries employed in 1881-1882, the year before its removal, ninety-five in 1883, one hundred and forty-four in 1884, one hundred and eighty-seven in 1885, two hundred and fifty-five in 1886, two hundred and eighty-seven in 1888, three hundred and twenty-four in 1889, and four hundred and six in 1891. Perhaps in no particular has the Board rendered more signal service than its agency in the creation of State mission Boards throughout the South, for these were the direct outgrowth of the work of the Home Board.[2] In many instances, these local organizations have been so efficient as to obviate the necessity of further operation of the Home Board in a number of the States.

A passing allusion has been made to the work of the Home Board among the Indians of the West. Fragments of original tribes still linger upon the western confines of our country to which the Home Board has been for many years devoted. Astonishing results have been achieved by the missionaries who have borne the gospel to the red men. Speaking of the Indians, Secretary Tichenor says in one of his reports:

> *The membership among them in proportion to population is now equal to that of our strongest Baptist States. They have been reclaimed from barbarism. They support a well-organized government. They have opened farms, built houses, established*

---

[1] Dr. A.H. Newman, *American Church History*, Baptist, Vol. 2, page 455.

[2] The name was changed to that of Home Mission Board in 1873

schools, and are prepared, if they so desired, to enter this great federation of States as a constituent member. Within the Indian Territory there are now sixteen Associations and three hundred and one churches, with a membership of thirteen thousand eight hundred and forty-four.

What was said of the work of the Board in Florida may be said equally of Texas. When the Home Board entered this wild region west of the Mississippi, there was a thinly scattered and mixed population in Texas; today the State has a Baptist membership of 111,138.

During the later years of its history the Board has accomplished remarkable results through its Cuban Mission. A captain in the insurgent army during the rebellion of 1868-73 was surrounded by a body of Spanish troopers upon a tongue of land that protruded into the waters of the gulf. Preferring the casualties of the deep to the apprehended cruelty of the Spanish soldiery, the captain with his sole companion seized a drifting plank and the two were borne far out at sea. Through a long dark night they were the plaything of the billows. The dawn of day found them still clinging to the friendly plank. Sick and exhausted the captain's companion relaxed his hold and rolled into the waters a dead man. Stretching himself as best he could across the supporting timber, the captain himself sank into unconsciousness and when he awoke found himself on board a fishing-boat, the crew of which had picked him up. Being conveyed to New York in a vessel to which he was transferred from the smaller boat, he became violently ill of pneumonia and was taken to a hospital where his case was pronounced hopeless. The youthful Cuban appealed strongly to the sympathy of Miss Alice Tucker, a young Christian woman, who led him to Christ by means of a Spanish New Testament. Baptized in the Willoughby Avenue Church, Brooklyn, N.Y., Alberto J. Diaz returned to his native land to preach the newly found truth.

Though rejected at first by kindred and friends, he continued to preach to the Cubans while he engaged in the practice of medicine, the art which he had acquired before leaving New York. In spite of persecution he laid under tribute every available agency for the furtherance of the truth on the island. A Baptist mission on the Florida coast at Key West, established in the interest of refugee Cubans attracted the attention of Diaz, which resulted in the establishment of a correspondence between him and Secretary Tichenor. Mutual interest led to the incorporation of Cuba into the field of the Home Mission Board. This action furnished the occasion of much enthusiasm on the part of Southern Baptists, which was equaled alone by the enthusiasm of the Cubans in behalf of their distinguished young countryman. Taking practical advantage of the prevailing interest in the Cuban mission throughout the South, Secretary Tichenor purchased a large theatre building at Havana, at a cost of $75,000, and converted it into a church. In addition to this interest there have been established by the Board a school for girls and a hospital for women. The mission in Cuba was achieving extraordinary results until the outbreak of the rebellion in 1895. In April, 1896, Diaz was arrested and no doubt would have been summarily dealt with but for demonstrations in his behalf throughout the South and to a large extent throughout the Union.

Another feature of the Home Mission Board is that of planting mission stations in such of the cities of the South as demand them. This is receiving notable emphasis in New Orleans. Here it has steadily fostered the work in the midst of prevailing difficulties and has been instrumental in maintaining permanent worship at the three Baptist strongholds of the city—Coliseum Place, First, and Valence Street Churches. For a number of years the Board published an organ known as *The Home Field*, which was consolidated with the *Foreign Mission Journal* in 1895, under the direction of the Southern Baptist Convention; but in 1896 the Convention again dissociated the journalistic interests of the two Boards, and left them to their discretion concerning the adoption of organs for the future. The result was that the Foreign Board re-established *The Foreign Mission Journal*, while the Home Board proposed to adopt the columns of the State denominational papers as a medium of communication with the masses of the people. In entering upon its special work in 1845, the Foreign Mission Board was relieved of much embarrassment by finding a field already open by reason of the peculiar relations which certain missionaries in China and Africa sustained to the Baptists of the South. Messrs. J.L. Shuck and I.J. Roberts, as a matter of choice personal to themselves, were transferred from the Northern Board to the Foreign Board of the Southern Baptist Convention.

The difficulties encountered by the Foreign Board in gaining headway in the South have already been noticed. Especially in the early stages of its history, it was largely dependent upon the missionary enlightenment imparted through the Home Board. During the first eighteen years of its history, the Foreign Board sent out twenty-two missionaries, viz.: Messrs. Clopton, James, Gaillard, Holmes, Bond, Roberts, Tobey, Whilden, Johnson, Shuck, Pearcy, Cabaniss, Burton, Yates, Crawford, Schielding, Hartwell, and Graves, together with Mrs. Shuck, Mrs. Graves, Mrs. James, Mrs. Whilden, Mrs. Bond, and Miss Baker. Within the period named five had died upon the field, Messrs. Clopton, James, Gaillard, Holmes, and Bond. Mrs. Whilden, Mrs. Shuck, Mrs. James, and Mrs. Bond had also passed away, and Mr. Roberts had retired from the service of the Board. Eight had returned permanently to America, viz., Messrs. Tobey, Whilden, Johnson, Shuck, Pearcy, Cabaniss, Burton, and Miss Baker. The China mission would have been reinforced in 1861 by three others, but the outbreak of the war interfered with their sailing. During the period named twelve missionaries were maintained upon the field: Messrs. Yates, Crawford, Schieling, Hartwell, and Graves, with their wives, together with Mrs. Gaillard and Mrs. Holmes. Meanwhile the labors of several native assistants were being enjoyed.

The first points occupied by the Board were Canton and Shanghai, to which were subsequently added the stations of Shin-Hing, Chefu, and Tung Chow. In addition to preaching the gospel, the missionaries were engaged in the establishment and direction of schools, the erection of chapels, and the distribution of literature. Tours were frequent into the interior of the empire, where the gospel was preached to many thousands. During the first eighteen years of the operations of the Board in China, more than one hundred converts had been received, but the faithful labors of the missionaries were regarded as prospective rather than as immediate in their results.

From 1849 to 1863 there had been appointed sixteen missionaries to Yoruba, Africa. In 1849 Missionary J.F. Bowen had founded this original mission in Africa and had opened the way for future operation. Among the earliest of the appointments of the Board upon the African field was Missionary Harden, a devoted colored preacher at Lagos, and Messrs. Goodale and Denmore, together with Mrs. Denmore, Mrs. Reid, and Mrs. Phillips, who died upon the mission field in Africa. Of the sixteen just alluded to, two were prevented from sailing. This reduced the force of the African Mission to Messrs. Harden and Stone and their wives, together with Messrs. Reid and Phillips. Missionary stations had been established at Lagos, Abbeokuta, Ijaye, Ogbomishaw, and Awyaw. Up to 1863 the missionaries upon the African field could number about fifty converts. Meanwhile an effort was made to found a mission in Brazil, and J.T. Bowen was assigned to that new field, but broken health forced him to abandon it. Early in the sixties arrangements were made for the establishment of a mission in Japan, and Messrs. C.H. Toy, Johnson, and Rhorer were appointed to that new field, but the Civil War interfered with the sailing of the first two, and the third perished at sea. The mission was abandoned until 1889.

The Liberian Mission had been the most fruitful in its results. It was among the earliest ventures of the Board, and was conducted almost exclusively by colored missionaries, though the Board had commissioned two white preachers, Messrs. Ball and Kingdon, as special assistants to the work of the mission. Mr. Ivingdon soon fell a martyr to the cause, as the African climate was entirely too severe for his constitution.

Up to 1863 twenty-four stations had been established in foreign parts by the Board, and twenty pastors and twenty-six teachers had been employed. Twelve hundred members had been gathered into all the churches upon the foreign field, and seven hundred pupils had been brought into the schools. This indicates the first work accomplished by the Board, and represents the period up to the closing of the Southern ports and the consequent suspension of communication with the outside world. It was a period of darkness and perplexity to the Board when, as a result of the great American war, its missionaries, laboring upon two distant continents, could not be communicated with. In China the missionaries were not only perplexed by the severance of communication with their native land because of an American War, but were harassed also by a prevailing Chinese war. With characteristic courage, Mr. Crawford, one of the devoted missionaries, wrote: "War or no war, the mission must go on. We can live notwithstanding the wars of China and America." Taking advantage of their positions, the Baptists of Maryland and of Kentucky transmitted funds, from time to time, to the members of the Chinese Mission. By means of this help and the makeshifts which the missionaries in China were enabled to adopt, they tided over the period covered by the years of conflict. The most formidable foe encountered by the missionaries of the Southern Board during this trying period was the Asiatic cholera, which served greatly to enhance the difficulties arising from the two wars from which the missionaries suffered. It was a dismal period for the China Mission—congregations were scattered, schools broken up, chapels burned, and one of the most devoted of the missionaries, J.L. Holmes, was murdered near Chefii.

With the restoration of peace came the enlargement of the missionary operations of the Foreign Board. After mature deliberation, the Board resolved upon the establishment of a mission in Italy in 1870. Dr. W.N. Cote, the son of a converted Roman Catholic priest, was the pioneer missionary to Italy. He succeeded in baptizing twelve converts during the first year of the mission, and near the close of the year was prepared to organize at Rome a Baptist church with eighteen members. Dr. John A. Broadus, who was at that time making a European tour, and was present at the organization of this original church, wrote from Rome in January, 1871: "I am thoroughly satisfied that the Board has acted wisely in establishing this mission, and I should exclaim vehemently against any idea of abandoning it." In 1873, Dr. Geo. B. Taylor, of Virginia, was appointed superintendent of Italian missions. He succeeded in opening a handsome chapel in Rome, in 1878, costing $27,000, since which time regular services have been held in that city. In November, 1880, Rev. J.H. Eager, of Mississippi, was sent to reinforce Dr. Taylor. The situation in Italy was portrayed thus by Mrs. Eager in 1887:

> *Before 1848 there was not one publicly declared Evangelical in the whole of Italy, except in the Waldensian Valleys. From 1848 to 1859, the gospel was preached in Piedmont only. Until 1870 not one Roman dared proclaim himself Evangelical, and no foreign Protestant could worship within the walls of Rome. Now, in 1887, there are eight thousand seven hundred and eighty-one church-members, one thousand two hundred and twenty-two catechumens, four thousand seven hundred and fifty-eight Sunday-school pupils, eighty-two colporters, one hundred and ninety-two preachers, two hundred and fifty-six churches and stations, five orphan asylums, and nine religious newspapers, either monthly or weekly.*

On leaving America, whither he had come in 1889 to raise money for the erection of chapels in Italy, Dr. J.H. Eager wrote: "Oh, for the one hundred thousand dollars spent in the churches of New York City on Easter Day for flowers!"

The Brazilian Mission being abandoned in 1860, in consequence of Missionary Bowen's health, it was not undertaken again until 1879, when E.H. Quillian was appointed a missionary at Santa Barbara. In 1881 the Brazilian Mission was reinforced by the appointment of W.B. Bagby and wife, and the next year after by Z.C. Taylor and wife, all of Texas. The mission has been a reasonably prosperous one.

The most fruitful and progressive department of work under the Foreign Mission Board is that of the Mexican Mission. The way for the occupation of that republic by the missionaries of the Southern Baptist Convention was providentially opened by the migration of a body of Texans into Mexico. Establishing a chain of settlements, they organized churches, and from the beginning received some accessions from the Mexican population. The leaders of this movement were the brothers, Westrup, both of whom had been previously supported in the State of Coahuila by the Texas Baptist State Convention. One of these, John O. Westrup, having been barbarously murdered by the Mexicans and Indians, his brother assumed direction of the entire work. Appealing to the Foreign Board for help, he was, in 1882, reinforced by W.M. Flourney and wife. During the same year, W.D. Powell and wife, of Texas, and Miss Annie J. Mayberry were appointed to the same work, and stationed at Saltillo. This was the beginning of a grand onward march into Mexico. According to a comprehensive and systematic plan, the region proposed to be evangelized was divided into missionary districts, and the missionaries were stationed at certain commanding points. In this way, a line of missions was established from the Rio Grande to the Pacific Ocean. Between the years 1882-1889, the following missionaries, together with Seniors Cardenas, Rodriguez, Gomez, and other natives, entered the field of the Mexican Mission— Misses Tupper and Barton, Mr. and Mrs. Wilson, Mr. and Mrs. McCormick, Miss Cabaniss, Mr. and Mrs. Mosely, Mr. and Mrs. Watkins, Mr. and Mrs. Chastain, and Mrs. Duggan. The qualities of leadership possessed by W.D. Powell made him the acknowledged director of the Mexican Mission. Wise in conception, resolute of purpose, courageous in execution, irresistible in energy, and yet gentle in disposition and consecrated at heart—Powell combines all the elements of a great missionary leader in a region like Mexico. From the beginning, his career in that new field of missions has been distinguished by the most signal success. He is able readily to respond to the emergencies which necessarily arise in such a region and amid such a people as the Mexicans. In the *adobe* hut of the lowly Mexican, upon the remote ranch, in the crowded mart, before the frenzied mob, in the presence of the highest officers of State, or in the most cultured assemblage—he is equally the master of the situation. Fired with a consecrated earnestness, he sways the Mexican mind with a magical power. Writing of his work in 1889, he says:

> *We have carried the work from the Texas border to the Pacific coast. Opposition is waning. I almost universally meet a warm welcome. The government gives us full protection. The leading dailies in the city of Mexico, and throughout the republic, expose Humanism and defend our cause. The clergy have lost ground rapidly during the past two years. All of our churches and mission stations report progress and prosperity. Our force of workers is insufficient to occupy the territory already open to us. We have eighteen American, and fifteen native, workers. There are eighteen organized churches and some six hundred members. "Truly this is the Lord's doing and marvelous in our eyes." . . . All our central stations have been established at fine strategic points.*

The youngest of the enterprises of the Foreign Mission Board is the Japanese Mission. It was undertaken in 1889 by Missionaries McCollum and Brunson, and their wives. Upon the retirement of Mr. Brunson, the mission was reinforced by the appointment of Messrs. Maine and Maynard, and their wives. Up to this period, the work has been of a preparatory character, but its progress had been most encouraging.

Among other efforts made by the Southern Baptist Convention was the organization, in 1851, of the Bible Board established for colportage purposes. Previous to this, efforts had been made in some of the States, notably in Alabama and Virginia, to establish and maintain local Bible Boards, but they had failed. Nor did this larger and more pretentious undertaking succeed. Publication work by a denomination is invariably attended by more or less peril. After a struggle of twelve years, the Bible Board of the Southern Baptist Convention was discontinued. The failure was largely due to the fact that with increased facilities of transportation, the American Bible Society established its auxiliaries and its colportage system throughout the South.

The Southern Baptist Publication Society never had organic connection with the Convention, but was a private enterprise. It never succeeded. As the American Baptist Publication Society came to supply the demands for denominational literature in the South, the other gradually retired and finally disappeared altogether. In 1863, the Sunday-school Board of the Southern Baptist Convention was born. It likewise perished, its span of life being measured by the period of a single decade. There was a revival of this suspended interest at the session of the Southern Baptist Convention in 1891. This was the result of the agitation of the question of Sunday-school literature, the Convention deciding to organize its own Board for the publication of this matter, but distinctly adopted the conservative proviso "that the fullest freedom of choice be accorded to everyone as to what literature he will use or support, and that no brother be disparaged in the slightest degree on account of what he may do in the exercise of his right as Christ's freeman." Dr. J.M. Frost, the author of the resolutions reviving the Board, became its first secretary, but retired after the lapse of a year, when Dr. T.P. Bell, then assistant secretary of the Foreign Mission Board, was elected secretary and treasurer of the Sunday-school Board. Retiring in the latter part of 1895, to take charge of the *Christian Index*, at Atlanta, Georgia, Dr. Bell was succeeded by Dr. Frost, who was called again to the charge of the affairs of the Board. The headquarters of the Board are in Nashville, Tennessee. Under its auspices are issued *The Teacher*, the quarterlies of different grades, leaflets and cards, together with *The Young People's Leader*. The receipts of the Sunday-school Board for the year ending May, 1896, were $62,841.12. The contributions to benevolence were made as follows: To the Foreign Board, $2,175.93; to the Home Board, $2,139.21; to Sunday-school Mission work, $3,887.50.

CHAPTER X
THE SOUTHERN BAPTIST THEOLOGICAL SEMINARY

As has already been shown, one of the matters of chief concern with the denomination builders of the South was that of preparing the way for a more enlightened and better qualified ministry. This subject engaged the attention of the most progressive of the Baptist ministry of the States of the South as early as the middle of the eighteenth century. With the opening years of the present century, the importance of a more intelligent ministry was emphasized by two imperative considerations— the growing intelligence of the masses, and the steady intellectual advancement of the ministry of other denominations. At this early period plans were devised for meeting existing demands, but they were necessarily crude, as has been shown in a previous chapter. From this desire to possess a more able ministry has grown all our denominational colleges for young men. Indeed this idea was the germ of most of our denominational advancement, for it was not dissociated from that of missions in the minds of the founders of our general denominational organizations in all the States.

While the denomination was getting in readiness for this onward movement, another event occurred in a distant quarter of the globe which contributed most materially to the enhancement of its importance. Adoniram Judson and Luther Rice decided in India that it would be necessary for one to return to America and organize means for the support of the other who might remain upon the foreign field. The return of Rice, in whose mind lay the associated ideas of intellectual advancement and denominational expansion, was most opportune for the promotion of a cherished purpose which had long engaged the attention of the most advanced elements of the denomination. Every Baptist college in the South took root in these early plans and endeavors. Founded originally upon the idea of a better prepared ministry, the earliest Baptist schools were soon forced to respond to a general demonstration to provide means for the education of those looking to other vocations than that of the ministry. This led to the next stage of development, that of providing a theological department in connection with a purely literary course. Provision was made for a single chair in connection with such a theological course as was given under such circumstances. This served the purpose, after a fashion, for a period of years; but it eventually became unsatisfactory. Baptist candidates for the ministry in search of the most comprehensive scholarship attainable, began to go North in order to avail themselves of the advanced instruction afforded at Newton, Hamilton, and Princeton.

Among such as sought these better facilities may be named J.P. Boyce, J.W.M. Williams, S.C. Clopton, H.A. Tapper Sr., E.T. Winkler, and Basil Manly Jr. The impression produced upon their minds of the incomparable advantages enjoyed in a theological seminary above those of a theological annex to a literary institution, made them earnest advocates of a seminary for the South. They found ready co-operators in such, men as J.B. Jeter, W.B. Johnson, and R.B.C. Howell.

The attention which had been devoted to the general subject for so long a time, and the attempts which had been made to meet the prevailing deficiency in the denomination, had created a profound conviction of the necessity of a separate institution for the training of the Baptist ministry of the South. Consequently one of the earliest questions considered, after the organization of the Southern Baptist Convention, was that of the possibility of founding a Southern seminary. At Augusta, Ga., in 1845, a conference of delegates from several States was held in the interest of the proposed institution. The question came up for consideration two years later, in 1847, at the meeting of the Indian Mission Association at Nashville, Tenn. Two years later still, Mr. W.B. Johnson sought to secure a meeting of the delegates to the Southern Baptist Convention from South Carolina, at Aiken, prior to the meeting of the general body in order to gain cooperation in urging the claims of the Furman Theological Institution as a nucleus of such seminary; but the effort failed. Similar attempts were afterward made by other institutions, among which was Mercer University, Georgia, but without success. The question gradually became one of general comment, and eventually led to a discussion in the denominational papers between Drs. R.B.C. Howell and Robert Ryland. The chief objection urged by Dr. Ryland against the founding of such an institution was that it would require an endowment of $100,000, and that could not be raised. .

When the Southern Baptist Convention met at Charleston in 1849, Dr. W.B. Johnson, the presiding officer of the body, presented before an educational meeting, in a learned and elaborate address, the claims of a theological seminary. He was supported by Basil Manly Jr. Still no practical action was taken.

In 1854 the General Association of Virginia proposed that at the meeting of the Southern Baptist Convention for that year, at Montgomery, Ala., "the friends of theological education" consider the claims of a seminary. This is understood to have emanated from Dr. J.B. Jeter, who was an earnest advocate of a theological seminary many years before the consummation of the enterprise. At Montgomery, resolutions were offered by Dr. A.M. Poindexter and unanimously adopted to the effect "that in the opinion of this meeting it is demanded by the interests of the cause of truth that the Baptists of the South and Southwest unite in establishing a theological institution of high grade." To this was given the practical sanction of a meeting solely in the interest of the proposed seminary, to be held the following April in Augusta, Ga. There came, to this last-named meeting, representatives from nine States and the District of Columbia. A large and able committee, of which Dr. Basil Manly Sr., was the chairman, reported "that from various causes they found the subject embarrassed by difficulties at every point, which it is useless here to discuss, as it is impossible to decide whether they are insuperable." But this declaration did not afford satisfaction to many who were intent upon the establishment of a seminary for theological instruction.

Another meeting still was appointed to be held a year later, and in order to afford ample time for the consideration of the matter, it was agreed to meet two days in advance of the Convention. To prepare the way for practical action, a committee, consisting of B. Manly Sr., A.M. Poindexter, and J.B. Jeter, was directed to report to the said meeting at Louisville:

> *1. What funds exist subject to the control of the Baptists for theological instruction in each of the institutions of the South and Southwest; whether the trustees or other parties holding legal control over these funds can and will contribute them in any form—and if any, what—to the uses of a common theological institution to be located at any other point within or without the limits of their own States severally, should the aforesaid Convention, to assemble at Louisville in 1857, adjudge such different location best for the common good; whether these funds, in case they are limited to a spot, can and will be placed within the control of such a Board of trustees as may be appointed by competent authority agreed upon for a common theological institution. Besides this the committee was authorized and requested,*

2. To use adequate means for ascertaining what efforts will be made in favor of any location, already occupied or not, by the inhabitants and friends thereof, and what pecuniary subscriptions or pledges will be given as a nucleus in case such location should be selected for the common institution; the object of all these inquiries being to ascertain, in the fullest manner possible, whether such a demand is felt for a common institution as may be a basis and encouragement for future united action.

The plan thus proposed was the product of the brain of James P. Boyce. Up to this time, the hope had been indulged that the departments for theological instruction connected with the Baptist institutions throughout the South might be combined into such an institution as was now contemplated. But this idea was now given up altogether.

When in July, 1856, the Baptist State Convention of South Carolina met at Greenville, Prof. James P. Boyce, of the theological department of Furman University, induced the Convention to propose to the contemplated Educational Convention to be held at Louisville, Kentucky, to establish at Greenville, South Carolina, a common theological institution, proposing to turn over the funds, to the amount of about $30,000, then held by the Board of Trustees for theological instruction, to the proposed institution. To this amount it was proposed to add such a sum as would make the total $100,000, to be raised in South Carolina, provided an additional $100,000 could be procured from the other States of the South.

The matter was now beginning to assume practical shape, the whole question, however, turning upon the possibility of collecting $70,000 within nine months in South Carolina.

In May, 1857, the Educational Convention which was to precede the meeting of the Southern Baptist Convention, at Louisville, Kentucky, was held. There were present eighty-eight delegates from the States of Maryland, Virginia, the Carolinas, Georgia, Alabama, Mississippi, Louisiana, Arkansas, Tennessee, and Kentucky. The proposal which came from the South Carolina Convention furnished the occasion for much enthusiasm, especially since Professor Boyce and others assured the delegates that the proposal as made by the South Carolina Baptists would be fully complied with. The interest deepened as the hope of founding a seminary grew brighter. At this juncture the executive skill of James P. Boyce for the first time became conspicuous. He formed a plan for the establishment of the seminary at Greenville, South Carolina, the following year, provided the sum of $100,000 be raised in that State by May 1, 1858, ready to be placed in the hands of the Board of Trustees. The interest accruing from this sum, $7,000, was to be used for the support of three professors, for the purchase of books (not exceeding $500 annually), and for paying a proper agency in other States to raise the additional $100,000; provided also, that recitation and lecture rooms could be secured in Greenville, for a number of years, free of rent. It was finally arranged that if the additional $100,000 should not be raised within the period of three years, then the amount furnished by South Carolina should revert to Furman University, to be devoted to theological purposes, and the contributions collected elsewhere, to their respective donors. The wisdom of such a plan is at once apparent. Here were checks and balances, bold inspiration and discreet protection at every point. A special educational meeting was provided for at Greenville, South Carolina, for May, 1858, to consummate the plans already indicated, provided the South Carolina Convention should accept the conditions. Committees were appointed, meanwhile, to prepare a plan of organization, to nominate a faculty, secure a charter from the legislature of South Carolina, provide for the canvass of the States of the South, and to issue an address to Southern Baptists. It is a noteworthy fact that the members of the committee on plan of organization, named by the venerable president of the meeting, Dr. Basil Manly Sr., were afterward elected to fill chairs in the seminary, viz., James P. Boyce, John A. Broadus, Basil Manly Jr., E.T. Winkler, and William Williams.

It fell to the lot of Dr. Jeter to prepare the address to the Baptists of the South. With his usual vigor of style, he showed that an institution like a theological seminary was needed, and that Southern Baptists had been seeking to found such for a number of years. He further showed the propriety of establishing the seminary at Greenville, South Carolina, because of its accessibility, healthfulness, and cheapness of living. In presenting the plan of organization, he insisted that the seminary:

> *being free from the shackles imposed by the old systems and established precedents, and having all the lights and experience and observation to guide us, we propose to found an institution suited to the genius, wants, and circumstances of our denomination, in which shall be taught, with special attention, the true principles of expounding the Scriptures, and the art of*

preaching efficiently the gospel of Christ.

Assurance was given that prevailing systems in the denominational colleges would not be interfered with, but would be encouraged by the proposed seminary.

The South Carolina Baptist State Convention met in July following the Louisville meeting, which gave birth to the seminary. The proposal made to the South Carolina Baptists to raise $70,000 was accepted, and James P. Boyce was appointed agent to raise the amount. Accompanied by a driver, he traveled South Carolina over in a two-horse buggy to raise the quota of that State. Though the task was a laborious one, it was cheerfully undertaken. In August, Messrs. Boyce, Broadus, and Manly met at the home of the last-named, in Richmond, to arrange an abstract of doctrinal principles to be signed by each professor, to devise the legal and practical arrangements in regard to trustees and professors, and to prepare an outline of a plan of instruction for the seminary.

The year went past and the last of the educational conventions held in the interest of the establishment of a seminary, met at Greenville, South Carolina, on May 1, 1858. Five days were spent in the discussion of plans proposed for the seminary, and the result was unanimity of sentiment and of action throughout. So harmonious was the body, after carefully reviewing each point, that every feature was adopted by a unanimous vote. Instead of the original plan of three professors, Dr. Boyce now advised the appointment of four. In every detail of outline and execution the hand of James P. Boyce was actively guiding. He had raised almost the entire amount of $70,000. Through his agency, the church building occupied by the Baptists at Greenville, previous to their entrance into their handsome edifice in another portion of the town, was procured for the use of the seminary. This building rendered valuable service for years, affording space for lecture rooms and a library. The wisdom of Dr. Boyce was conspicuous in that he pronounced against the idea of the consumption of funds in the erection of buildings until an ample endowment for instruction had been secured. Though the temptation was frequent to swerve from this purpose, Dr. Boyce held firmly to it, and the wisdom of such a course has been abundantly vindicated by the events of thirty-five years. In giving sanction to this pronounced expression of Dr. Boyce, Dr. Thomas Curtis, then the principal of Limeston (S.C.) Female Institute, said, with sonorous English tones and rolling Rs:

The requisites for an institution of learning are three b's— bricks, books, brains. Our brethren usually begin at the wrong end of the three b's; they spend all their money for bricks, have nothing to buy books, and must take such brains as they can pick up, but our brethren ought to begin at the other end of the three b's.

This expression was caught up and was soon spread all over the country.[1]

According to the modified plan, four professors were elected—J.P. Boyce, J.A. Broadus, B. Manly Jr., and E.T. Winkler. Two of these, Broadus and Winkler, declined. This together with other causes led to the delay of opening the seminary another year. In May, 1859, the Board of Trustees of the seminary met at Richmond, in connection with the Southern Baptist Convention. Drs. Broadus and Winkler were again elected to chairs in the seminary, and again Dr. Winkler declined, whereupon Dr. William Williams was chosen, and in the fall of 1859 the first session was opened. The leaders in the movement to establish a seminary, besides those mentioned were, J.L. Burrows, J.B. Taylor, G.W. Samson, R. Furman, J.W.M. Williams, J.O.B. Dargan, J.H. De Votie, D.P. Bestor, J.M. Pendleton, S.L. Helm, J.L. Dagg, and Samuel Henderson. These men represented the influential elements of the denomination throughout the South. From the outset the system of instruction in the seminary was made elective, and sufficiently flexible to be easily adjusted to the ability of any student who might desire to take the course. The first session opened prosperously with twenty-six matriculates. Of these, ten came from Virginia, nine from South Carolina, three from North Carolina, two from Alabama, one from Florida, and one from Missouri. "This was a far larger beginning than any theological seminary in America of whatever denomination had enjoyed for its first two years."[2] By a combination of the influence of the powerful factors already named, the additional hundred thousand dollars was secured from the other States of the South. This, together with the success which crowned the initial session of the seminary, secured its permanency. Before the close of the second session, the Civil War began, and from 1862 to 1865 the work of the seminary was necessari-

---

[1] Dr. J.A. Broadus, *Memoirs of James P. Boyce*, page 153.

[2] Dr. John A. Broadus, in *First Thirty Years of the Southern Baptist Theological Seminary*, page 11.

ly suspended. The professors were requested to retain their connection with the institution until the close of hostilities, to prevent the dissolution of the seminary.

Meanwhile, their salaries were continued, and were paid in Confederate money, the privilege, however, being granted them to engage in such other pursuits as they deemed advisable, while they should hold official, though nominal, connection with the institution. In consequence of this privilege, the faculty was dispersed in different directions, Dr. Boyce becoming chaplain of a Confederate regiment, and later, a member of the South Carolina legislature. Drs. Manly and Williams found partial employment as country pastors in the regions adjacent to Greenville, while Dr. Broadus divided his time between country pastorates, missionary work in General Lee's army, and the corresponding secretaryship of the Sunday-school Board, which was at that time located at Greenville.

During the summer following the capitulation of the Confederate armies, the members of the seminary faculty met at Greenville to consider the advisability of attempting to resume work in the fall of 1865. The endowment had been almost totally destroyed in consequence of the war, $5,000 alone remaining, and that was invested in Georgia Railroad bonds which could be sold for nearly par. In order to open the seminary in the fall, Dr. Boyce generously contributed $1,000 to the available resources of the seminary, although his own private affairs were critically deranged by the war, and the business outlook of the country was quite gloomy. Fortunately no incubus of debt was upon the seminary—a calamity which had been averted by the sagacity of Dr. Boyce.

With 1865 began, on the part of the seminary, a protracted struggle for life. Only seven students were enrolled during the first session after the close of the war. But the noble men of the faculty stood at their posts. One of them said, "The seminary may die, but suppose it be understood that we'll die first." Fully aware of the arduous and self-sacrificing labors which awaited them, the members of the faculty cheerfully resumed the direction of the affairs of the seminary. There was no abatement of interest nor the slightest indifference to instruction because of the slim attendance. Professors met their classes as promptly as they would have done had the lecture rooms been crowded. Dr. Broadus gave a pretty full course of instruction in homiletics to one student during the first session after the war, and that one was blind.

The number of students slowly increased, year by year, but the depressed condition of the country suggested only failure continually. Money was exceedingly scarce, and the spirit of progress seemed to have departed from the South. In the midst of these conditions, these brave and gifted men in the temporary quarters at Greenville were barely able sometimes to keep the wolf from the door. At one time, the payment of the salaries fell an entire year behind, and the worst of it was there was no assurance that they would ever be paid. Some of the professors would ride on horseback considerable distances across the country to serve rural churches, and not infrequently return laden with food for their families. The lesson of rigid economy learned during the years of the war was never more valuable than at this time. Nor were the few students who strayed through the halls, and occupied the seats of the lecture rooms, any more fortunate, for they were frequently reduced to very great straits. In this extremity, friends were not wanting. Occasionally the trying tension was relieved by the contribution of some generous soul. To the frequent appeals made by Dr. Boyce, favorable responses would now and then come, but oftener they would not. However, there were never lacking some who gave of their hard earnings to the seminary.

About 1870 a few generous Baptists at the North began to afford some aid. This was at first given to defray the personal expenses of some of the students, but afterward was contributed to the current expenses of the institution. As soon as the condition of the country would justify it, Dr. Boyce began the organization, at the meetings of the Southern Baptist Convention, of a general subscription for the payment of a given amount each year, for five years, to meet current expenses. This course was pursued at two sessions of the convention, and served the purpose admirably of assisting to tide the seminary over difficult straits. But it was evident that this could not long continue. One of two things soon became necessary—to give up the seminary altogether, with no probability of reviving it for a whole generation, or to endow it. If endowed, the seminary must be removed. The idea of endowment suggested that foundation work was as necessary as when the seminary was first instituted. It was clear that in order to endowment, the seminary would have to be removed to some State that would be willing to contribute at least one-half of the endowment fund. In the deplorable condition in which South Carolina then was, it would be impossible to realize the amount necessary for the proposed object. At that time Furman University was struggling to get upon its feet, and it stood in urgent need of every dollar which the denomination in South Carolina could command. While the question of removal was being discussed, offers were made by several cities in different States to secure for themselves the location of the seminary. It was finally decided to remove it to Louisville, Ky. South Carolina was being abandoned only in response to a call of stern necessity. All the members of the faculty were about to sunder their connection with their former surroundings, not without great grief. This was especially true of Dr. Boyce, who was devoted to his native State, and the more so now because of her prostrate condition. Dr. Boyce preceded the removal of the seminary to Louisville, where he had been engaged for several years in working up the endowment.

In 1887 the seminary opened its doors in its new home in the West. There was an increase in the attendance from the beginning. This has steadily continued from year to year. By degrees most of the great body of Kentucky Baptists came to appreciate the location of the seminary among them, and personal pledges were given to the amount of $300,000, of the half-million supposed to be necessary to maintain the institution.

Many of the pledges made by the denomination in Kentucky and elsewhere failing to be collected, and the expenses having been materially increased by reason of removal to a large city, a deficiency of funds ensued. Really it seemed, for several years after reaching Louisville, that the seminary might after all collapse. Just at this juncture, Gov. Joseph E. Brown, of Georgia, contributed to it $50,000. This was the occasion of much enthusiasm among the friends of the institution. Mr. George M. Norton, one of the leading businessmen of Louisville, was the next to act, and in such a way as to secure gifts, which when added to those already in hand would yield the increase necessary to sustain the school. Mr. Norton and his brother, W.F. Norton, had already been generous contributors to the seminary, but his plan now was to give in such a way as to secure $200,000 of invested funds. In order to command the confidence of the business public, and at the same time to secure any gifts to the seminary against any contingency, Mr. Norton proposed that such changes be made in the charter as to require that the principal of all contributions for endowment made subsequently to February 1, 1880, be held forever sacred and inviolate, only the income to be expended, and if any portion of the principal be used for expenses, then the whole should revert to the original donors. In order to give the greatest possible practical force to this measure, it was further proposed that a financial Board of the seminary, composed of five businessmen in Louisville, should be elected every year to invest the principal, hold the securities, and pay over the income to the treasurer of the seminary. The purpose was to protect the principal against all invasions, however urgent the need or grave the crisis. The legislature of Kentucky granted the amendment to the charter. Having accomplished this much, the Norton brothers now proposed to give each a generous sum toward securing the $200,000.

From this time the seminary took on new life. Without delay a vigorous canvass was begun. Dr. Broadus went North and procured about $40,000; and within two years the $200,000 was collected and invested and the seminary was saved. Up to this time the school had been quartered in rented buildings in Louisville, for the same policy was here adopted that had saved the seminary from wreck at Greenville, which was that building should not be undertaken until a permanent endowment was secured. For a period the students were quartered in a hotel of moderate dimensions, and lectures were delivered on the third and fourth floors of the Library Hall, which space had been rented for these purposes. The hotel and the two floors of the Library Hall were rented for the seminary for a term of years.

A substantial endowment being secured, Dr. Boyce, in 1884, began to devise plans for building. The Board of Trustees had appointed a committee of fifteen, including the faculty and a number of businessmen in Louisville, to select a location. A division of opinion existed respecting the location of the seminary—some contending for a suburban location where the property would gradually enhance in value; others, for a central location which would give the seminary an independent and respectable position from the beginning, and bring it frequently under the observation of its friends and supporters. Besides, it would give to the students the advantage of all that was best in the social life of the city, and place them within easy reach of the churches, Sunday-schools, and lecture halls of Louisville. A central location would enable the students to reach more readily the surrounding regions, where they might desire to preach on Sunday, as it would equally serve to enable them to resume more promptly their work on Monday. The question was the occasion of no little concern until President Boyce found property in the city which could be purchased at reasonable rates. This he quietly gained the consent of the committee to purchase. A judicious investment was made; the difficulty was at once solved; the seminary was located. So emphatically did the location commend itself to the business public that a number of gentlemen voluntarily contributed to the payment for the property.

The choice of location for the seminary was only the beginning of a new struggle on the part of President Boyce, who had now to raise $50,000 to pay for the purchased lots. Where should he look for the amount? Louisville, it would seem, had been drained of its generosity toward the seminary; the churches had grown weary of appeals, and the current expenses had still to be met. Matters were again brought to a standstill. The heart even of the great Boyce was sorely tried under such pressure. He needed $20,000 with which to make a payment for the property, and no means were in sight. Appealing to Mr. W.F. Norton to start the subscription with $2,500, Dr. Boyce wrote:

> *Getting this sum is really going to be fearful work; yet it is necessary to get it, if possible. If I can do this then the hope of buildings in the future may be reasonably entertained. Without it, I do not believe I shall ever see the day when these buildings can be completed. I do wish before I die to see the seminary fully equipped and at work. For this I have spent my whole life thus far, and am willing to spend the remainder, if I can attain the end. But my heart often sinks within me at the difficulties to be overcome. My faith in the enterprise fails. I begin to think I must leave it incomplete for some other man to finish. Oh, that I could get my brethren to see its possibilities for good, with an ample endowment! I know it could do ten times its present work.*

He was overwhelmed with the burden at this juncture because the time had arrived for making titles to the lots, and the payments due were indispensable.

From here and there the money came, sometimes from unconjectured sources. A visit from Dr. Edward Judson to Louisville about this time resulted in arousing his interest in behalf of the seminary. Returning to New York, he became the indirect means of awakening the interest of Mr. John D. Rockefeller, which found substantial expression somewhat later. Mr. J.A. Bostwick's sympathy was also quickened in consequence of a visit to Louisville. This was followed by a visit of

Dr. Broadus to New York, where generous gifts—largely conditioned upon local liberality in Louisville—were obtained. Notwithstanding his broken health, Dr. Boyce made gigantic efforts to meet the conditions named. Unchecked in his zeal even by harsh weather, which he had to encounter with shattered health, he toiled as never before. Slight dribbles gathered here and there gave but little hope of subsequent relief. Finally the amount was raised and $60,000 was realized in New York. Senator Brown, of Georgia, again came to the rescue, sending his check for $5,000 more for the contemplated building, and New York Hall was an assured success.

In 1885 two bequests were made to the seminary which greatly increased its resources. Mr. D.A. Chenault, of Madison County, Kentucky, bequeathed to it $15,000, the interest of which was to be used in aid of needy students in attendance. W.F. Norton, of Louisville, contributed $10,000 for the same purpose. On December 28, 1888, Dr. Boyce died at Pan, France, whither he had gone with the hope of procuring relief from the gout, from which he was a great sufferer. His loss was greatly lamented throughout the States of the South. His had been a career of remarkable activity, usefulness, and honor. Endowed with the highest qualities of intellect; with courage and a lofty spirit, a mastery of details which was phenomenal, a quick apprehension and an unerring judgment, indomitable firmness which never quailed before the most menacing exigency, promptness, punctuality, and perseverance which never failed; an energy rarely equaled, a capacity for labor which was herculean, and a poise of character which made him a prince among his fellows—James P. Boyce was pre-eminent among the Baptist leaders of the South.

Those elements in which he may not have been the peer of others, were compensated for manifoldly by the possession of other great qualities of which the owners of special gifts alone never dreamed. His qualities of mind and character were not only many, they were great. Jurist, financier, philosopher, theologian—he was all these to a pre-eminent degree. He was petty in nothing; he was great in all.

Dr. John A. Broadus succeeded Dr. Boyce as president of the seminary. Under his administration the work went successfully on. Side by side he had labored with Dr. Boyce from the inception of the great denominational enterprise. His last years were cheered by the decided progress which marked the career of the seminary. He had seen it grow from struggling infancy to the proportions of a giant; for in 1894 there were in attendance two hundred and seventy students taught by eleven instructors.

At that time the value of the grounds and buildings was estimated at $250,000, the endowment had grown to $475,000, and the library was valued at $50,000, there being twenty thousand volumes upon the shelves—the total valuation being $775,000.

On March 16, 1895, Dr. Broadus died. His successor to the presidential chair of the seminary, Dr. Whitsitt, in the historical address delivered at Washington, D.C., in May, 1895, on the occasion of the fiftieth anniversary of the Southern Baptist Convention, said of Dr. Broadus:

> *This year of our jubilee, with all its light and gladness, has been sadly darkened by his departure. On the seventeenth of March devout men carried him to his burial, and made great lamentation over him. The foremost leader of our history, great in the might of his greatness, has passed away from us, but his fame and usefulness shall go and grow throughout the years and ages. When you, who sit here, shall be aged and feeble men and women, little children will gather about your knees with reverence and delight to look upon one who has seen and heard and spoken with John A. Broadus.*

In May, 1875, Prof. W.H. Whitsitt, D.D., L.L., was elected by the Board of Trustees the president of the Southern Baptist Theological Seminary. The success of the first session of his administration was phenomenal, the attendance being three hundred and eighteen representing twenty-eight States, the District of Columbia, and the Indian Territory, together with one student each from China, England, Nova Scotia, and Persia, and four from Canada.

CHAPTER XI
SUNDAY-SCHOOL WORK

Information respecting the earliest Baptist Sunday-schools in the South is scant. That they existed in the earliest years of the present century is easily ascertained, but to locate them in every instance is not so easy. That so valuable an auxiliary should have been suggested to a people so alert respecting local evangelization as the Baptists of the South have ever been, is altogether natural.

In the opening years of the century great rivalry existed between the Baptists and Methodists of the South. Their local missionaries and pastors vied with each other in seeking to be the first upon the ground in every new settlement, and they were watchful of each other respecting any means which might be employed for denominational advancement. Any legitimate means which were laid under tribute by one were equally employed by the other if the cause was thereby promoted. It is a matter of record that a Sunday-school was organized in 1786, at the suggestion of Bishop Asbury in Hanover County, Virginia. This is the first school of that character of which we have an account in the South. Again, in 1790 a resolution favoring Sunday-schools was adopted by the Methodist Conference, in Charleston, South Carolina. Baptists have not been so careful to preserve their records as have other people, only as these records are embodied in the local proceedings of churches, and are therefore inaccessible to the general chronicler; hence we are left for data to the occasional glimpses that are afforded through indirect means rather than through documentary evidence.

The first third of the present century was a period preparatory to the Sunday-school interest which began to assume commanding proportions about 1840. The development of the interest was greatly hindered during the latter half of the time named, by the perpetual struggle between the progressive and the unprogressive elements of the denomination. And yet it must not be inferred that the young were left uninstructed in sacred things during this long period. While there were but few schools that approximated in efficiency the Sunday-school of today, there were organizations in which sacred instruction was given. In the centers of population, like Savannah and Charleston, where presided such denominational representatives as Holcombe and Furman, the young were regularly trained in catechetical instruction. During his Charleston pastorate, Dr. Richard Furman would, every quarter, assemble the young people of his charge for the purpose of having them recite from Keach's Baptist Catechism. Standing over the closed baptistery (which was then called the font) the honored pastor, in clerical robes and bands, having the boys ranged face to face with the girls, would alternately ply them with questions.[1]

This exercise was statedly and solemnly conducted in the presence of the assembled audience, and the recitation served to excite much interest, especially on the part of those most concerned in the reciters. The prominence thus given to the teaching of the youth of the church preserved a wide-awake interest in sacred instruction among the Baptist homes of Charleston. The lessons thus taught were never forgotten. It was a period of thorough indoctrination. Under such conditions men and women grew up robust Baptists. Though superior in many respects, the Sunday-school literature of today is not equal to that of the earlier periods with respect to denominational culture. At that time but little disposition was shown to simplify either the terms or thought of the catechism in accommodation to the capabilities of the youth. The cardinal doctrines were presented alike to the mind of the child and that of the matured theologian. It was not so much a matter of comprehension—that could be left to maturer years—it was a cramming process. Questions relative to the fundamental doctrines would be as glibly answered by boys and girls in the old First Church of Charleston, as by the thoughtful preacher in his study.

While these examinations in Keach were taking place quarterly, the Presbyterians, Methodists, and Baptists would unite in a weekly union Sunday-school. By degrees, however, each denomination withdrew and established its own school.

The first regularly organized Baptist Sunday-school in the South was in the Second Church of Baltimore. This organization took place in 1804, at the suggestion of Elder Healy, the pastor, who had emigrated from England in 1795, and was doubtless largely influenced by the Sunday-school activity then prevailing in Great Britain.

The next Baptist Sunday-school of which we have any record was that of the First Church of Charleston. It seems that prior to 1816, several denominations were united in Sunday-school instruction, as has already been shown. It was in 1816 that a distinctively Baptist Sunday-school was organized at Charleston. In 1819 still another was orga-

---

[1] Dr. O.F. Gregory, *History of First Baptist Church, Charleston, S.C.*, subject, Sunday-schools.

nized by Dr. Adiel Sherwood at Trail Creek Church, near Athens, Georgia. Dr. Sherwood had just removed from New England, where he no doubt had enjoyed the advantages which he was now seeking to impart to others.

After 1820 Sunday-schools became more numerous in different portions of the South, especially in the upper tier of the Southern States. Oftentimes they would continue until the winter months, when they would suspend until the reopening of spring. Again, they would be operated successfully for a period of months and then gradually become extinct. In the populous centers schools generally began as union organizations. The literature was such as could be gotten from any source, and usually embraced a few old catechisms.

The expansion of the denominations, however, compelled separate organizations to be made for the different Sunday-schools. Beginning first in the cities, schools gradually came to prevail in the town and village churches, and finally in the country. A Sunday-school in a rural church was rarely heard of before 1825. This marks the date of the beginning of the opposition to Sunday-schools on the part of the anti-missionary Baptists of the South, which opposition waxed in bitterness until 1838.

In some instances, ministers were silenced for advocating such institutions, and in others, members were excluded from the churches for suffering their children to attend them. The temper of the opponents of Sunday-schools at that time may be judged from an extract from the Minutes of an anti-missionary church in Alabama, the record bearing date, 1825:

> *Breastwork Church petitioned in her letter that this Association (the Alabama) take into consideration the propriety or impropriety and make consideration thereon, of a declaration made by that church declining an un-communion fellowship with the Baptist State Conventions, theological schools, Sunday-schools, Bible societies, tract societies, and all churches that hold members of such societies in fellowship with them.*

The organization of the American Sunday-school Union in 1824 gave an impulse to the Sunday-schools in the older States of the South. Agents were appointed to canvass the most populous sections, not only to organize schools, but to solicit funds for the furtherance of the objects fostered by the Union, as well as to nourish the schools organized under its auspices. In the rural districts of the South, these agents were not, at first, cordially received. Sunday-schools were regarded as an innovation, and they were adopted slowly and cautiously. The managers of the Sunday-school Union displayed great wisdom by appointing some of the denominational leaders in each of the older States of the South to represent its interests. For a long period it was difficult to maintain Sunday-schools with any degree of permanency outside of the churches of the cities.

As early as 1830 the North Carolina Baptists were advocating Sunday-schools through reports submitted to the general bodies. The Mississippi Baptist State Convention, as early as 1838, made this ringing deliverance:

> *Though the institution of Sabbath-schools is, as it were, in its infancy, its advantages have been tested by numberless experiments. It numbers now among its friends, the statesman, the philanthropist, and the pious of every name.*
>
> *And that the great Head of the church regards it with special favor is evident from the abundant success with which he has crowned it. Your committee would recommend it to the warmest sympathies and most hearty cooperation of this body as promising great good to the rising generation and the general advancement of the cause of Christ. We are aware of the discouragements under which its friends must labor in this State. Few comparatively are experienced in its operations; it is difficult to obtain books, and, in many parts, the population is so sparse as seemingly to forbid its successful introduction. But in every good cause obstacles yield to resolute perseverance. If we look about our State, we shall doubtless find that not one-sixth of the children attend preaching regularly on the Sabbath; so that it is to them the most idle day of the seven. It need not be said here that idleness is the parent of vice. But could the children be brought into a Sabbath-school, they would be restrained from profaning the Sabbath and be employed in a most valuable process of mental and moral culture.*
>
> *As an aid to the friends of Sabbath-schools, we would suggest to the Convention the expediency of establishing a Sabbath-school repository within the bounds of this State, believing that it would give birth to numbers of Sabbath-schools within the present year, be the means of securing the greater*

uniformity in books, and such books too as are generally approved by our denomination.

This admirable report, which was really a forecast of the system as it was afterward developed, closed with resolutions of high approval of the system of Sunday-school instruction, and urged its immediate attention upon the Baptist pastors throughout the State.

This report was submitted on the occasion of the second annual meeting of the Mississippi Baptist State Convention. A few years later we have the first expression concerning the Sunday-school from the Alabama Baptist State Convention. In 1844 a report was submitted for the first time, which report clearly indicates that schools have been for some time existing in the State, but the writer is led to regret "the absence of such statistical information as would contribute to the usefulness and interest of the report." In a closing resolution, the report provides that the "Convention, impressed with the value of the system of Sunday-schools, earnestly recommended that it claim the immediate attention of pastors, and that they be urged to constitute a school in each church as early as practicable." When, in 1831, Dr. William Vaughn was appointed the agent of the American Sunday-school Union in Kentucky, the cause began to excite public interest, though the schools were slow in forming. The agitations of that period, arising from the distractions occasioned by Alexander Campbell on the one hand and by the anti-missionary Baptists on the other, had made the Baptists of Kentucky reluctant to embrace any new measure. They looked askant upon the introduction of any innovation or departure, however great its promise of good results. This extreme caution delayed denominational endorsement of the Sunday-school for twenty years. It was not until 1854 that we find the General Association of Kentucky bestowing the slightest attention upon the institution. Even then the expression was a feeble and dubious one. A report upon the subject says: "From the best information we can obtain, we are of the opinion that Sunday-schools are not appreciated among our churches; that a very small proportion of the churches—probably not one-fourth—have Sunday-schools, and many of them in a very sickly condition, scarcely maintaining an existence." No positive action was taken, no aggressive interest manifested. In 1856, however, we find the General Association of Kentucky adopting the following:

Resolved, That we recommend to our churches the im-

portance of organizing Sunday-schools whenever it is practicable.

Resolved, That pastors of churches use their influence by presenting to their respective congregations the subject of Sabbath-schools and aid in organizing a healthy and efficient system.

This interest being at last aroused, an investigation of the literature which was being distributed by the agents of the American Sunday-school Union was had. The undenominational character of the literature at once aroused the opposition of the Kentucky Baptists, who were naturally sensitive at this particular juncture to the slightest evasion of a positive presentation of the principles of the Bible as they were held by Baptists. This investigation led to a vehement denunciation of the diluted character of the literature of the Sunday-school Union.

Now that interest was aroused, it was determined to constitute a new organization to be known as the Southern Sunday-school Union, which was established at Memphis, Tennessee, in November, 1858. While the depository was located at Memphis, the governing Board was appointed at Nashville. The resolutions which follow emanated from the General Association of Kentucky, and clearly show the sentiments which controlled the Baptists of the State at that time.

Resolved, That while we recognize the excellencies of the Sunday-school Union libraries, in the main we feel the defect of an entire silence on many points of divine truth, essential to the duty of Christians and to the union of God's people.

Resolved, That we approve the principle of supplying all our libraries with a literature entirely scriptural and expressive on all points of duty, both of doctrine and polity.

Resolved, That we recommend the patronage of the Southern Baptist Sunday-school Union.

This new turn in the tide of affairs served to quicken for a while denominational interest in the subject. L.B. Fish, becoming the general agent of the Memphis organization in 1860, succeeded in arousing more enthusiasm in the work than had previously existed. This brings fully before us the varying phases of the work within the territory under consideration, until the outbreak of the Civil War. Up to this time no uniformity characterized the work in the different portions of the

South where it existed. Wherever a school was established it adopted its own methods and its own course of study. Independent of uniformity of system or cooperative action Sunday-schools gradually multiplied each year until the establishment of a system under the auspices of the Southern Sunday-school Board. There were occasional general expressions of public interest in the work, such as was had at Richmond, Virginia; in 1853; when a Sunday-school convention of the Southern States met in that city.

The most that was accomplished by this meeting was that it gave increased vigor to the Institution. The subject did not claim the attention of the Southern Baptist Convention; however, until 1859. Repeated, but incidental, allusions had been made to Sunday-schools in the proceedings of the Convention from its inception; but they had not become sufficiently prominent to claim official attention until the session of the year just named. This is perhaps due to two chief causes—the Convention up to this period was engrossed in the formation of its plans for missionary work at home and in foreign fields, and the cause of Sunday-schools had not assumed sufficient prominence throughout the States constituting the Convention to challenge attention. In his annual report for 1859, as secretary of the Home Mission Board, R. Holman shows that that Board had already begun the work of the organization of Sunday-schools. He reported 114 schools as organized up to that date, with 601 teachers and 5,570 students. The same report alludes to the work previously done in the South and claims that as a result of such work 743 pupils had been converted and brought into the churches. From this time forth the Sunday-school interest claimed more the attention of the Southern Baptist Convention.

From the earliest years of the Convention Basil Manly Jr. had been greatly interested in the Sunday-school cause. He had made several ineffectual efforts to bring the matter to the attention of the general body. At last, in 1863, he procured the appointment of a committee of seven, composed of Basil Manly Jr., Sylvanus Landrum, I.T. Tichenor, T.E. planner, J.L. Burrows, C.J. Elford, E.T. Winkler, and W.T. Brantley, to report upon the expediency of a more vigorous effort in behalf of Sunday-schools. The result was an able and elaborate report which emphasized the importance of the Sunday-school as an auxiliary of church life. The report raised three questions: (1) Whether it is expedient for the Convention to attempt anything in the direction of promoting interest in Sunday-schools; (2) whether the present is the proper time; and (3) in what way the effort should be made. The conclusion was finally reached that a concentration and consolidation of the interest in all the States of the South would induce economy, uniformity, and an expansion of salutary results. The outcome of this action was the creation of a Board in the interest of the work, which Board was located at Greenville, South Carolina, with Basil Manly Jr. as president. At the same session of the Convention at which the Sunday-school Board was formed, the Bible Board was abolished. An arrangement was subsequently entered into for merging the Southern Baptist Publication Society, which sustained no connection with the Convention, into the Sunday-school Board. Hence the new organization came to be called the Sunday-school and Publication Board.

An address was at once issued to the Baptists of the South defining the object of the new Board, explaining its plans, and appealing for "voluntary agents and general help." Though beginning at a most inauspicious time, the Board began its work with confidence, and from the outset aroused great public respect, and soon laid under tribute many valuable agencies. Funds were raised for the support of the work of the Board; such pastors as could do so devoted much time to its interest; and the denominational press of the South rendered it most efficient aid. The Board was fortunate in being able to obtain a portion of the time of Dr. John A. Broadus as its corresponding secretary. Still the Board was greatly embarrassed because it had no printing facilities, and no means with which to obtain such. The Southern ports were now closed by a hostile fleet, and intercourse with the outside world being cut off, it was next to impossible to promote the interests of the Board. No literature was to be had except the remnants of stocks left on the shelves of the book dealers, together with an occasional useful book found here and there in a private house. But with the scanty material on hand, and much of that crude, the Board resolved upon the publication of a number of books.

10,000 Sunday-school primers were soon exhausted, and a second edition was issued; an edition of 14,000 *Little Sunday-school Hymn Books* was soon gone, and 70,000 more were called for. The *Confederate Sunday-school Hymn Book* was issued in an edition of 3,000, and afterward in an edition of 10,000, and they were rapidly taken. The best talent in the South was invoked in behalf of the struggling enterprise and some timely productions were issued. Among these were the *Infant Class Question Book*, by L.H. Shuck; *Little Lessons for Little*

People and the *Child's Question Book on the Four Gospels*, by B. Manly Jr., together with *A Brief Catechism of Bible Doctrine*, by James P. Boyce.

Just after the constitution of the Board, application was made to the brethren at Baltimore to arrange for the purchase of 25,000 Testaments for its work in the South. In response to this, the American Bible Society at New York made a donation of that number. These were sent under a flag of truce "for the use of the Sunday-schools of the Southern Baptist Convention." No such contribution had been thought of, but so soon as the American Bible Society learned of the destitution in the South, it promptly made liberal response. The society was informed that "the Board did not think proper to accept them as a donation, but informed the donors, with an acknowledgment of their Christian courtesy, that they would receive and distribute the Testaments, and would pay for them as soon as commercial intercourse should become practicable."[1] Even after the Board had come into the possession of these books, it found it difficult to distribute them. Mail facilities were inferior and shipment, as freight, was perilous. But most excellent results were reached by the Board. By means of a competent Sunday-school missionary in each State, much interest was aroused throughout the South. The secular press everywhere lent its potent aid, and every means possible was made to do the Board service. Among the active missionaries of the Board were: W.E. Hatcher, of Virginia; J.A. Chambliss, of South Carolina; W.T. Brantley, of Georgia; and A.W. Chambliss, of Alabama.

The exigency of the times contributed largely to the success of the cause, as parents found in the Sunday-school at least a partial means of education for their children, now that the secular schools were closed.

During this stormy period Baptists were alone in the prosecution of Sunday-school work in the South, and the schools organized by the agents of the Board were eagerly patronized by the people irrespective of name or denomination.

With the capitulation of the Southern armies came a cessation of the work of the Board. But in January, 1866, it began, in a limited way, again issuing the periodical known as *Kind Words*. This was a signal for a great demand upon the Board for Sunday-school literature. Appealing to the churches, the Board was able to get but meagre re-

---

[1] *Report of the Sunday-school and Publication Board*, for 1865.

sponse, because of the prostrate condition of the country. Unavailing to lose its hold upon the people, it promptly bought up what books it could from the Sunday-school Union, the American Baptist Publication Society, the American Tract Society, as well as from individual publishers. The brash efforts of the Board under such adverse conditions won for it sympathy, and efforts were made to restore it to its position of influence and power for good. When the Southern Baptist Convention met at Russellville, Kentucky, in May, 1866, while the South was in ruins, the following passage occurred in the report of the Sunday-school and Publication Board:

Sunday-schools for the colored people have, for many years past, been conducted in different sections of the South, particularly in the cities and towns. Their recent emancipation furnishes increased motives for establishing such schools, and there can be no longer any disposition to restrict them to oral instruction.[1] In the same connection the reasons were shown that it was timely to teach the Negroes the way of salvation more perfectly because of their increased responsibility. It was insisted too, that the people of the South were under obligation, as far as possible, to do this work for the emancipated black man. It was finally urged that the obligation was upon the Convention to organize schools for the Negroes.

The Sunday-school Board now began a wrestle for life. It had suffered in the common calamities of the war, and nothing was now left it to fall back upon but the affections of the people. An appeal for help was issued, but not a dollar came in response. A self-assumed indebtedness of $2,000 hung over the Board by reason of its refusal, in 1863, to accept the 25,000 Testaments which Dr. Fuller, of Baltimore, had been instrumental in procuring from the American Bible Society. Dr. Broadus having retired from the service of the Board, Rev. C.C. Bitting was elected to succeed him. With characteristic zeal he began laying his plans for an extensive work. The indebtedness of the Board had first to be wiped out.

Investigation showed that the Sunday-school Board possessed, at the time of the receipt of the Testaments, imperfect knowledge, and influenced by the highest dictates of Christian honor had assumed the obligation of making payment for the books. But the American Bible

---

[1] Some of the States of the South forbade by legal statute the education of slaves.

Society, on the other hand, insisted that it was a donation and begged that it be so considered. This led to a formal acknowledgment of the books as a donation, to which another was added by the American Bible Society in 1867.

Steps were now taken to enter anew upon the work of publication and missionary effort. In 1868 the Board was transferred from Greenville, South Carolina, to Memphis, Tennessee. By the consolidation of the Board with the Southern Baptist Sunday-school Union, Dr. S.H. Ford became the president of the new enterprise, and Dr. T.C. Teasdale was made secretary. The embarrassments of the Board by reason of its crippled condition were seriously enhanced by the occupation of the South at this time by the American Sunday-school Union, the American Bible Society, and the American Baptist Publication Society. Pressed on every hand for aid, Dr. Teasdale appealed to Dr. Griffith, of the American Baptist Publication Society, for relief. Dr. Griffith at once responded: "If you receive more applications than your Board can supply, encourage the applicants to appeal to us. We will cheerfully consider each case and make grants as long as we have anything to grant with."

Internal friction, complications, and inability to cope with agencies possessed of fertile resources, led to the extinction of the Sunday-school Board in 1873, by its being merged into the Domestic Mission Board. This led to the organization of Sunday-school Boards in some of the States of the South. Meanwhile the Domestic Board continued the publication of a cheap series of Sunday-school papers, of which *Kind Words* was the chief periodical, all of which were edited by Rev. Samuel Boykin.

With the returning tide of prosperity to the South came the creation of new enterprises of evangelistic endeavor. One of these was the State Boards throughout the States of the South, which Boards were based upon the Sunday-school work which had originally been done. These new agencies, without exception, were dependent upon the American Baptist Publication Society for the supplies necessary for their work. Without the timely aid of the Publication Society, Sunday-school and colportage work in the South would have been most seriously retarded if not effectually blocked. It was destined for almost a score of years to sustain the struggling Sunday-school interests of the South, both of the whites and of the blacks.

CHAPTER XII
COLLATERAL AGENCIES

The forces which have contributed to the denominational growth of the Baptists of the South have been supplemented by yet other forces. This last class, though subsidiary in character, have been none the less effective. They have come into operation, as occasion has demanded, and while the creature of denominational growth, they in turn have been productive of yet other means which have contributed to the same end. One of the most effective of these agencies in the South is the Baptist press. The Baptists are thought to be the pioneers of the religious press in the States of the South. The first undertaking of journalism as an engine of power in religious enterprises was by Henry Holcombe, of Georgia, who established, in 1801, *The Analytical Repository*. This was the first venture of Baptist journalism in the United States, the second being *The Massachusetts Baptist Missionary Magazine*, which appeared in 1803. Though it was a most effective agent while it lasted, *The Analytical Repository* was not long-lived. To the more advanced and progressive elements of the denomination in Georgia, it was most stimulative, but it was too far in advance of the conditions of the times to be effective with the masses of the denomination. It was doomed by its prematurity.

The Latter Day Luminary was one of the projects of Luther Rice for arousing an interest in foreign missions. The *Luminary* made its appearance in Washington, D.C., in 1816, first in the form of a quarterly, but afterward as a monthly. It ran a useful but brief course, but failed for want of support. This was followed by "The Columbian Star," which was ultimately resolved into *The Christian Index*, and removed first to Philadelphia then to Georgia. In its new sphere it became a powerful factor in the hands of Jesse Mercer, whose position and ability made him the champion of progress in that early period. At a time when plainness of speech and uncompromising principle were needed to turn back the tides of ignorance and prejudice, Jesse Mercer, with *The Christian Index,* most efficiently rendered the needed service. More than any other, he aroused and maintained among the Baptists of Georgia interest in missions and education. In 1840 he presented the *Index* to the Georgia Baptist State Convention, and through the subsequent eventful periods it has served as a great engine of progress, not in Georgia alone, but in the States adjacent as well.

For nearly three-quarters of a century *The Religious Herald* has rendered inestimable service to the denomination toward the East.

Started in 1828 by William Sands, a practical printer, it has laid under tribute the ablest pens of the denomination from that period to this. By its ability impelling the denomination toward the attainment of the highest development, it has been equally serviceable in restraining it by its conservatism. As an advocate of progress, *The Religious Herald* has inspired much zeal in the promotion of interest especially in behalf of education and missions. After the close of hostilities its tone of conservatism did much to allay sectional animosity and to restore a sentiment of co-fraternity between the North and South.

The Biblical Recorder was brought into being in response to a demand for such an organ in the progressive period of 1834. Thomas Meredith, the acknowledged leader of the North Carolina Baptists of that time, recognized the necessity of a State organ if he should expect to succeed in the accomplishment of the ends at which he aimed; hence *The Biblical Recorder*. It was a connecting link between *The Christian Index* on the one hand and *The Religious Herald* on the other during a period of years when they were the only denominational exponents along the Atlantic board of the South. These organs were simply indispensable during the formative period just succeeding the constitution of the Southern Baptist Convention.

To the strong and uncompromising denominational views of *The Biblical Recorder* are the Baptists of North Carolina largely due for their uniform stability and progress.

Among the most useful of the denominational organs in the western portion of the States of the South has been *The Western Recorder*. It had its germ in *The Baptist Banner*, which was begun in 1825, and was therefore the pioneer of Baptists journals west of the Alleghenies. The paper did not become *The Western Recorder* until 1851, being known by different names before that time, as it was shifted from point to point. During the troublous periods through which the denomination in that quarter of the South had been compelled to pass, *The Western Recorder* has been an invaluable ally to the maintenance of Baptist principles and a pronounced promoter of denominational progress.

Later appeared in the southwest *The Tennessee Baptist*, the chief representative of the extreme views of the Baptists of the South. It was the organ of "Old Landmarkism," and under the editorial direction of Dr. J.R. Graves, swayed a marvelous influence in the Mississippi Basin and in States bordering upon those watered by the great river, both east and west. Graves was a born polemicist, and his challenging tone, coupled with his ready utterance and forcible diction, won easily for him the popular eye and ear. He came upon the scene at a time when the conditions most favored his polemical spirit. The incoherent character of the bulk of the population reached by his paper, its ringing notes of controversy so congenial to a bustling and formative state of society, its fervid declarations against all forms of doctrinal error, at a time when both the South and the West were being swept by a storm of controversy, the location of the *Tennessee Baptist* just where many of these opposing influences met—these served to give alike to the editor and to his paper a prominence which they would not have enjoyed in calmer times. Indeed, when calmness began to prevail, the lustre of the editor as well as of his journal began to grow dim. But extreme as were the views advocated by J.R. Graves, there can be no doubt that he rendered some service in giving a proper setting to Baptist doctrine in a region where, if the sentiments had been less pronounced, they would not have been so effective.

The Southern Baptist, which was published so long at Tuskegee, Alabama, was a valuable ally to its denominational contemporaries. It had its origin at Wetumpka, Alabama, in 1838, where it was founded by Rev. John D. Williams. Removed to Marion, Alabama, where it was known as the *Alabama Baptist*, and then as the *Alabama Baptist Advocate*; thence to Montgomery, where it became the *Southwestern Baptist*; and again removed to Tuskegee, Alabama, the journal did much good in counteracting the extreme views of the *Tennessee Baptist*, while it was an able advocate of the enterprises of the denomination. The value of its contribution to Baptist interests in this newer region of the South and Southwest is beyond estimate; but it was not a whit less valuable in its stalwart defense of Baptist principles in a region where the Methodists were most progressive and aggressive. The *Southwestern Baptist* was merged into *The Christian Index*, as a result of the Civil War. One of the signs of the growth of denominational spirit in the lower basin of the Mississippi was the establishment of the *Southwestern Baptist Chronicle*, by Rev. W.C. Duncan, in 1847. The paper was ably conducted for three years, but was discontinued in consequence of the failing health of Dr. Duncan.

Feeling the need of a local organ in that quarter of the South, Mr. L.A. Duncan, brother to the former editor, undertook the establishment of the *New Orleans Baptist Chronicle* in 1852. This journal attained a considerable circulation in the States of Mississippi, Louisiana, and

Arkansas, but the paper was discontinued in 1852. Again in 1855 an effort was made to give the Baptists of the Pelican State an organ of intercommunication, hence Rev. Hanson Lee began the publication, at Mount Lebanon, of the *Louisiana Baptist*. This enterprise proved to be more successful than the others, for the paper attained the rank of one of the ablest of the Southern Baptist journals. The paper was continued throughout the dark days of the Civil War, even after the death of its gifted editor, in 1863, and was conducted subsequently by Rev. A.F. Worrell, W.F. Wells, Dr. Courtney, and W.E. Paxton, but in 1869 it was merged into the *Memphis Baptist*, the powerful organ of Dr. J.R. Graves.

Mr. J.L. Furman began the publication of *The Southern Messenger,* a semi-monthly periodical in 1876, but the enterprise was not a success for want of patronage and was soon discontinued.

The organs already named were the chief journals of the Baptists in the States of the South until the revival of interest following the cessation of hostilities. The concentration of resources and compactness of organization which became necessary after the social revolution wrought in the South, required a multiplication of educational agencies. Nothing could serve so effectually to meet prevailing demands as Baptist newspapers. Hence with the revival of suspended interests in the South came a reassertion of denominational spirit, which was voiced in each State through journals instituted for the purpose. One after another of the States began the publication of official organs, until there is one or more in each of those of the South.

Besides those already mentioned may be named *The Baptist Courier,* of South Carolina; *The Baptist and Reflector*, of Tennessee; *The Kentucky Baptist,* of Kentucky; *The Alabama Baptist*, of Alabama; *The Baptist Record*, of Mississippi; *The Baptist Chronicle*, of Louisiana; and *The Florida Baptist Witness*, of Florida.

All these have been valuable auxiliaries in denominational development in the Southern States during the last twenty-five years. In closest connection with the State Boards, these agencies have acted and reacted most helpfully upon each other, and for the general promotion of the cause of God.

Besides these, there have been periodicals of a more distinct character which have been cooperative with the State journals. Chief among such is, *The Foreign Mission Journal*, issued by the Foreign Board from Richmond, Virginia. Since its inception it has commanded a wide circle of readers throughout the South. It occupies a sphere peculiarly its own. By reason of its vital touch with the missionaries in foreign parts, it has been able to present to the churches just that information which has aroused sympathy and interest in our foreign mission work.

For a period of years the Home Mission Board issued a neat organ known as *Our Home Field*, which sustained the same relation to that Board that is sustained by *The Foreign Journal* to the Board of which it is the organ. An attempt was made in 1895 to unite these interests, but it proved impracticable and the Boards were left in 1896 to devise their own means of communication with the churches.

In the absence of a review in the South, the *Seminary Magazine*, of Louisville, Kentucky, somewhat supplies that deficiency. It is issued by the students of the Southern Baptist Theological Seminary, and by its elevated tone has done much to stimulate progress in theological thought in the States of the South.

Besides the press, there have been other potent agencies which have been closely allied to the denominational papers in the promotion of Baptist interests. The most conspicuous among these is the American Baptist Publication Society. In its origin, the Publication Society was Southern. With the expansion of the denomination in the South came, in due time, the suggestion of the imperative necessity of a general publishing agency, by means of which there might be presented, as well as perpetuated, the principles of Baptists. These principles were extending; thousands were every year embracing them, but they were presented almost exclusively by the preacher's lips.

It was not until 1824 that the matter of creating a publishing agency took shape. Four years before that time the subject had been considered in Philadelphia, but no definite action was taken. In 1823, Noah Davis, of Maryland, wrote a letter to his classmate, J.D. Knowles, of Washington, D.C., urging the formation of a tract society, to be operated under the auspices of the Baptists. The idea was suggested to Mr. Davis by seeing a tract fall to the ground from the hat of another. The letter just referred to suggested that a call be issued for a meeting to consider the feasibility of establishing a publishing interest, and the call was made through *The Columbian Star*. In response thereto, twenty-four persons met at the home of Mr. George Wood, in Washington, D.C., February 25, 1824. Among those present were William Staughton and Baron Stow, the latter being at that time a student in Columbian College.

A society was formed, George Wood became its agent, and it began operations at once. The necessity of such an agency was manifest from the readiness with which it was responded to throughout the States. Two years after its establishment, it was removed to Philadelphia, where it has since remained.

This is not the place to furnish a history of the American Baptist Publication Society; but it has thriven commensurately with the growth of the denomination and the prosperity of the country.

During the chaotic days subsequent to the close of the Civil War, when the Baptist denomination was seeking to rally its agencies, and when a new beginning was to be made in the reorganization of its work, the Publication Society came to its rescue. The work of the Sunday-school Board of the Southern Baptist Convention during the war showed where means would accomplish the greatest good. The inability of the Southern Board to meet these demands left the South in greatest need of supplies for this important department of Christian labor. Sentiment in favor of Sunday-schools had been rapidly growing since 1863. A most remarkable development of interest had been shown in this sphere during the ten years following the period just named. But just when the interest was most intense, the source of supplies was cut off by the necessary extinction of the Sunday-school Board. At that juncture, the American Baptist Publication Society turned its attention to the cultivation of the Sunday-schools in the South. It was a friend in need. With unstinted hand it gratuitously supplied hundreds of schools, both of the whites and of the blacks. Hundreds of Sunday-school libraries also were furnished in the same spirit. For more than fifteen years this work was prosecuted by the Society alone in the States of the South. Coupled with this was a colportage and missionary system conducted under the auspices of the Publication Society.

So great was the demand for Sunday-school and colportage supplies in the South, that it was determined in 1887 to establish a Branch House at Atlanta, Georgia. This was earnestly advocated by such men as Drs. Henry McDonald and H.H. Tucker. The enterprise was begun somewhat as a business venture, but when the receipts from sales for the first fiscal year amounted to more than $32,000 the experimental stage was passed, and Atlanta became the center of a great Sunday-school influence. A few years later, in response to a growing demand for the literature which the Publication Society was dispensing, another Branch House was located at Dallas, Texas, which, together with the one at St. Louis, constitutes the three in the States of the South. A fair estimate of the Society by Southern Baptists is expressed in an extract taken from an address delivered by Dr. J.B. Hawthorne at the opening of the new building of "The Salt Witness," at Ocala, Florida, in 1894:

> *The corrupting influence of the world's bad books is opposed by the purifying and the ennobling influence of millions of volumes in which there is not a taint of impurity. In this connection it gives me great pleasure to say that among the institutions which are providing the world with a wholesome literature, there is not one that deserves higher esteem and honor than the American Baptist Publication Society. It is the one Baptist institution of which every Baptist in the wide world can afford to be proud. Into every nook and corner of this great country its books and periodicals have gone to enlighten and elevate and save the people. With its magnificent facilities, directed by many of the brainiest and best men of the nation, and with the moral and material support of nearly four millions of Baptists, it is destined to accomplish wonderful transformations in this and in other countries. Working harmoniously with kindred institutions, it will do much to emancipate this land from the dominion of an unclean and debasing literature.*

Another benevolent agency in the South is the American Baptist Home Mission Society. Its work is chiefly confined to the colored people, and it is among them that work is most needed. It has created a spirit of self-respect among Southern Negroes by means of the establishment of schools. The Society has rendered the help which could not have been otherwise extended to the colored people of the South, and in the most critical period of their history. During the year 1893 alone it expended $12,562 in mission work among the colored Baptists of the South. It maintains for that people in the Southern States twenty-nine institutions of learning, of which fourteen are high schools and fifteen secondary. An important feature of the work of which the South has been a fortunate recipient from the Society is that of assisting, by gift and loan, in the erection of houses of worship.

The American Baptist Education Society was organized in 1888, possibly for the purpose of administering the educational gifts of Mr. John D. Rockefeller for the promotion of Baptist schools. Substantial and timely aid has been rendered to struggling institutions in the South in the payment of debts incurred and by the increase of their endowments. The Society serves as an eliciting agency by conditioning its donations, in almost every case, upon the raising of several times the amount donated from other and interested sources.

The Southern Baptist Young People's Union has just begun as an organization. It promises to accomplish much excellent work among the Baptist churches of the South. Through its Christian Culture Courses it is affording to the young of the denomination a more exalted and extensive view of the sacred literature, denominational history, and the history of missions.

The Southern Educational Conference is an organization which holds its sessions annually in connection with the meetings of the Southern Baptist Convention. It was organized at Birmingham, Alabama, in 1891. At its annual sessions papers of an educational character are read and discussed by the representatives who come as Baptist educators from the schools of the South.

CHAPTER XIII
WOMAN'S WORK

The general organization of Baptist women in the South into cooperative societies for missionary work, is of comparatively recent date. Long prior to this movement the women in different portions of the South were engaged, in numerous ways, in contributing to the cause of missions. Unpretentious local societies would, from time to time, be formed, and now and then a voluntary contribution would be made by some devout woman. Even as early as 1823, women's missionary societies existed in different portions of the then young State of Alabama. When the Baptist Convention of that State was organized, seven of the twenty delegates were there as representatives of these societies. These little societies were entirely independent of any general organization. Among the contributions made that year by the hands of devout women was, on the part of one, a watch and chain, and, on the part of another, two pairs of socks "knit with her own hands." There was a Woman's Missionary Society in Richmond, Virginia, as early as 1823, doubtless there were others scattered here and there through the South.

Even after new interest in woman's work had been kindled in the South, there was, in many quarters, a marked demonstration against it. The fears generally expressed were those of undue organization in the churches, which would exhaust itself in that alone, and that separation of the churches into different elements would tend to disintegration. And the further fear was not disguised that there was danger of according too great prominence to women in the churches. Even after the work of organization had begun in the South, in some quarters they were knocking in vain at the doors of Associations and State Conventions for permission and encouragement to join in the general work of the denomination. So persistent did these appeals become in some States, that efforts were made at conciliation by the adoption of certain complimentary resolutions as void of meaning as they were intended to be.

Under the inspiration of the new movement which had been transmitted from the Woman's Missionary Society of Newton Center, Massachusetts, of which Mrs. Gardner Colby was the president and Mrs. Alvah Hovey the corresponding secretary, Mrs. Ann J. Graves of Baltimore organized, in that city, in 1867, a woman's missionary prayer meeting for the support of native Bible women belonging to the Canton Baptist Mission. Mrs. Graves was the mother of Dr. R.H. Graves, the missionary to China. This meeting, certainly unpretentious enough, was steadily maintained until 1869, when Miss Brittan, of Calcutta, India, visited America, and was invited by Mrs. Graves to be present at one of the prayer meetings. So profound was the impression produced by Miss Brittan that great interest was aroused in behalf of women in heathen lands. This led to the formation of the Baltimore Auxiliary of the Woman's Union Missionary Society, which included a number of earnest women of the various Christian churches of that city. This society was constituted in 1870 with Mrs. J.W.M. Williams as president and Mrs. Ann J. Graves as secretary. Within a few years, the contributions of this local society grew from $600 to $1,000 annually.

In October, 1871, the Woman's Mission to Woman was organized, with Mrs. Franklin Wilson as president, Mrs. F. Crane as treasurer, Miss Jane W. Norris as recording secretary, and Mrs. Ann J. Graves as corresponding secretary. This work continued to grow in interest, which was not a little heightened by the marriage of Miss Norris and Dr. R.H. Graves, the missionary to China.

At the same date, October 23, 1871, Rev. John Stout, pastor of the Baptist Church at Newberry, South Carolina, organized a Woman's Missionary Society. Mr. Stout was the first in the South to undertake and to encourage such organization. Through successive years he was engaged in the organization of these societies in his native State.

Miss Edmonia Moon, of Virginia, having been accepted by the Foreign Mission Board as a missionary to China in 1872, the Baptist women of Richmond, Virginia, at once organized the Woman's Missionary Society of that city, for the support of Miss Moon. The contributions, the first year, amounted to $1,200.

In 1872, in his first annual report to the Southern Baptist Convention at Raleigh, North Carolina, as corresponding secretary of the Foreign Mission Board, Dr. Tupper alluded to the importance of organizing Bible women at our missionary stations and suggested that the women of our churches might be aroused to the importance of "redeeming their sister women from the degrading and destroying thraldom of paganism."

A report upon woman's work read at the session of the Convention in 1872, by Dr. J.W.M. Williams, appealed to the delegates present to take immediate steps to organize women's missionary societies. Rev. John Stout was present at this session of the Convention and was greatly interested in the woman's movement, as he had shown by his efficient work in the organization of societies in South Carolina. The work which was done in this direction for several years afterward was confined almost exclusively to South Carolina and to a single pastor— John Stout, the originator of the movement in the South. The matter claimed the attention of the Southern Baptist Convention again in 1875, when the work of organizing woman's missionary societies was formally commended. In 1876 the South Carolina Central Committee of Missions was constituted at the suggestion of Mr. Stout. This was the first central committee organized in the South. It received that year the sanction of the South Carolina Baptist State Convention.

In 1878 the matter was again before the Southern Convention, which met that year at Nashville, Tennessee. At this time the first positive step was taken by the Convention respecting this important work. In a report submitted by Dr. J.W.M. Williams, of which committee Mr. Stout was a member and who no doubt influenced the suggestion, it was urged that central committees be organized in each State to co-operate with the two general Boards, as auxiliary to the Southern Baptist Convention. The following year, 1879, the chairman of the committee on woman's work was Dr. T.T. Eaton. The committee emphasized the action of the one of the preceding year, repeating the importance of women's organizations.

Meanwhile the work was assuming greater proportions. Under the lead of Rev. John Stout, South Carolina was greatly in advance of the other States of the South, in some of which the Conventions declined to give encouragement to the movement. The segregated condition of the societies which had been formed throughout the South, suggested the propriety of a general cooperative organization, but it was not effected for several years.

In 1881, Secretary Tapper, in his annual report, called the attention of the Southern Baptist Convention to the movement going on in the South and stated that so far as could be ascertained, three hundred and fifty of these societies had been organized, and they had contributed to foreign missions $6,244.30.

Still the Convention was tardy about doing more than to give verbal endorsement. Resistance to the movement continued in a number of the Southern States, and difficulties were overcome only by the quiet organization of societies in almost all these States. In 1883 the question was again before the Southern Baptist Convention, at Waco, Texas. This time it aroused more interest than had previously prevailed, which interest found expression very soon afterward in the organization of central committees throughout the States of the South. Organization gave additional strength to the growing cause. The work grew apace until the occurrence of a little episode in the Southern Baptist Convention, in 1885, at Augusta, Georgia. At that session a portion of the Arkansas delegation to the Convention was composed of women. There was nothing in the constitution of the Convention to prevent their recognition as delegates. The ripple of agitation produced by the occurrence, was lulled by the reference of the matter to a committee of one from each State, of which Dr. J. William Jones, of Virginia, was the chairman. After due deliberation the committee reported the following:

> *Your committee to whom was referred the whole question of the eligibility of women to seats as delegates in this body, have considered the matter and have unanimously agreed to the following: As some doubt has arisen as to the proper construction of the Constitution, we recommend the following amendment: In Article III., of the constitution, strike out the word "members" in the first line, and insert instead thereof the word "brethren."*

The report was adopted, and the matter was set at rest. Many Baptist women from the South were present at this session of the Convention not with the view of being recognized as delegates but to confer together about the work throughout the South. Holding a meeting, in which the ladies from Arkansas heartily joined, all these noble women present at that time sent a communication to the Convention, disclaiming any purpose to form a separate and independent organization, and announcing as their purpose to work directly through the churches and through all the appointed channels of the Convention.

Whatever misapprehensions may have previously existed were removed by this action on the part of the women at Augusta, and a fresh impulse was given to the movement in every portion of the South. Prior to 1890 the general organization for the South was known as the Executive Committee of Woman's Mission Societies. Later, it assumed the more dignified designation of Woman's Missionary Union.

After the meeting of the Southern Baptist Convention at Augusta, Georgia, in 1885, woman's work received appropriate recognition. It became a prevailing custom for the representatives of the women's societies from each State to assemble at the same time and place of meeting of the Southern Baptist Convention. While auxiliary to the Convention, the women hold their meetings separately, and in another portion of the city. Partly through modesty, and partly because they wish to transact their business in a manner satisfactory to themselves, they forbid the attendance of members of the other sex. If one enters a meeting of the Union it is because he is invited to do so. The headquarters of the Woman's Missionary Union is in the city of Baltimore. Mrs. A.M. Gwatney is the president of the body, and Miss Annie W. Armstrong is the corresponding secretary. Besides the collected funds which are contributed directly to the treasuries of the two general Boards, much valuable service is rendered by the union in the distribution of religious and missionary literature, and in furnishing stores of supplies to the missionaries of the Home Board laboring upon the Western frontier. The organizations in some of the States assume the support of missionaries upon the foreign field, while others attend to the education of their children.

The year 1888 marks the date of the distinct organization of the woman's movement in the South. All the efforts which preceded that date were preparatory to a general organization. Within a few of the States the work had been thoroughly and efficiently organized long before that time, but the movement did not become general until the date named. As the organization increases in numerical strength, it gains in popularity and multiplies in its agencies for work. In the larger cities much missionary work is done, and much benevolence is expended among the poorer classes.

The following recommendations of the Executive Committee adopted at Washington, D.C., in 1895, clearly set forth the spirit and purpose of the Woman's Missionary Union.

1. Believing that through the influence and power of the Holy Spirit great things can be accomplished for the Lord, we suggest that the first week in January, 1895—the World's Week of Prayer—be observed by the woman's mission societies with special reference to the guidance of the Spirit in the extension of interest in missions; and to make our prayers more specific, that the Mission (Prayer) Card be more generally used. ...

3. That the recommendations of the Foreign and Home Boards asking for total collections from woman's mission societies of thirty thousand dollars and twenty-five thousand dollars respectively, be heartily commended; and we further sug-

gest, to give definiteness, that these sums be proportioned among the States.

4. Believing that in the young people is our future strength, we earnestly recommend that the work of organizing mission societies and bands among young women, girls, and boys be vigorously prosecuted. That central committees appoint one of their number, or elect one to be of their number, to take charge of this work in each State.

5. Encouraged by the enthusiasm with which the week of self-denial was entered upon, and the results following, it is again recommended that a week of self-denial be observed by the societies.

6. That mothers' meetings and industrial schools be organized among foreign populations and colored women and children; and that Sunday-schools be instituted for the Chinese wherever found, whether there be one or more.

Thus, from a crude and tangled form, doubtful of its issue in 1888, the woman's movement in the South has become one of the most efficient arms of sacred work. Foremost in the establishment of the success of the union has been Mrs. Ann J. Graves, Miss M.E. McIntosh (Mrs. Bell), Miss Annie W. Armstrong, Mrs. A.M. Hillman, Miss Fannie E. Heck, Mrs. M.D. Early, Mrs. Geo. B. Eager, Mrs. John Stout, and Mrs. J.P. Eagle. Many others there are whose names are known to the Master. The commendable aim of the union is understood to be "to make of every Baptist woman an intelligent and active friend of missions, and to induce in such a regular, systematic habit of remembering this work both in their prayers and gifts."[1]

---

[1] The development of woman's work in the South, so far as it pertains to the contributions of funds, is shown in the following woman's work table. Totals for home and foreign missions since organization:
1888 $21,039.16
1889 30,773.69
1890 31,237.76
1891 38,990.31
1892 44,282.80
1893 (Centennial Year) 62,336.75
1894 45,128.59
1895 48,449.25
Grand Total, $322,238.34

CHAPTER XIV
COLORED BAPTISTS AND THEIR WORK

One of the most interesting features of denominational history in the South is that of the colored Baptists. The beginning of their spiritual history antedates their political emancipation more than a century. True, the enslavement of the black man was a monstrous evil alike to slave and owner, and yet there were incidental advantages springing even from slavery that were incalculable to the Negro. American slavery is dead, never to be revived, and there could be no satisfaction derived from a reproduction of arguments in its defense, even if the disposition should exist; yet there were advantages incidentally derived from the institution, without which the colored people must have remained barbarians. While many thousands of them were subjected to the most exacting labor, and oftentimes to cruel treatment, there were yet many other thousands whose labor was light, who were exempt from cruel servitude, and who were favored by being brought into daily contact with the highest culture of the South. In the capacities of maids, housekeepers, seamstresses, and nurses, of hostlers, coachmen, and attendants, they served by the ten thousand in the most cultured of Southern homes. Docile, gentle, and impressible, these people became the unconscious possessors of innumerable advantages which rendered them excellent service when the period of emancipation came.

Associated with the youth of the whites, thousands not only secured the rudiments of an education, but many became musicians, speakers, reciters, and writers, and many were enabled to absorb the conventionalities of social life. Easily receptive and deeply emotional, many bright slave boys caught the spirit of oratory from the numerous rehearsals of the white youth, and when the restraints of slavery were lifted, they flashed into sudden prominence as preachers and as public speakers. To many of them the transition was an easy one from the incidental benefits of slavery to a response to the demands made upon them when they were thrown upon their own resources. Back of much of the phenomenal advancement of the black man lay the numerous small advantages enjoyed during his enslavement, which advantages, in the aggregate, were considerable; so that the Negro was not an untutored savage when liberation came. Many there were who had been imbruted by cruel masters; many who suffered from lack of the necessaries of life; many who were degraded by the most vicious impositions; still there was a large favored class whose gain was immense, and without the enjoyment of which the race would have been deplorably helpless when the boon of emancipation was received.

In recording these facts, there is no desire to rob the colored man of any merit which justly belongs to him. That he deserves much credit is true; that he deserves the need of praise for his prompt and appropriate use of means placed within his reach the fair-minded will not deny; and that he has been able to accomplish so much in the midst of adverse conditions is a matter of no small wonder and an occasion of much commendation.

In order to a proper estimate of the history of the evangelization of the colored people of the South, and in order fully to understand the nature of their work, we shall have to gather up the scattered threads of history and knit them together.

Just before the beginning of the Revolutionary War a colored man, and a slave, named George Liele, was converted in Burke County, Georgia, under the preaching of Matthew Moore, a pioneer Baptist preacher. Having been baptized, Liele was permitted to preach, and his efforts were attended with the happiest results. Liberated by his master, Henry Sharpe, about the time of the outbreak of the Revolution, Liele went to Savannah and began preaching with great acceptance at Bramton and Yamacraw, near the city, as well as upon the outlying plantations. Continuing his work in this region to the close of the Revolution, Liele accompanied the British to Jamaica as the body-servant of an English officer. Deeply moved by the degradation of the unchristian masses about him on the island, Liele began preaching to them. Wherever he could gather a crowd, whether upon the commons or the race-course, on the streets or in his own hired house, he earnestly presented the claims of the gospel. His efforts were rewarded by his ability to gather a church of four members, who, like himself, were refugees from America.

He now threw himself with consuming zeal into gospel work, and while he supported himself, was enabled within seven years to baptize five hundred converts. In 1793 he erected the first dissenting chapel ever built in Jamaica. Meanwhile he was the victim of much sore persecution, having been imprisoned and loaded with irons more than once, and once tried for his life. From Jamaica, George Liele was instrumental, through correspondence with Drs. Ryland and Rippon of England, in introducing the gospel into Africa.

Before leaving America for Jamaica, Liele baptized in the neighborhood of Savannah, Andrew Bryan, a slave who, nine months after his conversion, began preaching at Yamacraw.

Many converts were the result of his efforts. Obtaining permission to preach in a barn at Bramton, the good work went on until he was interfered with by some disreputable whites, who attacked the crowd under the pretense of suppressing sedition. This disturbance was summarily checked by the slave-owners of the community, and the meetings were encouraged to proceed. During all this time Bryan was not licensed to preach. Thomas Burton, an aged white minister, having heard of this work of grace among the slaves, visited them and baptized eighteen. Later, in 1788, Abraham Marshall, of Kiokee Church, accompanied by Jesse Peter, a young colored preacher of Augusta, visited the Bramton community and baptized forty-five more, organized a church, and ordained Bryan to the full work of the ministry. This became the parent of two other strong colored churches in Savannah. Bryan died at the age of ninety and was buried with marked respect by the white Christians of the city in which he had spent his life as a slave preacher. Slave though he was, Bryan left an estate of three thousand dollars when he died.

In recognition of the valuable services of this slave preacher, the Savannah Association (white) on the occasion of his death, in 1812, adopted the following resolutions:

> *The Association is sensibly affected by the death of the Rev. Andrew Bryan, a man of color, and pastor of the First Colored Church in Savannah. This son of Africa, after suffering inexpressible persecutions in the cause of his divine Master, was at length permitted to discharge the duties of the ministry among his colored friends in peace and quiet, hundreds of whom, through his instrumentality, were brought to a knowledge of the truth as "it is in Jesus." He closed his extensively useful and amazingly luminous course in the lively exercise of faith and in the joyful hope of a happy immortality.*

The mantle of Andrew Bryan fell upon his nephew, Andrew Marshall, who prosecuted with vigor the work in the midst of the slave population in Southern Georgia, until his death in 1856.

One of the most notable of the colored Baptists of the South was Lot Cary, who was the first colored missionary to go from America to Africa. Cary was born near the close of the eighteenth century, and in his early manhood was notoriously corrupt and vicious. In 1804 he was laboring as a common slave in a tobacco warehouse in Richmond, Virginia. Converted in 1807, he became a member of the First Baptist Church (white), of Richmond, there being at that time no organized colored churches in the South.[1]

From the galleries of the old First Church in Richmond, Cary heard a thrilling sermon based upon the conversation of our Lord with Nicodemus. Here was born in his heart a desire to preach, that he might tell this thrilling story to others. Finding a friendly tutor in a young white man, Cary was soon able to read the New Testament, and was licensed to preach. He became enthusiastic in his work among the blacks in Richmond, and was soon a controlling factor among them. His avidity for reading led him to purchase a small but indiscriminate lot of books which he usually picked up from the shelves of cheap venders. This scanty and heterogeneous library he kept within easy reach, that no opportunity might be lost for mental improvement. Every snatch of leisure in the warehouse was devoted to his books. A passer-by in the warehouse happened to pick up one of Cary's books on one occasion and found that he had been cudgeling his brain with Adam Smith's *Wealth of Nations*. It was a book—something to be read—and that was sufficient to the enslaved student. He had chanced upon it, no doubt, at some cheap book-stall, or at a miscellaneous auction, and was seeking to unravel its contents. Like his namesake, William Carey, he numbered among his possessions *The Voyages of Captain Cook*. Who can deny that in the unfolding of the life of this wonderful man God's hand was in the direction of his tutelage?

By a careful preservation of the bits of tobacco lying about the floor of the warehouse, which were given him, and by an economical hoarding of the generous "tips" of the merchants whom he served in diverse ways, Cary finally accumulated $850, with which he purchased his freedom and that of his children, his wife having been previously freed by the hand of death. He had no difficulty in obtaining work, as his reputation for honesty was well known in the business circles of Richmond. He was one of the principal agents in the formation of the African Missionary Society of Richmond, which society was organized in 1815—one of the first organized in America. Within

---

[1] When converts among the slaves began to multiply, galleries and adjoining compartments to the main audience rooms of the churches were provided for the accommodation of the colored people, who attended upon the same services with the whites.

five years this society raised $700, which was made up largely of the contributions of the Christian slaves.

Though the possessor of a pleasant home, which he had purchased, and though prosperous in business, Cary felt desirous of going to Africa as a missionary. His employer having learned of this desire, sought to dissuade him from such a purpose, and increased his wages by way of inducement to reconsider; but the consecrated preacher could not be moved. He surrendered his position, sold his attractive home, and offered himself to the Triennial Convention for work in Africa. In company with Colin Teage, another colored preacher, Cary sailed for Africa in January, 1821. These men began their labors among the Bassas, at Monrovia, Liberia, in 1822. After laboring for one year they baptized six, and the year succeeding nine more were baptized. Of the wonderful career of these ex-slaves more cannot be said than that a marvelous work was done in the conversion of many native Africans and in instructing them in the principles of government.

The numerical increase of the colored Baptists of the South is largely due to the interest which was manifested in the Negro in the early stages of Southern history. White missionaries were engaged by the district Associations to visit the populous plantations and to preach to the blacks. Many of our most devoted home missionaries were preachers to the slaves upon the plantations. Sometimes the owner of many slaves would engage, upon a stated salary, the services of such men, and again the churches and Associations would assign them to such work. Again, where ministerial gifts were developed among converted slaves they were sometimes liberated and appointed to labor as missionaries. Respectful consideration was not withheld from the Christian slaves even from the earliest periods of Southern history. So early as 1793 a church composed exclusively of colored people in the city of Williamsburg, Virginia, was admitted into the Dover Association, and they have continued all along to send delegates to the annual meetings of that body.[1]

In 1828, the Alabama Association purchased a slave named Caesar, at the cost of $625, and set him apart to the gospel ministry to labor among his people. This man of God, though as black as Erebus, was the companion in labors for many years of James McLemore, a

---

[1] Semple, *A History of the Rise and Progress of the Baptists in Virginia*, page 126.

white evangelist of local note in Alabama. Caesar was universally respected alike for his piety and his ability as a preacher, and not infrequently would address audiences composed entirely of whites.

Another slave, Dock Phillips, who was a preacher of power and of commanding influence among his people, the Tuskegee Association undertook to purchase in order that he might be appointed a missionary; but he declined to be severed from his master, who allowed him whatever time he might desire for preaching.

At this period there were but few separate organizations of the blacks in the South. In the centers of population an occasional colored church was to be met with. In Savannah, Georgia, there were three such churches, the pastors of which were sustained by one-third of the Negro population of the city, at salaries ranging from $800 to $1,000 a year.[1] At other points colored churches were presided over by white pastors, as was true of the Anthony Street Church, Mobile, Alabama, where Rev. Keidor Hawthorne was pastor. Another notable instance is afforded by the First African Church of Richmond, Virginia, of which Dr. Robert Ryland, then president of Richmond College, served as pastor. He sustained this relation for a period of twenty-five years, a fact that denotes devotion and affection on the part of both, and baptized during that time not less than three thousand blacks.

The custom of licensing and ordaining colored ministers was prevalent in the South up to 1825, after which date the practice was abandoned and in some of the States of the South, laws were enacted forbidding slaves to be taught to read.[2] This grew out of the apprehension that if thus taught they would chafe under the restraint of servitude, and possibly beget insurrectionary trouble. As has been seen, these statutes, however moderate or severe, were utterly ignored in thousands of instances, and housemaids and butlers were taught to read and write. The easily impressionable nature of the Negro has made him readily susceptible to the gospel, and he is usually a most enthusiastic auditor.

During slavery in the South Negroes attended in vast throngs services held on the plantations. Their stentorian melody of praise, unrestrained by conventionality, was often heard at considerable distances as they would heartily throw their souls into the worship. When the

---

[1] Edward Ingle, *Southern Sidelights.*

[2] The States of Alabama, Georgia, North Carolina, South Carolina, and Virginia had express provisions in their laws against the instruction of free Negroes.

slaves attended upon the same churches as the whites, the former generally outnumbered the latter, and when the Lord's Supper was observed, slaves communed with their masters. Among the notable instances of the devotion of colored Baptists to their principles may be mentioned the fact that, in portions of Louisiana which were completely under the domination of the French Catholics where the religion of the Romanist alone prevailed, the Negro slaves of these people were allowed to engage in no other form of worship than that of the Roman Catholic.

After their emancipation the fact became known that these enslaved people had secretly maintained Baptist worship for a long period of years. They had their regular organizations upon the plantations—their preachers, their deacons—all. Under the cover of darkness in unfrequented quarters these Baptist slaves would hold their services as noiselessly as possible, and observe the ordinances in due form. One feature of Romish worship greatly impressed these benighted slaves, and that was the baptism of infants. To the ignorant slave there was a fetich fascination in this ceremony, and long after the period of emancipation, colored Baptist preachers in some portions of Louisiana used the ceremony of the sprinkling of infants with water as an act of the consecration of the child to the Lord.

The records of the Baptist organizations in the South, prior to the Civil War, abound in allusions to provisions made for Christianizing the negro. Believing that more could be accomplished by members of their own race in Africa than by white missionaries, two colored men—J. Day and A.L. Jones—were sent in 1846, by the Southern Baptist Convention, to the Dark Continent. These were followed by others at later periods.

Considered as a body, the colored Baptists of the South, according to the eleventh census, 1890, constitute the most numerous section of Regular Baptists in the world. Multitudinous as these figures show the colored Baptists to be, they do not include all American Negro Baptists. Many of these reside in the North and are quite generally members of white churches and are counted with them without distinction, in the census aggregate.

There are many others who are not included in the great national count, because of obscure rural churches and of Associations of colored Baptists which were not reached by the census officers. Many again failed, for divers reasons, to respond to repeated requests made by the national officials to clerks or moderators for statistics. It is presumed that a third or more of the colored Baptist Associations of the South failed to furnish adequate statistics of numbers and of property. Notwithstanding this, we have the figures given below.[1]

For reasons already assigned, the colored Baptists of the South were not wholly unprepared to withdraw from the churches of the whites and to enter into independent organizations, when the period of emancipation came. This was clearly seen to be the wisest step possible on the part of the blacks, and yet they were not left wholly uncared for by the whites. Wherever aid was sought, and it could be extended, it was cordially given to the struggling blacks. In the work of organization, both of churches and of Associations, in the ordination of ministers and deacons, and in the erection of schoolhouses and church buildings, substantial aid was cheerfully rendered.

There has been, on the part of the colored Baptists, a most commendable progress in the development of church life. So soon as they were able to do so, they organized themselves into district Associations, then into the more general bodies of State and national Conven-

---

[1] Georgia leads with 200,510 colored Baptists; Virginia, 199,871; Alabama, 142,437; Mississippi, 130,647; North Carolina, 134,445; South Carolina, 125,572; Tennessee, 52,183; Kentucky, 50,245; Florida, 20,828; District of Columbia, 12,717; Maryland, 7,750; West Virginia, 4,233; Louisiana, 68,008. The grand aggregate for the States named, together with the District of Columbia, is 1,087,445. The following table furnishes additional data of interest respecting colored Baptists:

	Organizations	Meetinghouses	Seating Capacity	Property Value
Alabama	1,374	1,341	376,839	$795,384
D.C.	43	33	18,000	$383,150
Florida	329	295	61,588	$137,578
Georgia	1818	1,800	544,546	$1,045,310
Kentucky	378	359	109,030	$406,949
Lousiana	865	861	191,041	$609,890
Maryland	38	34	12,389	$150,475
Mississippi	1,385	1,333	371,115	$682,541
N. Carolina	1,173	1,164	362,946	$705,512
S. Carolina	860	836	275,529	$699,961
Tennessee	569	534	159,140	$519,923
Virginia	1,001	977	356,032	$1,192,035
W. Virginia	79	50	14,175	$59,090

tions. The colored Baptists of North Carolina were the first to organize a State Convention, which was done in 1866, with Alabama and Virginia following in 1867. Later, there came in point of time Arkansas and Kentucky, to be followed by the other States of the South still later.

As soon as this spirit of organization began to prevail in the States of the South, representative colored men came from the North to assist and direct in the matter of affiliation with the larger bodies.

In August, 1866, the twenty-sixth anniversary of the colored Missionary Convention was held in Richmond, Virginia, when it was determined to consolidate all of the general interests of colored Baptists—the Missionary, Northwestern, and Southern Conventions—into one body, which was called the Consolidated American Baptist Missionary Convention. Eleven years later, this consolidated body met again in Richmond, when some very decided differences of opinion arose respecting questions of management and extent of jurisdiction. Disruption for a time threatened the body, but it was preserved. Dissolution ultimately came, however, until now the field embraced by the States of the South is included in the Baptist Foreign Missionary Convention of the United States, which body was formed in 1880. In 1883, this Convention sent six missionaries to Africa—J.H. Presley and W.W. Colley, together with their wives, and J.J. Coles and H. McKinney.

The American National Baptist Convention was organized in 1886 in St. Louis. It was a large representative body of six hundred delegates from seventeen States. The advancement of the colored people was indicated by the fact that there were present "graduates in law, medicine, and theology; professors of philosophy, German, French, Latin, Greek, and Hebrew; a number of State ex-representatives and ex-sen- ators; two lieutenant-governors; editors and teachers, not a few; a Baptist senator from Mississippi; and a Baptist missionary from London, England." Rev. T.L. Johnson, one of the speakers of the occasion said: "Knox lifted up Scotland; Luther lifted up Germany; and it is for us to lift up the heathen in the land of our fathers."[1]

The genuine orthodoxy of this body was set forth in 1890, when a resolution was adopted recommending that the practice of receiving into membership persons immersed into Pedobaptist churches be dis-

---

[1] Dr. Cook's *Story of the Baptists*, page 423.

continued, on the ground that Pedobaptist organizations are not churches, and therefore have no power to administer baptism. The exchange of pulpits with Pedobaptists was also condemned as "inconsistent and erroneous."[1]

The colored Baptists of all the States of the South have nearly thirty schools of high grade, which are largely devoted to the preparation of preachers and teachers. The first of these to be organized was that of Roger Williams University, at Nashville, Tennessee, in 1864. It has a college property valued at $205,000. The next two schools were founded respectively at Raleigh, N.C., and Washington, D.C., in 1865; the first, Shaw University, having a property valued at $215,500, and the second, Wayland Seminary, the property of which is valued at $113,000. In 1867, the Atlanta Seminary was founded, and now it has a property, the total valuation of which is $85,500. The Benedict College, at Columbia, founded in 1870, has a property estimated at $112,000. In 1873, the Florida Institute was established at Live Oak, and its property valuation is $10,050. In Jackson, Mississippi, is Jackson College, organized in 1877, and its property is estimated to be worth $25,000. The Selma University was established at Selma, Alabama, in 1878, and it owns a property valued at $20,250. The college of Kentucky for colored Baptists, is located at Louisville, and is known as the State University. It was founded in 1879, and owns a property valued at $30,500. Spelman Seminary, of Atlanta, Georgia, was instituted in 1881, and owns a property the valuation of which is $153,000. Leland University was established in 1870 at New Orleans, Louisiana, and possesses a most valuable property, estimated to be worth $160,000. These are the principal schools which are under the management of the colored Baptists in the Southern States east of the Mississippi. Most of these schools are the result of Northern benefactions, and most of them, as well as others of less note, are maintained by the American Baptist Home Mission Society.

Among the periodicals owned and conducted by the colored Baptists of the region of country under consideration may be named: *The African Expositor*, Raleigh, N.C.; *American Baptist*, Louisville, Ky.; *Baptist Messenger*, Jackson, Miss.; *Georgia Baptist* and *Weekly Sentinel*, Augusta, Ga.; *Baptist Signal*, Greenville, Miss.; *The Living Way* and *Memphis Watchman*, Memphis, Tenn.; *Richmond Planet* and *Afri-*

---

[1] Dr. H.K. Carroll, *The Religious Forces of the United States*, page 28.

can Missions, Richmond, Va.; *West Virginia Enterprise*, Charlestown, W. Va.; *Baptist Tribune*, Columbia, S.C.; *Baptist Leader*, Montgomery, Ala.; and *Baptist Review*, Atlanta, Ga. The most of these are strictly denominational in character. A large number of papers are issued by the colored Baptists of the South which are politico-religious, while others are entirely political. One of the most promising features of the race is that they are omnivorous readers.

Allusion has been made to the fondness which the colored man has for meetings of a religious character. Coupled with this, was his equal fondness for the diversion afforded by the "shuffle" and "the breakdown." It was the care of many masters during the days of slavery that diversions be had by the slaves on Saturday night. In order to this, labor was often suspended before the close of the day. As a result the Negro quarters upon the plantations of the South would resound every Saturday night with the music of "the fiddle and the bow" the clapping of hands, the rattling of bones, and hilarious laughter. This was responded to by the shuffle and thump of agile dancers. Often till the wee sma' hours was this hilarity indulged in. But all this has changed. One rarely hears now the tumult of the dancers in the Negro quarters of the South. The rude frolic of former days has been almost entirely supplanted by the religious gathering. Instead of the strains of the banjo and violin, one hears now the song of praise and the voice of exhortation. The changes wrought in this people, and the progress made under such conditions, make them one of the most remarkable races of history.

In their religious inclinations, the Negroes are Baptists. Even when becoming members of other denominations they frequently insist upon immersion as the only baptism. In his work entitled "Men of Mark— Eminent, Professional, and Rising," Dr. W.J. Simmons, the well-known colored preacher, insists with evident satisfaction: "I claim that there are in the United States, more colored Baptists than white Baptists, and more colored Baptists than all Pedobaptists together."

CHAPTER XV
CONCLUSION

Having traced the development of the Baptist denomination in the Southern States east of the Mississippi, through a period of more than two hundred years, we are able, from the present ground of advantage, to review the eventful eras through which we have come, and to study with interest, and perhaps with profit, the causes which have contributed to our growth. Far beneath the movements of men and communities, of churches and conventions, lie the philosophy of deeds and the instruction of events

That on the stretched forefinger of all Time Sparkle forever.

It is a fact worthy of attention that, though in the beginning the principles of liberty advocated by Baptist pioneers in America were stoutly resisted at every step, they have become the fundamental law of the land. Consistent and meritorious aggression has overborne the most forbidding obstructions and has contributed, in the largest degree, to the freedom now enjoyed throughout this broad land of States. Along with the inculcation of these principles which underlie our national framework, has been a development of the people who were their chief supporters in the outset; and have been their uncompromising patrons to the present. Nay, the denomination has vastly outgrown the nation. While in the United States the population has increased sixteen-fold, the Baptists of the country have grown fifty-six-fold, or nearly four times as fast as the population of the country.

Nor can this marvelous growth be attributed to immigration, for statistics abundantly show that while other denominations have derived great numerical increase from immigration, Baptists have derived little or no benefit therefrom. In the section of States under review in this work, the number of regular Baptists alone has reached the enormous figure of 1,808,307.

In their relation to the outlying heathen world, Baptists sustain missionary facilities that do great honor to the wisdom of the fathers of the denomination. Systems well-constructed and properly adapted to the evangelization of the heathen have been founded and are in successful operation. Immense organizations established upon the most improved methods of success for eliciting, combining, and directing beneficent agencies, are under Baptist control, and are directed with methodical success. Missionary representatives are at work in the crowded centers, the neglected districts, and on the remote frontier regions of America—in Mexico, Cuba, Brazil, China, Italy, Africa, and Japan.

In the early settlement of the country and until a considerable period after the Revolution, American Baptists, as a body, were an illiterate folk. Their ignorance won for them the contempt of ecclesiastical opponents. But, at different times, there were developed a few great leaders like Manning and Maxey, and later, of Wayland at the North, and of Furman, Holcombe, and Mercer at the South, who combined scholarship with sturdy good sense, and were denomination builders, on the educational side. Directing with skill the scanty resources at command, and marshaling with adroitness every encouragement developed, these earnest men of God provided a leverage for the future elevation of the Baptists of America. While with a great people who had obtained a popular foothold in every State, there must needs have been blunders, especially where so much was undertaken in educational work; still the close of the second century of Baptist history finds the denomination with many institutions of high grade, attaining indeed to the highest, most widely distributed and deservedly popular throughout the country.

While in the South many of these interests were prostrated as a result of the Civil War, most of them have been revived, and are today among the most powerful and salutary forces of our civilization. With the freedom of the slave came the establishment of schools for his elevation in the scale of moral and intellectual excellence. These give to colored Baptists numerous advantages over those colored representatives of other denominations in the States most populous with that race.

Baptists were the first of the denominations of the South to lay hold of the press as an engine of strength and progress. As the region has grown in population and in prosperity, this agency has improved, and its influence has broadened, until it has become a stupendous factor in the States of the South.

Among the chief elements of success which have come into the possession of Baptists is that of wealth. Prior to the Civil War, many Baptists in the South were very wealthy; but with the crash of Southern institutions came the destruction of most of the wealth of this section. But there has been a gradual rehabilitation of thousands of estates together with the production of wealth from many new sources. In this, Baptists who constitute so large a percentage of the population have, of course, shared. By reason of their overwhelming numbers in some of the States, they own a preponderance of property as compared with other denominations. Combined with other advantageous elements, this gives to Baptists social position.

But the chief source of visible strength to the Baptists is the firm hold which they have upon the sturdy middle class of the country. They reach and control more of that class perhaps than any other denomination of Christians on the continent. From the beginning this has been a basal element of denominational strength, and to this fact may be largely attributed Baptist achievements in America.

Such are some of the chief advantages enjoyed by the Baptists of America. Should denominational success continue at the same ratio of increase to the close of the twentieth century, Baptist influence will be beyond competition.

But while these advantages exist, and they are considerable, are there no possible drawbacks to Baptist growth and influence? Are there no snares besetting the future? In a land of unparalleled prosperity there is grave danger arising from a spirit of worldliness. Baptists have endured the ordeal of struggle and affliction and have thriven; will they be able to thrive with the increasing prosperity of the country?

The solidity of church life has been preserved by the exercise of a wholesome discipline in the local organizations. The inroads of worldliness will inevitably impair this distinct feature of our churches and invite decay. One of the direct results of worldliness is a decline of benevolence. Should that spirit decline rather than increase with the material prosperity with which the churches are blessed, disastrous results will follow. Upon Baptists more than upon others rests the responsibility of meeting this strain. If so much has been accomplished in spite of persecution and opposition, how much greater should be denominational success with these obstructions entirely removed, and with immense prosperity at ready command.

Another danger springing from the spirit of the times is that of superficiality of results. The apprehension is not without foundation that as we increase numerically there is danger of a corresponding spiritual loss. Church progress has come to be estimated too much by the enrollment upon the church register. There is a widespread desire for increased numbers rather than for increased efficiency. Pastors are sought who "draw" rather than those who build. In the craze for large accessions, organization is neglected, discrimination and caution are not exercised in the reception of members, and convert culture goes for naught.

Krummacher is credited with the saying, "The Baptists have a future." The statement of the German theologian is suggestive of the fact that Baptists are charged with a peculiar mission which is as yet unfulfilled. They have succeeded as a people in making their impress upon the world alone by their fidelity to the sacred trusts committed to them. Their influence is discovered by the practical adoption of their views by a large number of Pedobaptist churches. The steady and consistent observance of the principles held all along by Baptists has gradually brought into disrepute infant baptism; and in proportion to the decline of this practice has been the growth of the doctrine of immersion. In consideration of their numbers, influence, resources, and opportunities, the possibility of future achievement seems boundless.

The story of the Baptists of the South for two hundred years is one unequaled by that of any other people in the annals of time. From a few struggling outposts along the Atlantic, in the beginning scarcely daring the deed of self-assertion lest a storm of persecution be invoked, they have become a people multitudinous in number, and of immense resources. Pitied and despised by an arrogance that accounted their forefathers the off-scouring of the earth, resisted by an intolerance whose self-devotion blinded it to the noblest elements of character, and overridden by a haughtiness whose selfishness withheld all suffrage save that doled out by stinted hands, Baptists have thriven in this goodly land and have expanded as the garden of the Lord. Opposition has made them great. The benediction has come to the reviled and persecuted.

Today we are confronted by the danger of undue consciousness of greatness that may be a reversal of the law by which we have attained the commanding heights. There is apprehension lest our humility be transformed into the very intolerance against which a humble spiritual ancestry strove and became great. Insidious pride follows fast upon human success, and multiplies pitfalls in exact proportion to achievement. The Chaldean monarch was within a single stride of the level of the grazing herds when puffed with vanity he paced his capital walls and gloried in his grandeur; while the Hebrew prophet was greatest in his dungeon with the command ringing in his ears: "Buy the field that is in Anathoth, for the right of redemption is thine to buy it."

Restraint of independent thought and an arbitrary erection of barriers against expressed individual opinion—barriers as inexorable as the ramparts of the sea, saying, "Thus far shalt thou go and no farther," is akin to the intolerance that built the Inquisition.

Questions and problems, grave and complicated, are destined to be raised in the future as in the past. These cannot be met with fiery zeal and impetuous intolerance. In matters of grave import the wise counsel of Gamaliel is suited alike to all times: "If this counsel or this work be of men, it will be overthrown: but if it is of God, ye will not be able to overthrow them; lest haply ye be found even to be fighting against God" (Acts 5:38-39., R.V.).

APPENDIX A
OTHER BAPTIST FAMILIES

Besides that great family of Baptists, the history of which is briefly presented in this volume, there are others, ten in number, each of which bears a distinct name, and are expressive of the professed principles of each. These are: the Seventh Day, Six Principle, Freewill, Original Freewill, General, Separate, United, Baptist Church of Christ, Anti-missionary, and Old Two-Seed-in-the-Spirit Predestinarian Baptists.

All these agree in two particulars, viz.:

1. That the only subjects of Christian baptism are those who have been converted and profess personal faith in Christ, and

2. That the only scriptural baptism is immersion.

It is hardly necessary to say that they reject infant baptism as invalid, and sprinkling or pouring as unscriptural.

There are still other denominations, akin to the Baptists, which accept these principles wholly, or in part, such as the Disciples of Christ, Christians, Mennonites, and others, but they are not Baptists, and are never so classified.

The Disciples of Christ accept the principles named, but they also insist that only through baptism does "divine assurance of remission of sins and acceptance with God" come. The Christians generally insist upon the immersion of believers, but will accept pouring or sprinkling. The Mennonites believe in pouring and usually adopt this. The Regular Baptists are divided into Northern, Southern, and Colored. In doctrine, they are Calvinistic. The Freewill Baptists, in both its branches, together with the General Baptists, and others, are Arminian. The Anti-mis- sionary Baptists, of which there are two or three bodies, are hyper-Calvinistic.

THE SEVENTH DAY BAPTISTS

They appeared in England in the latter part of the sixteenth century. They derive their name from the observance of Saturday as a sacred day, or as a day of rest. This body was known as Sabbatarians, or Sabbatarian Baptists, until the General Conference of the body in 1818, when the name was changed to that of Seventh Day Baptists. The first Seventh Day Baptist church established in America was founded at Newport, Rhode Island, in 1671. Stephen Mumford, of England, was its founder. From this colony have come all the people of that name to be found today in different portions of the United States. Reaching southward, Philadelphia, and Piscataway, New Jersey, became other distributing centers.

They entered the South in 1754, when Rev. John Gregory led a colony from Pennsylvania and New Jersey into South Carolina, and they organized a church on Broad River, in St. Mark's Parish. In 1769 or 1770, eight other families removed from Chester (now Delaware County), Pennsylvania, and joined them. A revival of religion followed this event, when twenty-four members were added to the church. At that time they were a prosperous community of eighteen families. This is as far as trustworthy records can trace them.

From this time they disappear from history. They were located possibly not far from the present town of Manning, South Carolina. The principal families of the colony were named Price, Hughes, Johnston, Owen, Jackson, Gregory, Nelly, Seymour, and Noble. Were they absorbed by the Regular Baptists of that region?

In 1759 Rev. Richard Gregory led a company of eight families into the Tuckaseeking region, about forty miles north of Savannah, and organized a Seventh Day Baptist church. Richard Gregory preceded Daniel Marshall at Kiokee about twelve years. This colony of Seventh Day Baptists left Kiokee in 1765 and returned across the Savannah River and settled at Edisto, South Carolina. Other traces of these people are found in North Carolina, but they are dim.

The Seventh Day Baptists hold the views generally held by the great Baptist family, and differ from the others chiefly by observing the seventh instead of the first day of the week, as a sacred day. "They believe that the seventh day is the Sabbath of the Lord, that it was instituted in Eden, promulgated at Sinai, made binding upon all men at all times and is, in the nature of its relation to God and to man, irrepealable. They hold that any attempt to connect the Sabbath law and obligation with any other day of the week is illogical, and tends to destroy the institution."[1]

These people have suffered persecution in some of the States for the disregard of Sunday as a sacred day. This has been true both in Tennessee and in Georgia.

They have two collegiate institutions, one located at Milton, Wisconsin, and the other at Alfred Center, New York. The denomination is represented in twenty-four States. Of the States which come within the compass of treatment in this volume, in which the Seventh Day Bap-

---

[1] Dr. H.K. Carroll, *Religious Forces in the United States*, page 31.

tists exist, are Alabama, Florida, Kentucky, Mississippi, North Carolina, West Virginia, Georgia, and Tennessee, having a total membership in the States named of nine hundred and thirty.

THE FREEWILL BAPTISTS

This organization sprang up in New Durham, New Hampshire, in 1780. Its representatives derive their name from the doctrine held by them concerning the will. The founder of the sect, Benjamin Randall was at first a Congregationalist, but his views undergoing a change, he became a Baptist. Refusing to accept the doctrines usually held by the Baptists at that time, concerning predestination, election, a limited atonement, and the final perseverance of the saints, he was accounted unsound and fellowship was promptly denied him. This occurred in 1779. The following year he secured ordination at the hands of two Baptist ministers who coincided with him in his views. The Freewill Baptist church which he forthwith organized was, like all others in New England at the time, spoken of simply as a Baptist church. Within the next twenty years, the members of these churches being popularly called "Freewillers," the distinctive name of "Freewill" was adopted. From New England, the Freewill Baptists gradually extended into the West. No doubt headway would have been made in the South in the early periods of the century, but the founders of the organization were vehemently opposed to slavery. This opposition found pronounced expression in 1835, when the general conference of the Freewill Baptists put the stamp of condemnation upon African slavery.

The Freewill Baptist churches multiplied from the beginning. After the lapse of half a century they had four hundred and fifty churches, with 21,000 members. In 1841 they united with the Free Communion Baptists of New York, and their numbers were increased by the addition of fifty-five churches and 2,500 members. Later, however, the Freewill Baptists sustained losses by local dissensions through the Adventist movement. They suffered also as a result of the war, as both ministers and members largely enlisted in the Union armies. Having a membership of 60,000 in 1845, they had the same number in 1870. During the intervening quarter of a century the denomination had grown, and yet, by varying fortune, it had lost. Since that time, its numbers have gradually increased until, in 1890, there were, in the United States, 87,898 Freewill Baptists. As early as 1791 women began to labor among this people as preachers. It is a custom with them to grant ordination to such women as desire to serve as ministers.

Freewill Baptists hold that while man cannot, in his fallen state, become a child of God by natural goodness and personal effort, redemption and regeneration are freely provided for him. This admits of application to everyone, for the "call of the gospel is coextensive with the atonement to all men" so that salvation is "equally possible to all." They insist that the "truly regenerate" are "through infirmity and manifold temptations" in "danger of falling," and "ought therefore to watch and pray lest they make shipwreck of faith." Their position upon baptism and the Lord's Supper is that they hold immersion alone as baptism, and insist upon it that it is the "privilege and duty of all who have spiritual union with Christ" to participate in the observance of the Supper.

With emphasis they declare that "no man has a right to forbid these tokens to the least of his disciples." This declaration, of course, indicates that the denomination advocates what is usually known as "open communion."

The Articles of Faith provided for the churches declare that the "human will" is "free and self-determined, having power to yield to gracious influences and live, or resist them and perish." They declare that the doctrine of election is not an "unconditional decree" which fixes the future state of man, but that it is simply God's determination "from the beginning to save all who should comply with the conditions of salvation."

The general meetings of the Freewill Baptists are called conferences. They hold quarterly and yearly conferences, and a general Conference, which meets every two years. These are representative bodies. A quarterly Conference represents a restricted territory embracing a given number of churches. Its functions are almost altogether advisory.

The quarterly Conference inquires into the condition of the churches and is empowered to advise, admonish, or withdraw fellowship from them. It may not, however, "deprive a church of its independent form of government, nor its right to discipline its members nor labor with individual members of churches as such"; to deal with the churches only as churches and not with individuals, is what is provided for in the polity of the denomination. The quarterly Conference selects delegates for the annual Conference. It sustains the same relation to the quarterly Conference that the quarterly Conference does to the individual churches. The general Conference, which has the oversight of all the interests of the denomination, derives its delegates from the annual Conference. While it has a general oversight of the denomination, its disciplinary jurisdiction is limited to the yearly meeting. It cannot reach beyond these and interfere with the action either of the quarterly meeting or of the churches. It is absolutely without power to reverse the decisions of any of the subordinate bodies. Candidates for the ministry derive licenses, for a year only, from the quarterly meeting. Ordination is granted by a council of the quarterly meeting. The church officers are those of pastor, clerk, and treasurer, together with an elected Board of deacons who, besides attending to the temporalities of the church, assist at baptism, serve at the Lord's Supper, and take charge of meetings during the absence of the pastor. The strength of the denomination is chiefly in the North and West. Of the States under review in this volume, the statistics are as follows: Alabama has a membership of 847; Florida, a membership of 22; Kentucky, a membership of 1,641; Maryland, a membership of 98; Mississippi, a membership of 1,339; North Carolina, a membership of 11; Tennessee, a membership of 2,864; Virginia, a membership of 478; and West Virginia, a membership of 1,668.

THE ORIGINAL FREEWILL BAPTISTS

These are a remnant of the General Baptists who settled in North Carolina in the first half of the eighteenth century. The territory in North Carolina occupied by them lay contiguous to that which was occupied by the General Baptists in Virginia.

In each of these colonies they formed an Association. In 1787, the General and Regular Baptists united upon a Calvinistic basis. There were a few Freewillers who did not go into the coalition. Eventually they came to be known as Original Freewill Baptists. Probably the term "original" carries with it the idea that they precede, in point of time, the existence of those who afterward came to be known as Freewill Baptists.

In doctrine they declare that Christ "freely gave himself a ransom for all, tasting death for every man"; that God desires that all come to repentance; that "all men, at one time or another are found in such capacity as that through the grace of God they may be eternally saved"; that those "ordained to condemnation" are only the unrighteous who refuse to accept the gospel offer of salvation; that infants who die are not subject to the second death; that God has not decreed any person to everlasting death or everlasting life out of respect or mere choice, only as he appoints "the godly unto life and the ungodly who die in sin unto death"; that only believers are to be baptized, and that immersion alone is baptism. They also observe foot-washing, and anoint the sick with oil. Foot-washing and communion arc observed every quarter.

Conference for church business is held quarterly. Every member is allowed a voice in the transaction of the business of the church. The officers of a church are a pastor, clerk, treasurer, and deacons who look after the temporal affairs and prepare for quarterly communion. Besides these, they have a sort of judicial eldership, the members of which are called "ruling elders" whose duty it is to settle controversies. Discipline is theoretically rigid. Members of churches are not allowed to frequent the "race track, the card table, shooting matches, or any other place of disorder." In the administration of discipline it is provided that "no person of color within the pale of the church shall give testimony against any person" (except one) "of color." Provision is made whereby only male members shall hold office in the church. Once a year a general conference is held for settlement of church difficulties, for the reception of new churches, and for the trial and discontinuance of elders, or pastors. This yearly conference is composed of all the pastors, or elders, ministers, (ordained) preachers, (licentiates) in good standing, and of delegates chosen by the churches.

Besides the work already named, this annual conference alone has power to silence preachers. The churches of the Original Freewill Baptists are confined to North and South Carolina. In the former, there is a membership of 10,254; in the latter, there is a membership of 1,640.

The General Baptists

The name of this body is meant to imply its liberality in contradistinction from the Particular or Regular Baptists who are Calvinistic. The General Baptists are Arminian in creed. They have eliminated every vestige of Calvinism from their articles of faith.

We find General Baptists in New England at the close of the seventeenth century. Near the beginning of the century following they organized themselves into a General Association. A little later, we find them establishing churches in Maryland, Virginia, and the Carolinas. A marked revolution was effected in the last-named States by the visits of such missionaries as Gano, Van Horn, Miller, and others. Under the instruction of such men the most of them became Calvinistic in faith.

During the first quarter of the present century the drift of the General Baptists was toward the West, where they are now concentrated. The first Association of the General Baptists organized in the West was the Liberty, of Kentucky, in 1824. They adopted the practice of open communion in 1830, and fifteen years afterward so changed one of their articles of faith as to embrace idiots and infants in the covenant of grace. It seems that in the creed formulated at the constitution of the Liberty Association, this specification had been omitted. In order to give more emphasis to the tone of Arminianism, another article was changed so as to declare that "He that shall endure to the end shall be saved" instead of saying, "the saints will finally persevere from grace to glory." The purpose of these changes evidently was to wipe out from the creed the last vestige of Calvinism.

In 1870 they formed a General Association in which all the Associations of the general body are represented. The object of such organization is declared to be that of bringing "into more intimate and fraternal relation and effective co-operation various bodies of literal Baptists."

So closely akin are the General and the Freewill Baptists that each readily receives into its communion and fellowship the churches of the other. The growth of the General Baptists, has within the last quarter of a century been rapid. In 1870 they numbered 8,000; ten years later, 12,367; and ten years later still, 21,362.

They are scattered through the States of Indiana, Illinois, Kentucky, Tennessee, Missouri, Arkansas, and Nebraska. One fails to discover but slight difference between the General Baptists and the Freewill Baptists from a comparison of the Confessions of Faith. They hold that the Bible is the only rule of faith and practice; that there is one God, the Father, Son, and Holy Ghost; that man is "fallen and depraved," and is totally unable to save himself; that he that endures to the end shall be saved; that reward and punishment are eternal; that immersion alone is baptism; that only believers are proper subjects of baptism; that none can share in the benefits of the atonement, though made for all, except through repentance and faith, save idiots and infants only.

In Kentucky the General Baptists have 4,455 members; in Tennessee, 1,008 members.

THE UNITED BAPTISTS

This is a small body of communicants who retain the designation assumed when the Separate and Regular Baptists were united in Virginia, Kentucky, and elsewhere. But there was such general concession to the principles of the Regular Baptists, that the sections thus combined were eventually called Regular Baptists.

Later, they were additionally called Missionary Baptists to distinguish them from the Anti-missionary. Some have persisted in clinging to the name United Baptists and have preserved a continual existence in that way.

An additional reason for their independent existence is found in the fact that in Kentucky the fusion of the Separates and Regulars was not upon a purely Calvinistic basis. While in their doctrinal platform they did declare the final perseverance of the saints, they did not distinctly set forth election or reprobation. However, the fusionists did stipulate that the doctrine of a general atonement, as declared in the fact that "Christ did taste death for every man," should be "no bar to communion."

As a distinct denomination the United Baptists are moderate Calvinists. They hold that Christ "suffered and died to make atonement for sin," but do not say whether this atonement was general or particular. They further declare that though the gospel is to be preached to all nations, and men everywhere are to be urged to repentance, such is their opposition to the gospel that they deliberately and voluntarily choose a state of sin.

They further insist that God in his "mere good pleasure" elected or chose in Christ a great multitude among all nations, and that through the operation of the Holy Spirit, God "effectually calls them" and they "freely choose Christ for their Savior." They urge that those who are united to God by a living faith are forgiven and justified "solely on account of the merits of Christ," and that those who are justified and regenerated will persevere to the end. On the subject of baptism their views are in common with all other Baptists— immersion of believers only. Concerning the Lord's Supper they claim that it should be "observed by those who have been regenerated, regularly baptized, and become members of a gospel church." They also hold to the observance of washing the saints' feet.

The United Baptists are found in Alabama, Arkansas, Kentucky, Missouri, and Tennessee. There are in Alabama 702 members; in Kentucky, 6,443 members; and in Tennessee, 3,180 members.

The Baptist Church of Christ

This is a small body, the majority of the members of which are to be found in Tennessee. The first two Associations of the Baptist Church of Christ were the Elk River and the Duck River, both of which were organized in Tennessee in 1808. They assert that they are the oldest body of Baptists, and that no others existed in Tennessee until 1825, "when the Two-Seed churches came into existence as the result of what is known as the Antinomian Controversy."

The Articles of Faith of the Baptist Church of Christ are conservative in tone. They hold that "Christ tasted death for every man," and so conditioned the means of grace as to make it possible for God to exercise mercy toward all who come unto him on the terms of the gospel; that justification is by faith; that saints will persevere. They agree with the entire Baptist brotherhood upon the subject of immersion, and believer's baptism. They insist upon three ordinances—baptism, the Lord's Supper, and washing the feet of the saints. These are to be observed until the second coming of Christ. A few members of this body are to be met with in the States of Alabama, Arkansas, Mississippi, Missouri, North Carolina, Tennessee, and Texas. In Alabama there are 782 members; in Mississippi, 368 members; in North Carolina, 659 members; and in Tennessee, 5,065 members.

THE ANTI-MISSION BAPTISTS

This body of Baptists is known by a variety of names, such as "Primitive," "Old School," "Anti-Mission," and "Hard Shell." Their tenets are characterized by narrowness and rigidity. They owe their existence as a distinct body to their pronounced opposition, begun more than fifty years ago, to missions, Sunday-schools, Bible societies, and all similar institutions. They denounce them as human institutions, modern innovations, as unauthorized by the Scriptures, and unnecessary.

The severance of the anti-effort Baptists from the missionary organizations was a gradual process. It found open expression in the Chemung Association, the churches of which were partly in New York and partly in Pennsylvania, as early as 1835. It adopted a resolution insisting that as associational bodies with which it had been in correspondence had "departed from the simplicity of the doctrine and practice of the gospel of Christ, uniting with the world and what are falsely called benevolent societies, founded upon a moneyed basis," and engaged in preaching a gospel "differing from the gospel of Christ," it declined further fellowship with them. It followed up this declaration with an earnest appeal to all Baptists who did not approve these innovations to withdraw from those holding them. A year later this was followed by a similar protest from the Baltimore Association of Maryland.

Set over against these deliverances was a declaration from the Warwick Association, New York, in 1840. By this time the battle was waxing hot, as the tenor of the Warwick declaration shows. Expressing itself in a circular letter, the Warwick Association, in opposition to the Anti-missionary element, charges them with entertaining Hyper-Calvinistic doctrines, and insists that such views of predestination as they held practically relieved man of any responsibility for his conduct or condition. It charges upon them that they insist that God executes his plans "without the least instrumentality whatever," and that "all the preaching from John the Baptist until now, if made to bear on one unregenerated sinner" could not "quicken his poor, dead soul."

What was taking place in the East at this time was also taking place in the West and South. The separation was finally brought about by the withdrawal of the Anti-mission elements of the denomination. No objection exists on the part of the Anti-mission forces to the preaching of the gospel, but they stoutly hold that God will convert the world in his own way, and in his own good time, independent of human agency.

It has been popularly supposed that the inaction which such views necessarily engender, is leading to a gradual extinction of this people. This is corroborated by the fact that the masses of the Anti-mission Baptists being illiterate, attach no importance to denominational statistics. But the supposition of their gradual disappearance is erroneous. They are endowed with amazing vitality. We are indebted to the national census for the information, which we possibly would not otherwise have, concerning this peculiar people. In his admirable work, *The Religious Forces of the United States*, in the American Church History Series, Dr. H.K. Carroll conclusively shows that if past statistics concerning this people are correct, the census of 1890 exhibits a remarkable increase.

In their Articles of Faith the Anti-mission Baptists declare that by the fall of Adam "all his posterity become sinners in the sight of God"; that the "corruption of human nature" prevents man by the exercise of his own will and ability from reinstating "himself in the favor of God"; that "God elected, or chose, his people in Christ before the foundation of the world"; "that sinners are justified only by the righteousness of

Christ imparted to them"; that the saints will finally persevere and "not one of them will ever be finally lost"; that baptism, the Lord's Supper, and washing the saints' feet, are ordinances of the gospel, and should be continued until Christ's second coming; that "the institutions of the day are works of man"; and that it is "wrong to join them." They further insist that no fellowship should be had with churches which favor these human agencies. Indeed an article of the constitution declines fellowship with any church or churches which support any "missionary, Bible, tract, or Sunday-school union society, or advocates State Conventions, or theological schools," or "any other society formed under the pretense of circulating the gospel of Christ."

As may be readily judged from the foregoing, the Anti-mission Baptists have no State Conventions or theological seminaries. They vehemently oppose the preparation of their ministry for more effectively preaching the gospel. They are one with all Baptists respecting immersion and the precedence of faith to baptism, and that this is a prerequisite to the Lord's Supper. They further contend that no minister has authority to administer the ordinances unless he has been "called of God," "come under the imposition of hands by a presbytery," and is "in fellowship with the church of which he is a member."

The denomination is distributed through twenty-eight States. It is strongest in Georgia, Alabama, Tennessee, North Carolina, and Kentucky. It has disappeared from almost every Northern State except Indiana and Illinois. The denomination aggregates 121,347.[1]

THE TWO-SEED-IN-THE-SPIRIT PREDESTINARIAN BAPTISTS

This is the most peculiar and distinctive of all the bodies called Baptist. They hold no fellowship with any other body of that name. They entertain the most extreme views upon the subject of Calvinism, giving great emphasis to the doctrine of predestination, as their name indicates. Their conception of good and evil is expressed by the phrase "Two seed." One of these represents good, and the other, evil. Daniel Parker, of Virginia, is regarded the founder of this branch. In 1826 he

---

[1] Of the Anti-mission Baptists there are in Alabama a membership of 14,903; in the District of Columbia, a membership of 34; in Florida, a membership of 1,997; in Georgia, a membership of 18,535; in Kentucky, a membership of 10,605; in Maryland, a membership of 373; in Mississippi, a membership of 3,259; in North Carolina, a membership of 11,740; in South Carolina, a membership of 531; in Tennessee, a membership of 13,972; in Virginia, a membership of 9,950; in West Virginia, a membership of 2,777.

published a pamphlet in which were embodied the doctrines of this denomination. In 1829 another pamphlet appeared from his pen, entitled *Second Dose of the Doctrine of Two Seeds*.

The following is supposed to embody the views held by the Old Two-Seed-in-the-Spirit Predestinarian Baptists.

> *The essence of good is God; the essence of evil is the devil. Good angels are emanations from, or particles of, God; evil angels are particles of the devil. When God created Adam and Eve, they were endowed with an emanation from himself, or particles of God were included in their constitution. They were wholly good. Satan, however, infused into them particles of his essence, by which they were corrupted. In the beginning, God had appointed that Eve should bring forth only a certain number of offspring; the same provision applied to each of her daughters. But when the particles of evil essence had been infused by Satan, the conception of Eve and her daughters was increased. They were now required to bear the original number, who were styled the seed of God, and an additional number who were called the seed of the serpent. The seed of God constituted a part of the body of Christ. For them the atonement was absolute; they would all be saved. The seed of the serpent did not partake of the benefits of the atonement and would all be lost. All the manifestations of good or evil in men are but displays of the essence that had been infused into them. The Christian warfare is a conflict between these essences.*

This body is known by other names than the one already given. Some of the representatives call themselves "Regular," others are called "Regular Predestinarian," still others designate themselves, "Regular Two-Seed Predestinarian Primitive Baptists." The Articles of Faith held by these different divisions vary somewhat. One set declares that God is the Creator of all things and governs all things in righteousness; that man was created holy, but by reason of sin fell, and became corrupted, from which corruption he was unable to recover himself; that the elect were chosen in Christ before the world began, and "appointed to faith and obedience in love" by the Spirit of God because of the "righteousness, life, death, resurrection, and ascension" of Christ; that God's elect will, in due time, be effectually called and regenerated, the righteousness of God being imputed to them; that they will never finally fall away; that good works are the fruits of faith and grace in the heart, and follow regeneration; that ministers should receive "legal authority" through the imposition of hands of the presbytery acting for a gospel church, and should be subject to the discipline of the church; that the "eternal work of the Holy Spirit" is manifested externally as well as internally, in experimental religion and the call to the ministry, and the true church should distinguish itself from all "false sects" and have no fellowship with them; that the church is a spiritual kingdom which men in a state of nature cannot see, and it should therefore receive as members only those who have hope in Christ and experimental knowledge of salvation; that the ceremony of footwashing ought to be observed, and that the joys of the righteous and the punishment of the wicked will be endless.

We have said that the Two-Seed Predestinarian Baptists are unlike all others. They seem more nearly to approximate the Anti-mission Baptists in the doctrine of predestination, and yet they differ from them in that which seems to bring them more nearly together.

The Two-Seed Predestinarian Baptists hold that God predestined all his children to eternal life, and the devil and all his spiritual children to the eternal kingdom of darkness; that he foreordained all events whatever, from the creation to the consummation of all things, not suffering, in his infinite wisdom and perfect knowledge anything to occur to change his plans. The Anti-mission Baptists do not go so far. They hold that while God predestinated some to eternal life, his predestination did not extend absolutely to all things, for this doctrine would, they insist, blasphemously impute to the Almighty the existence of evil and do away with sin and human accountability. Among the claims of the Old Two-Seed Baptists is that of including Waldo, Calvin, Bunyan, Wycliffe, and Knox as "elders" who held the views of the Two-seed doctrine. They regard Arminius as a perverter and corrupter of the faith. Generally the Two-seed Baptists are opposed to a salaried ministry. Their interpretation of the all-sufficiency of Christ is that human agency is not needed to effect the redemption of men. They are purely antinomian in belief. Their idea of the function of the ministry is that of comforting Zion, feeding the flock, and contending earnestly for the faith once delivered to the saints.

They agree fully with the Anti-mission Baptists in their opposition to "modern institutions," by which are meant Sunday-schools, theological seminaries, Bible societies, missionary Boards, as well as missionary endeavor. They are scattered through twenty-four States of the Union, but are strongest in the South. The States in which they are most numerous are Texas, Tennessee, Kentucky, Mississippi, and Arkansas.[1]

---

[1] In the States represented in the group, the history of which is considered in this volume, they are numbered as follows: Alabama has 538 members; Florida, 39 members; Georgia, 330 members; Kentucky, 2,401 members; Mississippi, 840 members; North Carolina, 183 members; Tennessee, 1,270 members; Virginia, 142 members; and West Virginia, 806 members.

APPENDIX B
INSTITUTIONS FOR WOMEN AND VALUE OF PROPERTIES

VIRGINIA

Hollins Institute, founded in 1842; located at Botetourt Springs; Charles L. Cocke, A.M., president; value of property, $150,000; value of library and apparatus, $2,500.

Roanoke Female College, founded 1859; located at Danville; C.F. James, D.D., president; value of property, $25,000; value of library and apparatus, $1,500; number of volumes in library, 1,000.

Southside Female Institute, founded 1888; located at Burkeville; Rev. R.W. Cridlin, president; value of property, $15,000; value of library and apparatus, $2,000; number of volumes in library, 1,200.

Southwest Virginia Institute, founded 1884; located at Bristol; Samuel D. Jones, B. L., president; value of property, $150,000; amount of endowment, $7,500; value of library and apparatus, $1,000; number of volumes in library, 712.

Woman's College, founded 1854; located at Richmond; value of property, $65,000; number of volumes in library, 400.

NORTH CAROLINA

Chowan Female Institute, founded 1848; located at Murfreesboro; value of property, $50,000.

SOUTH CAROLINA

Cooper-Limestone Institute, founded 1880; located at Gaffney City; H.P. Griffith, president; value of property, $50,000; value of library and apparatus, $2,000; number of volumes in library, 250.

Greenville Female College, founded 1854; located at Greenville; Rev. M.M. Riley, D.D., president; value of property, $20,000; value of library and apparatus, $500.

GEORGIA

Monroe Female College, founded 1840; located at Forsyth; value of property, $15,000; value of library and apparatus, $500.

Shorter College, founded 1880; located at Borne; A.J. Battle, D.D., LL.D., president; value of property, $130,000; amount of endowment, $45,000; value of library and apparatus, $3,000; number of volumes in library, 1,500.

Southern Female College, founded 1843; located at La Grange; G.A. Nunnelly, D.D., president. This school has been located in the town of La Grange for fifty-two years. For many years it was conducted by Prof. I.F. Cox, A.M., who had control of the institution from 1857 to 1887, at which date he died. He was worthily succeeded by his son, Prof. C.C. Cox, who conducted the school with signal success until 1895, when he removed with his faculty and outfit to the handsome college building at College Park, near Atlanta. The new institution is known as Cox College. It is a magnificent structure and handsomely equipped.

KENTUCKY

Bethel Female College, founded 1854; located at Hopkinsville; Rev. T.S. McCall, A.M., president; value of property, $30,000; value of library and apparatus, $1,000; number of volumes in library, 1,000.

TENNESSEE

Boscobel, founded 1889; located at Nashville; J.G. Patey, A.B., president; value of property, $75,000; value of library and apparatus, $1,500; number of volumes in library, 1,000.

Brownsville Female College, founded 1851; located at Brownsville; value of property, $20,000; value of library and apparatus, $500.

Sweetwater Seminary, founded 1886; located at Sweetwater; William Shelton, D.D., LL.D., president; value of property, $20,000; value of library and apparatus, $2,000; number of volumes in library, 500.

ALABAMA

Judson Institute, founded 1839; located at Marion; S.W. Werett, LL.D., president; value of property, $61,000; amount of endowment, $540; value of library and apparatus, $20,000: number of volumes in library, 1,400.

MISSISSIPPI

Blue Mountain Female College, founded 1873; located at Blue Mountain; W.T. Lowry, D.D., president; value of property, $25,000; value of library and apparatus, $5,000; number of volumes in library, 1,500.

Hillman College, founded 1853; located at Clinton; Walter Hillman, D.D., president; value of property, $30,000; value of library and apparatus, $3,000; total value of property, $33,000.

In addition to these, there are many schools of a minor grade such as academies, institutes, and seminaries under the care of the denominational local bodies in all the States of the South.